A Swift and Deadly Maelstrom: The Great Norwich Flood of 1963, A Survivors Story

A Swift and Deadly Maelstrom: The Great Norwich Flood of 1963, A Survivors Story

Thomas Moody, Jr.

Copyright © 2013 by Thomas Moody, Jr.

Library of Congress Control Number:		2012921290
ISBN:	Hardcover	978-1-4797-4863-1
	Softcover	978-1-4797-4862-4
	Ebook	978-1-4797-4864-8

This book was printed in the United States of America.

To order additional copies of this book, contact:
Xlibris Corporation
1-888-795-4274
www.Xlibris.com
Orders@Xlibris.com
125804

TABLE OF CONTENTS

This book is dedicated to

Mom, Dad, Tony, and Nana . . . life givers and life savers all.

To Dad, Tony and Nana:

I am eternally grateful to them not only for being there to save and to then define my life but also for giving me the story of Mom and adding a dimension to my very limited memory of her that I wouldn't have otherwise had.

To Nana:

As cliché as it sounds, words cannot begin to express how much Jimmy, Shawn and I are forever beholden to her for how she raised us. The notion of her taking in three very young and rambunctious children at an advanced age, while suffering immeasurable sorrow and grief of her own is still incomprehensible to me, especially as I now approach that advanced age. She was truly incredible and our love and admiration for her is eternal.

To my dad:

I remain eternally thankful for the passing on of his interminable rectitude and for coming through as a parent under obviously indomitable circumstances—circumstances that took me far too long to fully understand. His lifetime influence on me, his voice and his steadfast fraternal personality will live with me forever. For that and untold other occurrences too numerous to mention here, I will always love and admire him.

Finally, to D'Ann, my guiding force, inherent inspiration and best friend . . . I could not have done this without you. I love you beyond what any words can describe. Here we go babe . . .

"Try to learn to let what is unfair teach you."
—David Foster Wallace, *Infinite Jest*

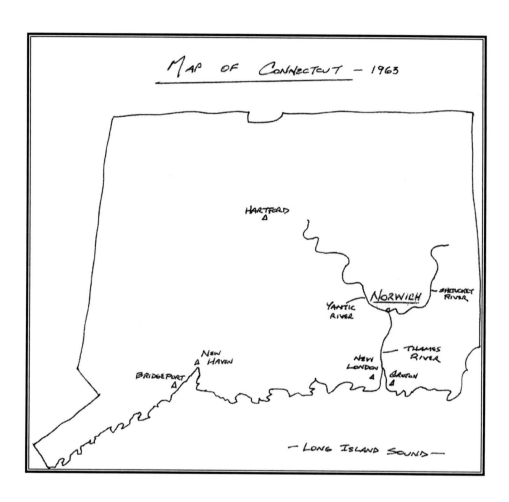

MAP OF CONNECTICUT — 1963

HARTFORD

NORWICH

SHETUCKET RIVER

YANTIC RIVER

THAMES RIVER

NEW HAVEN

BRIDGEPORT

NEW LONDON

GROTON

— LONG ISLAND SOUND —

CHAPTER 1

"The Dam Burst!"

I T HAD BEEN one of the most severe winters in recent memory for the people of Norwich, Connecticut, that season of 1962-1963. Those who would describe it simply as a typical New England winter were not giving it its due since it was the harbinger, in the end, of the most fatal disaster that the town would witness in at least the previous twenty five years.

The air temperature, most of the time, hovered incessantly below freezing with many of the daytime lows even approaching zero. The town, which is located in southeastern Connecticut at the mouth of the Thames River and situated only twelve miles north of Long Island Sound, annually has a dreary, dense and often ocean fed wind whipped winter effect that makes the period from November to March seem unendingly dreary.

This winter in particular, snow and freezing rain had dominated most days, pounding an area already accustomed to receiving its share of winter misery. This abnormally adverse weather had already been responsible for an above average precipitation amount, which was usually snow and which, as it fell day after day, only added to the girding and gloomy New England winter effect.

And for the majority of the time, there had been an accompanying blanket of ice perpetuating the three rivers that converge to make up the town (the Thames, Shetucket and Yantic rivers) while most of the surrounding lakes and ponds had been correspondingly frozen over. Even into early March, with the promise of spring only a month and a half away, the freezing cold and pounding precipitation would still not let up. Unwaveringly, it had been raining again heavily this Wednesday, March 5 (1.7 inches would fall overall), and this seemingly unending bad-weather would only add further to the already brimming lakes and ponds, causing repeated and chronic low lying flooding.

Spaulding Pond, the large man-made expanse in Mohegan Park, a large wooded enclave in the northern section of town, still had a glacial layer of ice this day that, notwithstanding the recent melting rains, was still two feet thick in places and, as in the past when extreme weather caused ice or water level to increase, posed a challenge to the aging earthen dam by which it was held in place. This dam, called eloquently enough, the "Spaulding Pond Dam" was being maintained under the jurisdiction of the Norwich City Public Works Department and was found to be leaking again this afternoon, a condition that had been observed at infrequent but increasing intervals in recent years, this time seeping water through its earthen core at approximately two-thirds upward from its rock-wall base.

Norwich Public Works director Harold Walz, the resolute city appointed manager and principal who had actually witnessed this seep through previously and was the responsible official for building the eight-foot high rock-wall on its south face eight years ago to help alleviate this seepage, responded to this latest report of dam leakage from his city foreman by personally inspecting it at 6:15 p.m. Although confirming that leakage was in fact occurring, he saw no noticeable erosion or other conditions symptomatic of imminent damage and, confident that this was simply another episode of minor and previously observed leakage, instead went home for dinner.

But with this seemingly informed judgment, Walz suddenly and indeed naively, now put into motion a series of deadly events that, sadly, allowed no going back. He and the myriad others who would play a crucial role in the delineations of the dam's health that evening were, instead, and also indistinguishable to them, suddenly engaged in a sort of native hopefulness that would ultimately prove catastrophic to the downtown area while further exposing a glaring untrained and severely limited knowledge of the dynamics of their dam.

Farther down in the city, meanwhile, at the Tom and Margaret Moody residence, life was, for the moment, calm and routine. The Moodys resided at 55 Lake Street, a gray shingled two-story house, just north of the center of town, at a time in Norwich's history when the downtown and areas surrounding it were still somewhat vibrant and industrious.

Lake Street, in March 1963, was a seemingly genial place to live, and families here were friendly to and supportive of each other; indeed the large Italian influence of the area lent itself to a strong, family oriented neighborhood.

Tom Moody (having just turned twenty-seven years old in February), and called "Ronnie" by his friends and family, arrived home from work at about 9:30 p.m. He was employed at the American Optical Company, a nationally known and acclaimed eyeglass-producing corporation that had many branches throughout the country with the Norwich locale specializing specifically in safety glasses. This particular office building was located on Broadway, one of the original colonial north/south roads in the town; and it was a job that Ronnie mostly disliked, thought mundane, but would, nevertheless, endure for thirty-eight long and rather fruitless years.

An engagingly simple and quiet man (almost to a fault) whose uncommon sense of fairness and right and wrong was laudable given his upbringing and which was exceeded only by his disdain for those who didn't share these principles, Ronnie, at this point, was at the very pinnacle of his life. At an age when many men were beginning to exhibit the onset of inevitable middle age expanse, Ronnie, who had been agonizingly thin all his life, was still very spare. At five feet ten and a half inches, he weighed perhaps 120 pounds, had thick dark hair combed in the late '50s DA/Elvis style and was the youngest of five children born to Katherine Kirby and Clifford Moody.

His parents were also unique in that, although being raised "city" and exposed to all that this implied, they were able to pass on to Ronnie and his siblings a seeming "un-city" maturity somewhat beyond their years, bolstered with an enormous sense of humor and self-deprecating wit that were characteristic in both their lineage. Katherine Kirby Moody was, in particular, a very beautiful woman who was known for wearing ostentatious hats, making marvelous fudge and who bore a striking resemblance to the actress Vivian Leigh.

Ronnie's father, Clifford, would be best described as a tough disciplinarian and taskmaster who "only had to reach for his belt at the dinner table and the volatile chatter would suddenly quiet." Clifford, who would bear a striking physical resemblance to his son Ronnie in middle age, or perhaps it was the other way around, was a seemingly proud, stoic man who wore his hair short and clean cut; a surviving picture shows him exiting a car with wireless glasses, a fedora, and a white shirt with knotted tie and fitted overcoat. A bemused smile is on his face as he appears to be both earnest and satisfied in his business matter of the moment.

Both Clifford and Katherine would die at very young ages however (she at forty-two years of uterus cancer in 1948, and he at forty-one years, also of cancer, in 1946). Upon this untimely and unexpected death of both his father and mother, Ronnie suddenly would become thrust with a maturity and independence at a predominantly early age, and he would proceed to develop, predictably, as one does with little adult supervision.

While having no relatives willing to take him in, Ronnie was instead raised by his sister Virginia and although she would run a reasonably disciplined house, she of course could not provide the required parental oversight that a young preteen requires, having to oversee four boys ranging in age between midteens to barely ten; and as a result, Ronnie would grow into the proverbial "street kid." Learning to smoke, drink and stay out to late hours, even on school nights, he would, however, still never forget and would always maintain that engrained and instinctive sense of right and wrong that was, throughout his life, exceedingly superimposed onto his personality.

This boyhood struggle and the inner conflict that it undoubtedly perpetuated was in all likelihood the genesis of an almost maniacal attention and devotion to education that he would later embrace and preach to his children as the eternal Holy Grail to life's success. This message became the virtual "house rule" when they were in elementary school, although educationally Ronnie never went beyond high school and was, at best, an average student at the Norwich Free Academy high school where he would struggle to graduate in 1954.

If Ronnie Moody had an inkling of an intellectual side, it would revolve around sports; and what he lacked in formal education, he made up for in a profound zeal for sports information and conversation. A somewhat fanatical Cleveland sports fan, he even went so far as to name his second son after the Cleveland Browns star running back of the time, Jim Brown—"Brown" being, coincidently, the maiden name of his mother-in-law, a fact that he deftly used in convincing his wife that the name was really to honor her.

Ronnie's wife was Margaret "Honey" Moody who was then just twenty-four years old. They had been married for six years at this point and a more-loving couple would have been hard to find. Stunningly beautiful with short brown hair and at five-feet-eight inches tall, resembling a fashion model, Ronnie found it still amazing, even after all this time, that she had married him, always thinking that she was "way out of his league." She, for her part, always loved his dark good looks and innate shyness, which drew her to him and which also instinctively told her that this was a man who would be a loyal and dedicated husband and father.

Having an amazingly magnetic personality, Honey seemed destined to travel a larger landscape in life and this infectious aura seemed to make people naturally drawn to her. With big, bright eyes and a constant smile, she was engaging, humble, and beautiful all at the same time and fiercely adored by all who knew her.

Honey, by 1963, had three children and was a stay-at-home mother who, aside from devoting her life to them, was an avid reader with a brilliant mind. Having completed her high-school curriculum in only three and a half years and graduating from the same Norwich Free Academy as her husband in 1956, she most certainly would have excelled academically at the collegiate level had she not met and fallen in love with Ronnie in 1954.

After their marriage, but before having children, she worked briefly as a telephone operator for the Southern New England Telephone Company where she would become known as an avid socializer; among her many friends was her sister-in-law Jackie Shea who was married to Honey's brother Paul. Jackie, also twenty-four, and Honey were young women embarking on married life together and remarkably alike in temperament and devotion to family. Both would ultimately have three children and all at nearly the same time . . . it was Jackie, in fact, who was pregnant with her last child Lynnsie and while visiting Honey following the birth of her last child Shawn, who would wearily tell her, "This is the last one, Honey . . . three's enough." Honey, also emotionally and physically spent, quickly agreed (although she had revealed to Ronnie on numerous occasions, both before and after the birth of Shawn, that she wasn't going to stop until she had a daughter).

Another predominate feature of Honey's personality was her total and unconditional devotion to her mother, Marguerite "Nana" Shea. Honey, as the youngest child of a large family, grew to depend on her mother both as a parent and as a friend and Nana, in turn, adored her daughter and clung to her as a mother often does to her youngest child. Nana, sixty years old in March, 1963, was a widower having lost her husband and Honey's father, William B. Shea to cancer in 1955.

Born in 1902, Marguerite Henrietta Brown would know only hard times as a child. A baby conceived out of wedlock to Effie Louise Martin and Thomas Henry Brown, she would be ostracized by the Brown family and called the "bastard child" by Thomas's mother until her parents divorce in 1907.

Nana's mother, Effie, would ultimately find employment at the newly opened Norwich State Hospital for the mentally ill, south of the city halfway between it and Groton about eight miles away, following the divorce and would visit Nana on only one afternoon a week (her only off-duty time) wearing the pre requisite hospital long nurses outfit. Being resigned to an attic in the gloomy mental hospital, Effie noticeably descended into decreasing mental health and one day simply stopped visiting Nana altogether and was curiously never heard from by the family again.

Her father, Thomas Henry, was far from a loving or caring parent and, although having custody, knew little of raising a small child. Getting little help from his otherwise financially capable parents, he instead boarded Nana at a Catholic convent in Baltic, Connecticut, where she was ultimately raised. Receiving the hard convent prerequisites as a child, kneeling on raw rice to "pray to Jesus for forgiveness for being a Protestant" she nonetheless grew to love the tough convent life and the equally strident nuns and would ultimately reside there into early adulthood where she would meet William Shea through her friend and fellow convent student Helen Shea (no relation to William).

Married in 1923, Nana and "Bill" would have seven children and would prosper in Norwich, with William being an important and influential business leader in the town, opening a meat-packing plant and becoming prominent in local politics. Nana conversely would become a stay-at-home mother, although possessing an astute intellect of her own that she would pass on to her children. Settling on Mount Pleasant Street on the west side of town, she and Bill enjoyed a remarkable life together, which was suddenly transformed when Bill died of cancer in 1955.

With all of her children now in adulthood and with most having their own families, Nana and Honey would become even closer after William's death. With a pension from his World War I military service and savings garnered from his successful meat-packing business, Nana now had time and could afford to travel to places like Florida to visit her eldest daughter, Mary. When Honey was eighteen, in 1956, and not yet married, Nana had a willing travel partner; and they would both make this trip by car more than once, which undoubtedly further solidified their relationship.

This shared devotion would become so binding that on the fourth birthday party of Honey's firstborn son, Tommy, while she was bending over to remove the birthday cake from the oven in her Lake Street home, Honey suddenly stood up straight and looked at her mother with an almost morbid stare and said, "Mom, if anything should ever happen to me, I want you to take care of and raise my kids." Nana, obviously shocked at this abrupt disclosure, assured Honey that of course she would. "You're just being silly', she told her. "You have a long life ahead of you. Just enjoy your baby's party", Nana urged.

Honey and Ronnie also had two other children at this point: the previously mentioned Jimmy Brown aged two and a half and the newborn Shawn, born the preceding October. By the time Ronnie had arrived home from work that night, all of the children had been asleep for a while.

Above the Moodys in the two-story house meanwhile, young Tony Orsini, a nineteen year old, lived with his mother Henrietta and father Pasquale, both strong Italian descendants who had migrated to Lake Street for the large Italian ethnic culture of the area. Tony, who worked at the Norwich State Hospital as an occupational therapy aide, was a small man at five feet five inches but in possession of a wiry athletic build. With dark thin hair, olive skin and prominent Italian features, Tony very much resembled his father at this very same age.

Tony had arrived home this evening after playing basketball in the Norwich City League and was extremely tired. A young man who loved sports (like Ronnie), he had also graduated from NFA, in 1961, and was a serious athlete, playing both basketball and baseball for many local teams. Tony, in fact, was an extremely impressive area baseball player. Playing, the previous summer, for the Jewett City Falcons of the then still-popular Norwich City League, Tony was a versatile infielder playing second base, third base and shortstop while consistently hitting over .300. Consistently being acknowledged as one of the top defensive players in the area, it was during the previous summer that his team won the Norwich Lions Club Tournament along with the Southern Rhode Island Summer League. Later, he would go on to play and coach on many top Norwich teams all the while adhering to a searing devotion to the New York Yankees—a dedication that would define him far into his later life. This night, however, Tony ate a quick meal and went immediately to bed.

Downstairs, after arriving home, Ronnie turned on the television while Honey checked on the children. Their small apartment-sized home had a small kitchen that one entered from a single outside entrance. This entrance was enclosed by a large porch that the children loved to race across and where Honey, when needing to bring them outside, could keep a close eye on them. Periodically, though, when she wasn't looking, one of the two older boys would inevitably slam the outside door closed, locking them all out which required Ronnie to come home from work, worrying and shaking his head, to break through a lower window to let them all back in again.

This porch entrance also had a stairway that descended to a small yard which then sloped down through a small wooded area and into the Lake Street playground, a large flat field with swingsets, baseball fields and basketball courts that all the neighborhood children spent most of their outdoor time at and was an area that the local parents depended on as a diversion when they needed to have their children occupied outside of the house.

Honey would occasionally bring her small children here as well whenever cabin fever or the need for exercise overtook her. Young Tommy, three years old at this point, thought that the playground was built just for him, however, and would sometimes feel the overwhelming need to, on his own, leave the porch and go down to the playground to play on the swing set. Honey, upon discovery of his absence and in a state of panic, would sprint down there and it was then that the youngster would learn the consequences of such "independent" actions.

The living room of the small home opened directly from the kitchen and was unique in that the floor sloped noticeably downward toward the rear of the house. The TV was at the "low" end of the room giving one the impression of looking downward into an almost theater like effect.

Tommy and Jimmy had beds in the rear of the children's bedroom, which was to the immediate left of the front door as one entered the house and the baby Shawn had a crib near the bedroom entrance. When Ronnie and Honey went for a rare night out, young Tommy took advantage of Nana, who became the de facto babysitter, by overloading his brother Shawn's crib with toys in an attempt to stop him from crying. Gradually the accumulated toys in the crib were such that the baby had nowhere to lie down and he inevitably continued screaming louder and louder until Nana came and rectified the situation.

After checking on the children, Honey now joined Ronnie in the living room as both planned to watch the local evening news. Channel 3 in Hartford was the CBS affiliate and preferred news source in southeastern New England with the venerable Walter Cronkite as the national news anchor. The news headlines in late 1962 and early 1963 were fraught with many shaping and polemical moments in US history, with certainly some of the most harrowing. The nation at this time was still reeling from the Cold War showdown with the Soviet Union after a US military U2 spy plane photographed nuclear warhead capable missiles in Cuba the previous October.

Following that dramatic international confrontation, the Cuban Missile Crisis, that lasted sixteen days in October 1962, the weapons had been subsequently removed from the island with verification by the United Nations. By early 1963, this standoff, although ending nonviolently, would have the undeniable longer-term effect of dividing relations with the Soviet Union and other Communist Bloc countries and would foretell, ultimately, the skewed military policy and flawed foreign policy thinking adopted by the country in the upcoming Vietnam War.

On the domestic front, the country was deep in the throes of a major civil rights crisis. James Meredith, a black US Air Force veteran from Mississippi, attempted enrollment at the state university in Oxford in October 1962, sparking race riots and violence on that campus that would resonate throughout the country. Federal involvement to quell this racial storm, suddenly and unexpectedly, became a priority for the young president John Kennedy and his equally youthful brother Robert, the attorney general.

Meredith, who was, against much protest, ultimately allowed to attend classes at the school, was forced nonetheless to move about campus each day with an armed contingent to protect him, all the while personally witnessing racially tinged and disparaging acts directed toward him and his race. Keeping his strength and perseverance however, he would go on to graduate from Mississippi in August 1963.

While Meredith was enduring these racial affronts on campus, Medgar Evers, a civil rights activist also from Mississippi and a man who was, ironically, influential in obtaining legal proclivity for Meredith to attend the university at Mississippi, was horrifically gunned down outside his home in full view of his wife and children in June 1963 by a member of the Ku Klux Klan, an act that again served to inflame activists and spark violent protestation, leading movement leaders to formulate the now-famous "March on Washington" where the renowned Martin Luther King gave his "I Have a Dream" speech.

The entertainment world was witness to its own tragic history as well, as country singer Patsy Cline died on March 5th at thirty-one years when the plane that carried her and her manager along with two other performers crashed in a remote part of Tennessee near Camden. On the entertainment front, Alfred Hitchcock released his suspense film *The Birds* in March to large audiences; and in England, a largely unknown musical quartet called the Beatles were at the dawn of producing their unique brand of rock 'n' roll, which would later lead to their first number-one hit record "I Want to Hold Your Hand."

Young partiers meanwhile were still doing the "Twist" while Ed Sullivan held a monopoly on the broadcasting of major entertainment events with his Sunday evening television variety show, which would peak early in 1964 with the first of three consecutive appearances by these same Beatles causing teen mayhem and chaos in the studio heretofore unseen by the conservative host.

Around 9:45 p.m. now, while still watching television, Ronnie and Honey heard a sudden and loud banging on the window in their living room. Startled, Ronnie quizzically looked over at Honey before jumping up and going toward the window. Someone outside (still unknown to this day, although, likely a local teenager sent by Public Works director Walz to warn residents on Lake St.) was shouting something to the effect that "the dam burst" and to evacuate at once. Looking out the window into the darkness he saw that the informant had disappeared, but he now noticed that a small rivulet of water was, curiously, flowing down Lake Street. He still didn't quite know what to make of all this, but heeding this warning and seeing water where it wasn't supposed to be, he asked Honey to call her mother and explain the evacuation warning; he was thinking that it would be safest if they got out of here and went over to Nana's house immediately.

Nana's small home (she had moved into a modest but charming white rent house behind her old home on Mount Pleasant Street after her husband died) was on Elizabeth Street and far removed from what was about to occur downtown. To get there though would require Ronnie and Honey to drive down Lake Street, in the direction of this water flow, past the large playground at the bottom of the road and onward down Pond Street and towards Franklin Street, the lowest point in the city in terms of sea level. Gathering the three pajama-clad children now and wrapping them in blankets for extra warmth, Honey led them outside to their 1957 Ford Fairlane parked on the street, while Ronnie turned to race up the outside stairway of their two-story gray house to warn Tony and his parents.

The water flow meanwhile had noticeably quickened and was already shin deep as the children were being loaded into the car. Honey quickly attended to them while Ronnie knocked on the door to the Orsinis' upstairs apartment. Pasquale quickly answered, and Ronnie breathlessly told him of the dam break and evacuation warning and asked if Tony could help them. They were headed toward the west side of town and may need a hand if they ran into any floodwaters. Pasquale quickly went to awaken Tony who had been asleep for only a short time following his basketball game. Getting dressed immediately,

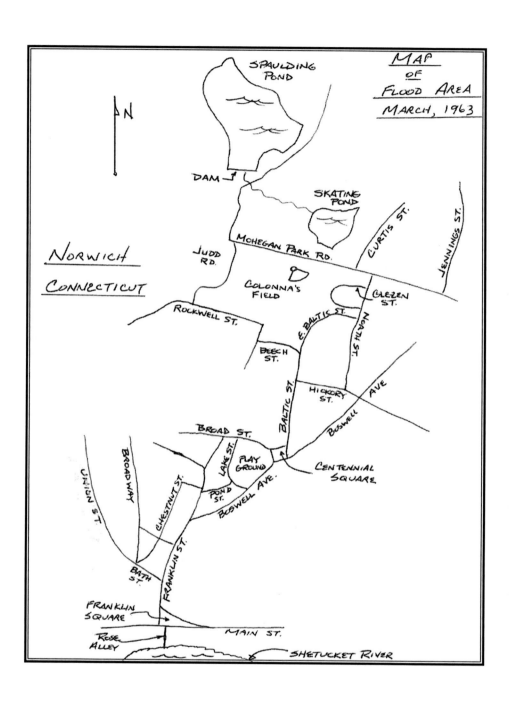

Tony implored his father to come with them, but Pasquale, a stubborn Italian in the fullest sense, refused to leave as he felt that it would be safer for everyone to remain in the safety of their home.

Tony, frustrated at his father's intransigence and not willing to argue further, came down to the street with Ronnie as Honey was finished loading the kids into the car. Agreeing to ride with them to Nana's house on Elizabeth Street, Tony and young Tommy now sat in the backseat while Honey sat in the front passenger seat holding onto the baby Shawn with Jimmy between her and Ronnie. None of them wore seat belts, as the culture of the times had not yet caught up to the present-day safety standards and which, as it turned out, may have saved their lives.

The group now proceeded quickly down Lake Street where at about one hundred yards from their house the road veered sharply to the left. After making this curve and heading east now, the car was moving past the open south end of the playground when suddenly Honey screamed out, "RON!"

CHAPTER 2

The Town, the Park, the Dam

A TOWN ABUNDANTLY rich in New England culture and history, Norwich, Connecticut was founded as a dominion of colonial expansion in 1659 when English colonists, arrayed across Connecticut's southern underbelly, assembled in Old Saybrook on the shores of Long Island Sound and continued to pursue the ingrained colonial doctrine of expansion. Sending intrepid explorers to the north along the banks of the Thames River, they came upon, after much exploration and physical hardship, land at the mouth of this river and happily noted that two other separate and large rivers converged into it. These colonists, led by Major John Mason and Rev James Fitch, went on to purchase this immediate river confluence and much of the surrounding area, "nine miles square" from Chief Uncas of the local Mohegan Indian tribe and established a settlement just north of this river confluence around what is now called the Norwichtown Green which, to this day, is a beautifully maintained area, by the town, in pristine seventeenth century architecture and ambience.

Here the colonists set up a provincial and highly religious sect, symbolizing the parochial colonial aesthetic that New England would become known for and, in the most visceral prophetic form, resemble the puritan townships of the Massachusetts Bay Colony. While earnestly working to establish the colony, these displaced Englishmen learned to deal with the many hardships of the time and location. Having to confront the vastly disparate seasons and the immense cold of the winter, they were, nonetheless, amazingly adept at forming peaceful relations with the area Indian tribes who taught these colonists the varied methods of keeping warm and producing food from the land. The Mohegans, from whom the area was purchased, were at their core, a remarkably peaceful tribe while, incongruously, at constant war with a neighboring group of Indians from Rhode Island, the Narragansetts.

It was during one of these many internecine tribal battles in 1643 that Norwich gained a measure of mythology and endowment to which a noted landmark stands symbolizing it to this day. In this battle, the Mohegans had been successful in pushing back an invasion by the Narragansetts such that many of these Rhode Island warriors were forced to retreat quickly onto the path from which they had come. These retreating forces were, however, able to somehow trap the Mohegan leader Uncas and enclose him in an area that is today known as the Uncas Falls. Here, in retreat, Uncas amazingly leaped a forty-foot chasm over the Yantic River which has a deep cavernous and rock-strewn geology to its makeup still to this day. After performing this "Uncas Leap" and while observing from the other side, Uncas now saw that the pursuing Narragansetts weren't so fortunate with many of them leaping to their death in pursuit. This area today remains a well-maintained historical site with the "leap" area still able to be prominently viewed from a bridge over these majestic falls.

Eventually, the ever-expanding colonial township slowly changed from the farming and agricultural foothold that had defined its inception and adopted, instead, the industrialized model of many of the large neighboring cities in New England. The centralized location in the small downtown stretch at the intersection of the Thames River with the Yantic and Shetucket soon became known as Chelsea and was occupationally connected to the Norwichtown Green by two main roads carved out of the thick wooded landscape running north (named East and West roads in the 1600s and 1700s and known today as Broadway and Washington streets).

These colloquial thruways soon enabled regular travel to the river from the Green area and the other newly formed settlements in and around it and allowed the town to import and export efficiently, with easy waterway access to New York and Boston while also enjoying unparalleled access to and trade relationships with England that became suddenly and irreparably damaged with the Stamp Act of 1764.

As the seeds of revolution were slowly being sown, Norwich would become an active participant in the growing revolutionary counterculture and agitation with particular notoriety being added to the area by it being adjoined with the "Sons of Liberty"—that very same formidable assemblage headed by Revolutionary luminaries Samuel and John Adams. Local icons would soon become influential also in the Revolutionary movement and would create a historical legacy that Norwich could forever be proud of.

Samuel Huntington who, little known to history and certainly to the average contemporary, could be, technically, considered the first executive president of the United States. As the reigning president of the Continental Congress, as it was embodied in the early 1780s, Huntington at the time commanded the legislature and held sway over the armed forces. These, of course, are duties now clearly outlined in the present-day Constitution for the nationally elected president, but while in the early 1780s, when the Articles of Confederation were in effect, they dictated that this position be the eponymous executive leader of the country; in fact, a movement by the local Norwich Historical Society in 2005 attempted to raise national awareness for Huntington's legacy to be so endowed.

Huntington, prior to this and when a member of the Continental Congress, was also an original signer of the Declaration of Independence and influential in many of the policies that led to the adoption of the US Constitution in 1787.

Another Norwich historical beacon was the infamous Benedict Arnold, "traitor" to the revolutionary cause in 1778 but, unknown to only the most scrupulous of historians, a remarkable soldier who was overtly instrumental in many of the early military successes for the colonials in the Revolutionary War. Commanding the retaking of New York's Fort Ticonderoga in 1776 (a momentum shifting early victory) and militarily leading the stunning victory for the rebellion at the battle of Saratoga in 1777, Arnold was an amazing field tactician and leader while receiving little notoriety historically for his military capabilities. While seeing no upward mobility in the confused ranks of Washington's command, his sensitive psyche led him to revert to his English advocacy and to ultimately defect in 1779, forever embodying his name with the "traitor" sobriquet.

Both Huntington and Arnold would go on to be renowned Revolutionary War personalities and are acclaimed Norwich natives.

After the war, in 1784, Norwich would finally be established officially as a township and would witness a gradual but, nonetheless, impressive industrial buildup that would spread throughout the early nineteenth century. Numerous mills and other industrial pillars were established, and the area suddenly found itself enjoying prosperity never before realized, using its three-river makeup as the primary driver for its economic advancement.

By the time of the Civil War in 1861, Norwich had progressed economically and industrially such that it had become a New England industrial stalwart while still exuding a small-town charm, a trait separating it from the larger surrounding New England cities. The war effort, meanwhile, and its need for armaments and textiles and other supplies ensured that the town would continue to remain salient even with many of its young, sadly, dying on far-off southern battlefields.

With the town supporting the war and stridently maintaining its standing as a leading northern abolitionist institution, it would also claim, as a native son incredibly, a future vice president.

Lafayette Foster, a US Senator from Norwich elected in 1854, so happened to be the Senate president pro tempore in 1865 when President Abraham Lincoln was assassinated. The line of presidential succession in that era had the Senate pro tempore following the vice-president (the Speaker of the House now follows the vice president in the modern lineage of presidential succession), thus Foster became technically the standing vice president under the new commander in chief, Andrew Johnson. Further, and amazingly, had the assassination plot that John Wilkes Booth envisioned been successful and Vice President Johnson also murdered as planned, Norwich's Foster would then have been elevated to president, and history as we now know it would certainly have been altered.

While the political intrigue was playing out at the national level, Norwich was still progressing impressively on the economic front. Adding to the town's industrial boom was the advent of the national railroad system. Local rail lines were soon springing up and being rapidly established from the center of town north to Massachusetts, south to New London and, eventually, outward to New Haven, Bridgeport and New York making Norwich a recognized and significant rail hub by the 1870s.

This forming of a railway stronghold helped to further promote the town as a leader in Connecticut industry but would give it a short-lived prominence and stature that endured only as long as this opaque "pre-technology" age lasted.

Once the late nineteenth and early twentieth century technological explosion occurred, and it became clear that this expansion was beyond

Norwich's capability to maintain, it would soon become evident that the extreme industrial standard that just a short while ago seemed so assured for the town was now also, sadly, evidence of its downfall. This gradual and inevitable onset of economic decline would now become more and more prominent in the city as the twentieth century progressed.

In the meantime though, while the town's huge import/export business was still at its zenith, Norwich would find it necessary to expand its compact physical borders to account for the large immigrant influx that had begun to manifest. Stretching both to the east and northeast, where communities developed to become today's suburbs of Taftville, Greenville, and Preston and also to the west, where many new ethnic neighborhoods would congeal to form a melting pot of social and cultural diversity, Norwich found itself rapidly growing, particularly westward, such that its confines now broadened all the way to the upper Yantic River.

Later, and as automobile travel predominated local transportation, an intricate highway access system was built and later expanded upon to the west and northwest side of town, becoming the acknowledged starting points in southeastern Connecticut for trips to Hartford and areas west and south while ultimately intersecting with the serpentine Interstate 95 as it stretched across Connecticut's southern border.

And as with all strong urban, economic, and social expansion, leisure activities would soon come to take on an increasingly important social and cultural significance with the Norwich townspeople proving to be no exception. For the growing populous, it seemed, a need for recreation and relaxation would not only act to further the overall perception of a city enjoying economic growth but would also provide a more-satisfactory outlay for their tax dollars, all the while furnishing a rather majestic and picturesque symbol of their government investment.

Parks and smaller areas for respite now started to spring up around town with the largest being Mohegan Park, named after the native inhabitants that the area was originally purchased from. For many years, prior to becoming the vast recreational retreat that it's become today, this area was a privately owned, tree-filled enclave encompassing approximately five hundred acres. Situated in the northern part of the township and at the extreme high point in terms of elevation (approximately 244 feet above sea level and 234 feet above the downtown area), the northernmost part of the park harbors an abundant supply of natural springs and creeks, with the largest being a substantial rock outcropping brook at the northwest part of the area. These natural headwaters all converge in the general middle park area and course naturally to the south end where they combine and flow downward in a general southerly direction toward the center of downtown as the natural land contour lowers, ultimately allowing this outflow to continue through the center of town and emptying into the Shetucket River.

Before today's strict flood control measures had been established, unabated brook flow had established a comparatively smaller pond area southeast of the park (later called the "skating pond" by the locals), which continued farther into an area that is today occupied by the Mohegan apartment complex, but, back then, made up Moore's ice pond (a place where winter ice was expeditiously smashed and cut up to supply the local area ice boxes) and became (later) land that a local philanthropist, Salvatore Colonna, purchased and converted into a baseball field.

A comparatively small pond, called Turner's Pond, which accepted Moore's pond flow via a waterfall located at present-day Brook Street flowed via a brook past today's Centennial Square, where a small business called Ossawan Mill would use an offshoot to feed its waterwheel. This brook then flowed down to form two small "lakes" where the Lake Street playground now resides. These lakes were collectively and ironically called "Spaulding Pond" (similarly named but geographically different from the name of the large expanse currently at Mohegan Park), and the outflow from these small bodies of water continued down present-day Pond Street and onto Franklin Street where yet another pond was formed as the town elevation now stabilized at approximately ten feet above sea level.

From this upper Franklin Street pond location, flows would continue to meander along today's Franklin Street at about where D'Elia's Bakery currently resides and eventually downward into present day Franklin Square to accumulate into the expanse currently encompassed by the large traffic circle. This area, in the early nineteenth century, was called, genuinely enough, "Swallow-All" as during these early days it would become the natural location for all of the abundant downtown drainage waters and the spot where most spring and summer floodwaters would also amass, causing such high water levels that the area was sometimes questionably able to "swallow" all of the water. From here, the inevitable body of water in the square would take the short and narrow path to the Shetucket River via the circuit that would eventually become the present-day city street called Rose Alley.

In 1853, two prescient but otherwise small-time Norwich entrepreneurs saw an opportunity to enhance their diminutive downtown enterprises by enlarging a small wooden dam that had been erected in 1833 at the south end of the park. This new and significantly larger earthen dam was ultimately created to be able to hold back the plentiful spring-fed headwaters, thus creating a large body of water that would allow a continuous controlled flow out of the park and which would allow an endless source of water for the downtown area to be used, as needed, by the businesses there.

Pedediah Spaulding and Henry Allen owned both a wood-turning business and machine shop in the general area of what is now upper Franklin Street and Chestnut Street and by using what would be this abundant source of water, sought to greatly enhance their business efficiency. By harvesting these outflows as a hydraulic driving force for water wheels, this power would in turn drive machinery and, in their grand concept, remove the human element from the manufacturing equation, thus greatly expanding the capability of both enterprises.

After Spaulding and Allen purchased the park area and built their large earthen dam, they left a small pipe opening at the bottom of the structure for this continuous outflow.

Nowhere in the record[1] however, is there any discussion or conclusion regarding specific design criteria, safety for the downtown area, or contingencies if this dam were to fail. Further, there is no available record of this dam ever being required to meet any local, state or federal code requirements or of any program of inspections or of persons being responsible for its integrity.

From this, one can only conclude then that this dam was built strictly for business purposes, with structural integrity or failure circumstances downstream, either secondary or not considered. Combined with the

---

[1]   This is the 'record' as far as my research would allow me to go.

avoidance of some seemingly common structural requirements such as saturation instrumentation, this dam looks to have had little in the way of essentials for a structure of this size and, when later sold to the city, would continue to be ignored in terms of inspections or maintenance that could have possibly avoided the 1963 break. All of these conjectures would later be discussed as significant and ultimately life-costing measures by the victim's families and town officials during the post flood investigation. None of it, unfortunately, would be addressed legally until the post-collapse jurisprudence nearly three years later.

After completion of the dam, Spaulding and Allen then used the ponds at Lake Street (which were, as mentioned, fed continuously from this park outflow) for their water supply, and for over a half century, the businesses in the upper Franklin and Chestnut Street areas enjoyed this natural hydraulic power that "furnished energy for the running of various contrivances . . ."

After the turn of the century and on into the early part of the 1900s, these water franchises (as the lakes and their supply flows were then known) would become less and less important. Electricity was slowly replacing water as the conventional power source, and these brooks and lakes became, instead, a dumping ground for raw sewage.

As the town inevitably expanded, the city decided that routing this Spaulding Pond outflow through underground piping would not only greatly enhance the available area for housing development, as urban expansion was booming at an enormous rate, but would also solve the growing health issues associated with the raw sewage.

Ultimately then, the pond areas on Lake Street were filled in and the brooks that fed it from the park were piped underground. Now and for all the years to come, the pond outflow would traverse underground to its outlet into the Shetucket River at Rose Alley.

But before this decision to re-pipe the pond outflows had occurred and sometime in the late nineteenth century, Spaulding would sell his business and his interests in the water franchise to a Charles W. Comstock. Henry Allen, meanwhile, had already sold his interests to a George Reynolds who, in turn, sold his rights and his interests in Spaulding Pond to a team of brothers from the city. It was Comstock who partnered with these brothers

(Nathan S., Alpheus, and Nathan G. Gilbert), new owners themselves of a prosperous wood-turning business on Chestnut Street, that sold the land that included Spaulding Pond to the city in 1906. Their rationale for selling at this point was that the pond and dam had outlived its usefulness; electricity was now the rage and used abundantly for business power, while the sanitation issues associated with the large open water areas went beyond the Gilbert's desire or means to deal with.

And so it was, in the charmingly overwrought legal language of the era, that these brothers were able to deed this land to the city:

TO ALL PEOPLE TO WHOM THESE PRESENTS SHALL COME GREETING:

KNOW YE that we NATHAN S. GILBERT, S. ALPHEUS GILBERT and NATHAN G. GILBERT from the Town of Norwich in the County of New London, State of Connecticut for the consideration of One Hundred Dollars received to our full satisfaction from the City of Norwich, a body corporate and incorporated, and located in New London County, State of Connecticut do give, grant, bargain, sell and confirm unto said City of Norwich an undivided half part of two certain tracts or parcels of land bounded and described as follows, to wit . . . etc.

It was after paying this astronomical sum of $100 and signing that magnificently baroque document that the city, as its first action under the new ownership, decided to enclose the brooks and fill in the lakes while also piping the water flow underground.

Also, with the town now owning the park and its vast area for expansion, the search was on for its potential use. Soon realizing the virtues that a large park would bring, city leaders decided to make this beautifully forested area a retreat for recreation and relaxation. Carved dirt roads soon abounded throughout the area appended with large pine trees dwarfing them while an abundance of forested woodland surrounded the large pond, giving it the feel of a mountain retreat. A large gazebo pavilion on the west end of the pond was soon erected, which hosted numerous family parties, and soon a small zoo was built to enrapture the young. In just a short time, this park became not only a getaway but also a rather majestic symbol of the town's prosperity. The pond itself would become a magnet for the swimming and fishing crowd as the townspeople all seemed to flock here, regardless of the time of week, to enjoy this forested retreat right in the middle of their booming city.

While the city suddenly had this beatific area for enjoyment, it now also had to contend with the rather large unknown dam that Spaulding and Allen had quickly erected sixty years hence. This earthen dam, which was sometimes called a "gravity dam" and had been supplemented in its construction with rock, stone, and the afore mentioned riprap, held little in the way of official documentation or design paperwork for the city to base any meaningful inspection criteria on.

For fortification, it had piles of earthen content sloping downward at an approximate forty-five degree angle from the top of its wall. After it had been built in 1853, the total pond area encompassed thirteen acres and held over forty-five million gallons of water. The dam, at the time the town purchased it in 1906, was over fifty years old but was still considered quite significant as a water control structure, as it was over forty feet wide at its base and tapered to a twelve-foot-wide causeway at the top, maintaining a height of approximately twenty feet and a length of 217 feet.

Again, what was notable and important was that no saturation monitoring instrumentation was ever installed, a feature that had become common for large earthen dams in the early twentieth century. This instrumentation, when properly installed and monitored, measured the amount of moisture that could inevitably saturate the earthen content and was equipment that would allow sooner diagnosis of any "seep through," thus avoiding more-serious problems (a calculated 4 percent saturation content was considered lethal. Engineers later estimated that the percentage of saturation at the time of the dam break was greater than 10 percent). Unfortunately, and as it happened, this lack of monitoring instrumentation would prove fatal over a half century later.

CHAPTER 3

"Well, It's Seeped Before . . ."

THROUGHOUT THE YEARS prior to and after the 1906 purchase of the park, occurrences of severe weather that would cause leak through and minor seepage had been observed from time to time at the dam structure. One particularly harrowing scare came in 1889 when heavy downpours throughout the area caused park workers to panic about overflow, dam leakage, and collapse. George Reynolds, a Norwich businessman who still had a small monetary investment in the dam at this time, reassured the city that its integrity was sound in a letter published in the Norwich newspaper:

> I found the dam as firm and safe as ever. As there are no ponds above it and as the stream which supplies it drains only a very small area, the reservoir does not feel the effect of large rains nor is it subject to sudden freshets (flooding). Even the continuous rains of the past week raised the water only a foot. The water which runs out from under the dam and which many are apt to think comes from a leak, comes from the gateway which is usually allowed to remain open a few inches to supply water to the factories below.

Since none of these leakage or seepage events had any evidence of the unified engineering belief that coincident erosion brought, no concern was raised nor, significantly, was anything done to address it. It was seemingly taken for granted by all involved that earthen dams "sometimes seep."

Starting, though, in 1949, significant changes to the dam's geometry would begin to occur that would have latent affects on its integrity. The city would decide, that year, to build a three-foot-by-eighteen-inch block wall at the top of its concrete spillway; this concrete spillway had replaced a natural earthen spillway that had been a part of the original structure in 1930. A dam spillway is a normally constructed component (either interior or part of its exterior physical structure) to remove water in the event of large rainfalls or ice melts that add significant water inventory behind the dam, posing a pressure threat to its bounding face. The resurfacing of the Spaulding Pond Dam spillway to concrete from its previous earthen body meant that any natural overflow would now proceed much more smoothly and with far less "system resistance" than its earthen counterpart would have provided.

Also, that same year (1949), a small wading pool to the west of the pond was constructed, which required the building of a concrete retaining wall along the west end of the pond, a wall that would extend north of the dam approximately one hundred feet. To accomplish this, the pond was necessarily drained to approximately half its inventory.

When the retaining wall was completed, the pond level was raised again, but now elevated nearly eighteen inches higher, taking credit for the new block wall attached to the spillway. These changes, all told, had the longer-term effect of raising total pressure felt by the dam's north face by 94 psi. True, this block wall and subsequent level increase added total water area to the pond proper and furthered recreational activities but, it was later estimated, increased pressure on the dam beyond its true design capability and figured greatly in the overall weakening of the structure.

Another factor added by this pressure increase was the case of the "east side crest." Designed as a part of the original structure, if one were to stand on the west side of the north face and look due east along the interior of the dam's top surface, one would notice a concavity or crest southward about three-fourths of the way down your viewing point. It "dipped in" and came back out before completing its course at its termination at the east end. This concavity, it was also later estimated, would take the brunt of this new pressure increase on the north face and was located exactly where the dam ultimately breached.

In 1955, in an effort to preclude further "seepage" of the brown-murky water that had been perpetually leaking from the base of the downstream side of the dam, a rock wall, eight-feet in height, was built. This gave the visceral image of the downstream earthen content now sloping to the top of this new wall and, it was thought, more stability. But what it accomplished, in reality, was to literally "push" the leakage pressure upwards to the extent that the earthen content above it now had to deal with this additional force.

Thirteen years later, in September 1962, work was initiated to replace an old cedar post fence, which had been part of a wooden stockade of rose arbors making up a scenic passageway across the top of the dam. When this replacement work commenced, suddenly the first real clue as to the accumulated saturation of the dam and the eventual failure became blatantly evident, albeit unannounced. The old fence had postholes that had penetrated the dam's top surface by approximately two to three feet. As these old rotted cedar posts were removed, mud and water was observed in several of the holes, a sure and disturbing sign of earthen saturation.

Also, beginning at about this time, the city had decided to install a water pipeline in a west-to-east run across the causeway to establish a water feed to the eastern side of the pond area that would provide flow for a fountain on that side. The trench that would house this pipeline was designed to penetrate the top surface of the dam approximately three feet and would be excavated about two feet in width. Once digging began however, mud and water, again, was observed. Pictures post breach show that large rocks, incredibly, were removed from the earthen content as this trench was dug; engineers later agreed that these accumulated actions had the overall effect of severely weakening the dam's integrity.

This pipeline trench was curiously abandoned in December 1962 (it's not clear from the existing record what caused its termination), and it was never filled back in; however, it later became full of spoil and rainwater. In the winter, only a few months before the dam breached, this trench, with the back-fill water, became frozen, causing expansion of the earthen area around it and undoubtedly added to the overall weakening of the structure in that specific area.[2]

---

2   This certainly is conjecture on my part but a later discussion with Dr. Steven Poulos, a Harvard soils professor at the time, confirmed that this trench, in fact, did abundantly add to the weakening of the structure in the exact location of the breach. His rationale was that if this trench was three feet in depth and never filled in and water subsequently settled into it, it would be only reasonable to conclude that the moisture would also invade farther down into the earthen content. The breach occurred only three more feet directly below this area so with the cold weather freezing this moisture and thus expanding it . . .

THOMAS MOODY, JR.

All of these instances of mud and water found within the dam's core were either dismissed or categorized within the sphere of the overall seepage occurrences—things that were seemingly just a part of the earthen dam's makeup.

Another completely misunderstood and entirely dangerous challenge to the dam's dynamic was the allowance of trees and other wild shrubs to grow unabated on its earthen southern face. Some of these outgrowths would extend and have root structures of a comparatively significant size, being allowed to expand unchecked essentially since the original 1853 construction. Engineers would later point to this seemingly innocuous occurrence as only adding to the deterioration of the dam's integrity.

In 1966, after having studied the geological aesthetics of the collapse and testifying under oath in Norwich Superior court, a soil mechanics professor from Harvard, Dr. Steven Poulos, warned that these blatant symptoms should have been enough, clearly, to alarm the Public Works Department and city leaders as to the disturbing situation at the dam. Nothing, however, was ever documented that addressed the moisture found during the posthole or trench digging in 1962. Neither was anything brought out that observed the tree outgrowth on the southern face as potentially damaging.

Separate engineers meanwhile, specifically contracted to analyze the collapse of the dam and abundantly knowledgeable in this type of earthen structure, agreed that without the aforementioned saturation instrumentation, the dam, with all of these past instances of saturation evident, could have easily come apart structurally, at any moment, essentially, from 1949 on.

And so it was on this Wednesday, March 6, 1963, that Norwich Public Works foreman Monroe Cilley first noticed leakage coming from the southeast side of the dam. After a day of digging ditches in and around the park and checking catch basins throughout the area, Cilley, along with fellow employee Clarence Vantour, returned to the dam at around 4:00 p.m. to check the spillway for trees, debris, or other obstructions following the day's saturating rains.

The spillway, still with its 1949 modified eighteen-inch extension block at the top, was found this afternoon, by Cilley and Vantour, to be mired in leaves and branches from the heavy rains, requiring a quick and thorough cleanout. This they proceeded to do as daylight was rapidly waning.

Farther downstream, the "skating pond" a large, flat area that was the natural overflow reservoir approximately a quarter mile southeast of the dam and was originally part of the primary brook flow out of the park, was also very full this day.

Completed in 1911 by the city after recognizing the need for additional flood control, this area became a rather large water expanse, and it was not long after this 1911 work that the site adopted its sobriquet as it seemed perfectly sized and suited for the area youth to enjoy winter ice-skating activities.

The small dam controlling its size tapered in height from approximately four feet to six running west-to-east at a length of approximately fifty feet and had a two-foot diameter drainage pipe at the bottom along with a concrete spillway at its west side, which acted to abate the overflow from running onto Mohegan Park Road, an alternate entrance (from the "main" park entry road from Reynolds Road) that ran northwest to southeast out of the park and one that would play a telling role in the coming tragedy.

This dam had a concrete face on its water side and earthen filler downstream as the land contour tapered drastically downward from this point, thus it protruded upward when viewed from the northern portion of Mohegan Park Road. It also had slabs embedded atop the concrete portion for the addition of two-by-four wooden boards that would, ostensibly, add height to the structure in times of minor overflow. This man-made addition also, of course, allowed the area youth to mischievously remove the boards, thereby allowing the overflow to trickle down Mohegan Park Road causing minor flooding and antagonizing the area residents.

Much had been made in recent years about the extensive cracking in the concrete on the pond side of the structure, however. This concrete slab, part of the original 1911 configuration, tapered from the top at an approximate thirty degree angle inward to the pond about twenty feet giving it a base thickness of approximately thirty feet. Worries about a break of this dam concerned the area residents such that many "inspections" had been mandated and conducted, all, though, by non qualified officials. If the Connecticut State Water Resources Commission didn't have qualified resources available for the "big dam" at Spaulding Pond, they certainly couldn't spare experts for this smaller, minor one.

As it turned out, city engineers would conclude over and over again that this dam was safe and that the cracking, although obvious, was only surface and not deep enough to cause leak-by. Nevertheless, it became a constant source of complaints for the Public Works Department and, in the end, an ironic twist to the coming disaster.

Now as Cilley and Vantour continued to remove debris from the Spaulding Pond spillway, they did note, however, that the water level was rushing over the block wall and flowing rapidly, undoubtedly due to the heavy recent rains. Although a little worrisome to witness water flowing this briskly and essentially burying the spillway block wall, they both also agreed, at this point, that it was not destructive enough to raise an alarm.

In the immediate downstream area of the dam, there was a small, gravel-based, square duck pond, which now, upon closer observation, was also immensely flooded over. The two men initially attributed this to the recent torrential rains, as indeed it was sprinkling even now; but observing the dam up close, Cilley now noticed that water was clearly trickling through it on the eastern end at a point above the southern retaining wall and down the south face and into the small pond. Somewhat alarmed, he now suggested that he and Vantour get out of their truck and perform an inspection at closer range.

The south face of the dam, as mentioned earlier, sloped at approximately forty degrees from its top down to the top of the rock wall base. With the total height of the dam being twenty feet and the rock wall being eight, this slope encompassed twelve feet of earthen content. This day, with snow and ice still perpetuating most of the slope and with the aforementioned tree and brush population, it was rather observant of Cilley to determine this leakage point so quickly.

The two men now climbed to the eastern end of the structure where they observed, even in that thin layer of snow that still attached itself to the surface and in the ever increasing darkness, unmistakable seepage coming through at a point about six feet down from the top of the dam at a small, thin gap in the dirt; a small rupture of about five inches in length.

Returning to their truck, Cilley and Vantour now decided that some relief should be quickly established to ease pressure on the inside face of the dam and that notification to their superiors of this finding was essential.

The valve at the bottom of the dam (the one that had been the original gateway to control water flow to the city in 1853) was still, at this point, the one used to control level in Spaulding Pond and, when opened, drained it into the duck pond and further onto a small road south of it. The opening of this valve, it was hoped, would also relieve pressure from the northern face of the structure and when Vantour, this afternoon, manually opened it, the brisk water flow that ensued served to optimistically alleviate the seepage.

While Vantour was at the bottom of the dam attending to the valve, Cilley, now back in the truck, radioed ahead to city foreman Patsy Ferra whose office was at the Public Works garage on Brook Street about a mile and half away. Ferra, a man in his sixties and near retirement, was a short, round man with striking Italian features and had been a hardened city employee nearly all his adult life.

Explaining the small rupture and their actions taken thus far, Cilley recommended that Ferra personally come to the park and inspect the dam himself. Arriving approximately ten minutes later, Ferra was led out to the leakage point by Cilley where Ferra himself, having personally observed dam seepage previously, commented somewhat benignly, "Well, it's seeped before."

Observing the small hole for a few minutes more and discussing it with his workers, Ferra attributed this new leakage episode to the recent extreme weather. Asking them to keep an eye on it for the remainder of their shift and discussing the spillway and catch basins around the park, he then got back into his truck and returned to the garage on Brook Street.

At the downtown office of the *Hartford Times* newspaper, meanwhile (on 46 Broadway, across the street from today's Dime Savings Bank building), young Norwich affiliate reporter Dennis Riley was at his desk, routinely forwarding teletypes to his main Hartford office for that day's deadline when the telephone suddenly rang. Picking it up, he heard the familiar voice of Jim Riley (no relation) who was the radio dispatcher for the Norwich Public Works Department up at the Brooks Street garage. Jim Riley was a known and useful source to Dennis, one who had helped him many times previously with various leads on public works projects that were either in the preliminary stages and would cost untold amounts of unbudgeted money or, more newspaper worthy, "in the ditch and over budget." Proving to be true on most counts, Jim became a legitimate and trusted source of information and one Dennis listened to intently for new information.

Today, however, Jim seemed very agitated and unusually excited: he was going on and on about the Spaulding Pond Dam and that the on-duty foreman (Ferra) had just come back from Mohegan Park talking about it and that it was leaking and that Ferra's workers there thought it could rupture. Dennis, perhaps distracted by his work, or most probably not taking Jim seriously due to his overexcited tone, placated him as best he could and, asking him to keep him posted, soon hung up.

Frank Majewski, a young Public Works employee, was out in his city truck driving through town this late afternoon, finishing up his assignments for the day and heading back toward the Brook Street garage when he started to hear some mildly disturbing radio chatter concerning the dam at Mohegan Park. These reports seemed to be more pointed than the usual monotone radio conversations, and this caught Frank's attention. This traffic between the office and Mohegan Park workers sounded as if they were discussing a leak at the dam and that inspections by park workers were confirming it. After an hour or so of silence, subsequently, and not hearing any crucial follow-up information as he neared the Brook Street office, he decided to give it no further thought and he dropped off his truck and went home.

Norwich Public Works director Harold Walz, meanwhile, had started this day with a conference in Hamden which he attended with his assistant William Gallagher, a town about sixty miles west of Norwich. After adjournment of this meeting (which included Public Works directors from other neighboring towns) and as he was returning to Norwich, he made contact with the Brooks Street garage for an update. The city car that he was driving had been outfitted with a two-way radio system, and Walz was now concerned that the day's additional rains had caused even more flooding in the city. And as he was briefed, by radio dispatcher Jim Riley, on the current conditions, he was worried that these additional rains had exacerbated the efforts that his team had already proffered to alleviate this flooding. The local lakes and ponds were already brimming to full capacity, and any addition, he knew, could cause further flooding. No mention of Spaulding Pond or its condition, however, was reported in this radio briefing.

Arriving in town at about 5:45 p.m., Walz proceeded directly to the Brook Street garage where, in a conversation with foreman Ferra, he learned of, in addition to the local flooding problems, the situation at the dam. Told that Ferra had witnessed minor seepage and rapid overflow of the spillway, Walz immediately got back into his car and made his way up to the park, arriving there at about 6:15 p.m. Once there, Walz noticed Cilley and another park employee, Arthur Aldi, placing road block barriers and flares on both sides of the small road south of the duck pond (the road that was now flooded after Clarence Vantour had earlier opened the dam relief valve).

Walz now got out of his car and made his way out to the top of the dam on the east side. Venturing over the side, he later reported that the footing was "hazardous" as the slope still had a layer of ice and snow. Nevertheless, he climbed down to just above the leakage point. Looking through that same snow cover, he now saw the seepage coming from the spot that Cilley, Vantour, and Ferra had earlier observed. Having also seen leakage previously (as Ferra had) and noticing, with his flashlight, that there was a notable lack of earthen erosion on the south face, Walz was not immediately alarmed. Inspecting the leak and its immediate surroundings for about five minutes, he then got back into his car and drove down to where Cilley and Aldi were working. Arriving there, the park workers informed Walz that no observable change in the dam dynamic or physical makeup had occurred throughout the remainder of the day from when they had first spotted the leakage and the only thing that concerned them was the still abundant spillway flow, currently roaring past the dam and causing the duck-pond to overflow and the road south of it to become flooded.

Convinced now that this dam seepage was not something out of the ordinary, Walz decided that he would go home for dinner and then return to the city afterward to continue monitoring it and other areas locally for any evidence of flood induced damage.

While leaving the park, Walz overheard a radio call asking for assistance with locating barricades for flooded areas on New London Turnpike in the Thamesville section south of town. Arriving there, he spoke with a Connecticut state trooper and personally inspected these flood conditions. Convinced that everything was under control here, he then drove his city-owned car back to town where his personal car was parked on 505 Main Street. This was on the other side of the city, and here he now switched vehicles to drive to his home in Preston for dinner.

Now at home and at about 7:30 p.m. while eating his dinner, Walz's wife answered a phone call from the *Norwich Bulletin* newspaper inquiring about a reported leak at the Spaulding Pond Dam. Immediately wondering how the local press got wind of this, he nevertheless called them back after his meal and told them that the leak was minor and of no immediate concern. He did, however, tell them that he planned to monitor the dam and other flooded areas in town throughout the night.

Following dinner and at about 8:00 p.m., Walz picked up his son-in-law John Peck and left his home in Preston for an inspection of the town and the dam. Meeting acting city manager Orrin Carashick by chance at about 8:30 p.m. Walz discussed the local flood damage with him. Neither at this point made mention of the situation at Spaulding Pond. After leaving Carashick and performing some additional local inspections, Walz finally made his way up to Mohegan Park shortly after 9:00 p.m.

As he entered the park on Mohegan Park Road, driving past the skating pond and travelling north to the immediate east of the dam, he suddenly heard a sound that gave him pause. Slowing his car and opening his window, he heard the unmistakable and unnerving sound of rushing water. Clearly concerned, he quickly maneuvered his headlights onto the south face of the dam, and there he now saw water gushing out of a fist-sized hole above the base rock wall. This breach was in a different location from where he had observed the earlier seepage; it was lower and more easterly and thus presented a whole new and dangerous development in the dam's integrity.

Instantly understanding that he had a catastrophic problem on his hands, one with enormous consequences, Walz, again in his personal car and with no radio, immediately raced into action. Turning his car around and dashing down to the Public Works garage on Brook Street., he rushed in and spoke with night foreman Angelo Yeitz, immediately ordering him to send a worker back up to the dam. "I just came down from the dam and we might lose it." he exclaimed.

Yeitz immediately got on the garage's radio system and called worker Charles Phoenix, requesting his location. Phoenix responded that he was in his city truck headed north-east on Eighth Street in the Greenville section of town. Realizing that this was very close to Mohegan Park, Yeitz then ordered him to go up there with specific instructions to report all damages, however minor, at once, concerning the dam.

With Phoenix now rapidly en route to the park, Walz then placed a call at about 9:20 p.m. to the Norwich City Police Station. On-duty captain James Casey took the call and listened as Walz fervently informed him of the dam leakage ("It might go!") while adding an adamant recommendation that an alert be sent out to the townspeople living in the immediate downstream areas of North Street, East Baltic Street, and Curtis Street. The dam was now leaking severely and could possibly collapse, therefore the folks in these areas should be ready to evacuate quickly.

While speaking with Casey, Walz received another important phone call at the garage. This was from Monroe Cilley, he of the original leak discovery, who was now calling after having gone home following his normal shift and who had returned later to check on the leak. His frantic phone call now was to inform anyone at the garage that he had just left the dam and saw "a white foam-like stream" jetting from it. "When I saw that, I was scared and got out of there," he reported later. When Walz spoke with him on the phone, he told him that he had also just returned from the dam and knew about the "stream from the dam."

Walz, clearly flustered and in a fury now, then called the city manager's office where he spoke with alderman Martin Rutchik and then he called the *Norwich Bulletin* back, this time to inform them that the situation was, contrary to his earlier report, in fact dire; Phoenix, meanwhile, had arrived at the dam and was now radioing back to the garage that "the situation was bad."

Casey, at the police station, immediately started placing phone calls to people on Curtis Street with whom he was personally acquainted and asked them to spread the word of the potential dam collapse in and around that area. He then radioed Norwich Police cruiser #2 driven by officer Richard Paradis with orders to pick up fellow officer Joseph Dluzniewski who was on foot duty downtown and proceed to Mohegan Park Road to broadcast an alert over his cruiser loud speaker. Paradis soon reported back that his loud speaker in cruiser #2 was not having much effect; Casey ordered him, instead, to patrol up and down Mohegan Park Road with his siren "wide open" while using his loud speaker, which Paradis soon confirmed seemed to be working better.

At the Bermuda green residence of young Pat (Kirby) Pellegrini at 79 Mohegan Park Road, the youthful mother of three was somewhat concerned this afternoon. A pretty redheaded woman who was just twenty-four years old and living in a house that she and her husband Americo "Chic" Pellegrini had built in 1958, her home was located on two spacious lots approximately three hundred yards southeast of the skating pond and encompassed about 1,300 square feet. The property had been in the Pellegrini family for some time having been given to Chic by his uncle John DePucchio. Chic's mother (his father was killed in a worksite blast in 1936) and second husband Nicola "Poppy" Romano would actually drive up to these lots (a journey of about a mile and a half from downtown) to visit Pat and Chic and tend to the gardens of which "Momma" Pellegrini annually maintained for many years thereafter.

Outgoing, gregarious, and a wonderfully engaging woman, Pat was Ronnie's cousin on his mother's side and had three of her own children: Danny at five and a half years, Tommy three and a half years and Joey who was an infant at three and a half months old and ill with the flu on this cold and rainy March 6. Patti, as she liked to be called, was an outspoken proponent herself of "right and wrong," a seemingly ingrained quality of Ronnie's side of the family, and one who had actively pursued improvement and betterment of her area (she had badgered the city, for example, to install light poles in the vicinity of the skating pond so that the area children would have some light and would therefore be safe while skating at the pond) as well as being an immensely intelligent woman who would later make a significant discovery and impact for her family with genealogy research leading to a revelation of Mayflower ancestors and Revolutionary War patriots.

This day, however, Patti had been on watch, observing through her large front window the brook flow across the street, which was the drainage point from the upstream skating pond, as it was now reaching flood conditions from the mercilessly inundating rains of the past few days. In immediate danger were her friends, the Marceau family, who had a small home on the south side of this brook and who were now victim to the rising water becoming more and more of an obstacle for escape down their long driveway to Glezan Street which was immediately southeast of Patti's house.

She also noticed, curiously, that many of the city Public Works Department trucks had been travelling rapidly on the Mohegan Park Road today in a much more frequent interval than normal. Racing to and from the park, this steady continuity became disconcerting and brought on a dread that, for the moment, was difficult for her to pinpoint.

Patti's husband, Chic, arrived home from work that day late in the afternoon and, while driving to his house from downtown, also noticed the heavy city truck traffic going to and from the park area. As he neared his house, he also observed that the intertwining brook network south of the skating pond and onward toward Colonna's field and North Street was very high with rain water and, in some spots, overflowing.

Chic was employed at Lamperell's Plumbing (ironically a business that would play a unique part in the evening's events), and as he now stepped out of his Lamperell-owned company truck, he surveyed the area surrounding his home. Walking up Curtis Street, he noted, with some neighbors as observation partners, that the fields between Curtis and Jennings streets to the east were curiously overfilled with rainwater. Backtracking now down Curtis Street to Mohegan Park Road and proceeding up to the skating pond dam outlet, he noticed that the brook outflow from the skating pond dam outlet piping was roaring with water, and the level was almost up to the road.

Upon entering his house, he said to Patti, "I've never seen rain and flooding like this before. I wonder if we should cancel the card game." The Pellegrinis had a weekly date with their friends for a game of cards. Tonight it was their turn to host, and Patti had been working all day preparing baked goodies for the game. Deciding that the weather wasn't quite so severe as to cancel the game, they ate a quick meal and prepared for their guests.

As guests arrived and the card game began, Patti, more concerned about Joey's illness and less about socializing, settled in instead to watch TV in the corner den. The *Dick Van Dyke* variety show was on that evening, and she was watching the comedy master employ a rendition of a classic Laurel and Hardy routine. Her two older children were asleep in their rooms, and young Joey was in a carriage in the hallway that connected the TV room with the kitchen. Patti wanted him close by, since he had been suffering from that bothersome cold most of the day and would only sleep sporadically. Now like most of the city residents, the Pellegrinis were settling in for a placid Wednesday evening, unaware that it was about to profoundly and unalterably change.

Back down in the city, meanwhile, Norwich police captain Casey, responding to Director Walz's specific pleas, called radio station WICH at about 9:25 p.m. to request that a citywide alert be broadcast. Casey was told, however, that since only one engineer was on duty, it would be problematic for it to happen immediately. This engineer, however, in a heroic act of industriousness, contacted the station management and explained the emergency situation to them such that they consequently contacted veteran station news director Ed Leonard.

Leonard, from his home in Montville, telephoned the Norwich police station and spoke directly with Captain Casey. Learning the details of the dam leak as it had progresses thus far, Leonard then called the radio station back and broadcast his alert, from his home, that went out over the airways at about 9:30 p.m.

Meanwhile, as Casey finished discussing the radio alert with Leonard, Director Walz now radioed back to the police station that Charles Phoenix was back on the line and reporting from the park that the dam "looked bad and seemed ready to go." Within minutes, Phoenix reported that the dam had, in fact, just collapsed, and both Walz and Casey, still on the line, went silent momentarily.

It was 9:37 p.m.

Engineers from the Connecticut State Water Resources Commission would later estimate that the consolidated pressure on the dam face at the time of the break was on the order of 360 million pounds or 180,000 tons. That force had clearly reached a point where the saturated dam structure could no longer stand it, and the wall, for all practical purposes, collapsed.

Although the contemporary record doesn't indicate Phoenix's observation, which assuredly was hindered by the lack of daylight, an observation made by one John Parke of the Pennsylvania South Fork Dam Company who witnessed the collapse of the similar earthen South Fork Dam near Pittsburgh, Pennsylvania, in 1889, and which is marvelously documented in David McCullough's seminal work *The Johnstown Flood* (Simon and Shuster, 1968), most likely and most succinctly describes Phoenix's view: "It is an erroneous opinion that the dam burst. It simply moved away. The whole dam seemed to push out at once. No, not a break, just one big push."

This breach now allowed a massive flow that resembled a wall of water being set free. The break would ultimately carve out a huge V-shaped hole in the eastern portion of the dam and would instantly destroy the rock wall in that section beneath it. A wall of water immediately dispersed through the area just south of it and then cascaded through the small duck pond while, in seconds, screamed through the canyons at the south end of the park, methodically tearing through the wooded terrain ahead of it, snapping trees, tossing large rocks, and picking up debris in its race southeasterly toward the skating pond.

If an observer were to be standing atop the small dam just south of the skating pond at just this point and looking northwest into the trees, he would see a cataclysmic wall of water suddenly crashing out of the heavy wilderness like a misplaced waterfall. This wave then pounded violently onto the skating pond and, as it had new and ample space to expand, pulverized the two-foot-thick ice blanket that had frozen onto it and sent the shattered ice upward and outward, ultimately crashing back down and sailing along now in its deadly flow as it rapidly filled this pond while heading toward the small earthen dam south of it.

THOMAS MOODY, JR.

As this rushing flow followed the natural land contour, a small portion of it diverted to the east where a smallish river, still with many of these ice chunks riding along the top, headed toward a tree-lined drop-off that made up the western side of Curtis Street. The freezing water in this offshoot then poured through the trees and down the slope, through the properties owned by the Viadella and Konikowski families, and turned southward now down Curtis Street, trapping officer Paradis in his police cruiser #2 after he had turned onto this road to sound the alarm.

This portion of the wave would ultimately cause immense flooding of the area, but due to the contour of the landscape, the large ice cakes that had been captured in its initial separation flow were gratefully left behind, trapped in the thick tree line back up on the slope. Had these chunks been able to flow down the hill and onto Curtis Street unimpeded, the Viadellas, Konikowskis and other homes here would have undoubtedly experienced major structure and property damage, along with potential fatalities.

The main flood flow meanwhile, still attempting to reclaim its hundred-year-old flow path that the dam had nullified, shifted somewhat and moved now in a more southerly direction. Inundating the wooded area south and east of the skating pond, the wave then rolled over the small concrete-earthen dam that was intended to control its level, all the while gathering ammunition to its already deadly arsenal as trees in and around this area were uprooted, while large boulders, which before the flood were haphazardly strewn about the landscape, now became joined in its battering flow.

As the water wave poured over the dam, part of this main flow cascaded southeasterly and came within thirty feet of the Algonquin Natural Gas supply station, which was built on a rather significant upturn in the terrain north of Mohegan Park Road. Supplying many homes in the area, this station, even today, is a regulating arm of the local gas service with a small house-shed with valves and gas lines routed into and out of it. Had the flood smashed into this station with any force at all, with its trees and ice chunks, structural damage could have created potential electrical sparks, which could have caused an explosion of immense proportions, enormously complicating an already disastrous situation.

At the Pellegrini residence just down the road, meanwhile, the kitchen card game was suddenly interrupted by a loud knocking on the door; Stanley Pawlak Jr. the Pellegrinis' next-door neighbor, was suddenly there warning them that the dam had let go. With the outside door open, everyone now heard the unmistakable roaring sounds of the floodwaters to their west. Patti, in the den, heard the commotion in the kitchen and, stepping into the hall, saw her husband and a couple of his friends coming rapidly toward her. "The dam let go, we have to get out," Chic said. The dam let go? Patti was confused as her immediate thought was that the skating pond dam, which was only a relatively small structure, had come apart (undoubtedly due to all that cracking concrete) and was causing all this excitement.

The men all rushed into the children's room to gather them up and just as quickly turned to hurry outside. As Patti watched, she quickly looked toward the baby carriage and saw that it was empty. "Where's the baby? Who has the baby?" she screamed. Chic urged her outside, assuring her that someone had gathered little Joey and was making their way toward the cars. "We heard the water rushing past. We grabbed kids that were in the house and just got out," card guest Paul Lamperell later reported.

As they made their way out the front door and onto the porch, they now heard and felt the ground shake from the amplified sound of the roaring water, very frightening now, as it raced through the skating pond and over the small dam. Watching in amazement as the ice, which moments ago had made up the smooth solidified frozen top layer of the skating pond, came crashing over the road and into the trees across the street, Patti, obliquely, observed one of her guests running down the front lawn toward the road with a bundle in his arms—this bundle clearly being the baby Joey.

In a panic, she now raced from the porch toward the man, "Pops" Fatone, one of the card playing guests. Pops had apparently grabbed the baby out of the carriage in his haste to get out and had now fallen near the edge of Mohegan Park Road. Struggling to regain his feet, Patti arrived just in time, ripping the baby from his arms while grabbing his shirt, desperately trying to pull him away as the floodwaters approached.

"Run! The water is bearing down on us!" she exclaimed. Rushing away from the road and with their backs now toward the oncoming water, the entire household, guests and all, rushed down Mohegan Park

Road to their neighbor's front lawn, the forewarning Pawlak's. Seeing the oncoming floodwaters pouring down Curtis Street in front of them, and still in dreadful anticipation of the waters inundating them from behind, Patti and the group suddenly feared that they would be trapped now from both sides. The Pawlaks' front lawn was, gratefully, on significantly higher ground, though; but it was still unclear to them to what extent the flood behind them would cover—would it wash all of them away?

While earnestly clutching to her youngest child, the indomitable and instinctively ironclad emotion felt by all mothers and one that would surface again only a short time later, this time with far different consequences, forced Patti to now look around frantically for her other two boys. One guest, wandering onto the Pawlaks' property now, held a large bundle wrapped in blankets—here thankfully was the second child; now where was the third?

The water, meanwhile, had become a river of destruction as it raced over Mohegan Park Road, ripping up chunks of road surface and, with all its damaging weapons, now poured onto the property south of the Pellegrini residence. Chic, meanwhile, concerned about his last unaccounted-for child as well, ran back towards his house, stepping through the now-numerous low-lying flooded expanses in the short distance, and after navigating this puddled minefield, noticed another figure running toward him, holding what appeared to be the third child. Relieved that everyone was safe and accounted for, they both turned and made their way back to the Pawlaks to be with the group and await the next episode in this unbelievable tragedy.

As the random violence and destruction of this tragic event was just now beginning, the Pellegrinis were the recipients of what little good fortune would come this night. The Pawlaks' house, where the group had amassed, was on a large-enough rise in the terrain that they were essentially on an island as flood flow careened to their left down Curtis Street, while to their right, the main flow surged over the road onward toward the city. The flood, it seemed, was going to gratefully flow right around them, and later, when they returned to their house, the Pellegrinis noted that there was, miraculously, nary a drop of water in their house.

Down in his Broadway office, *Hartford Times* reporter Dennis Riley was still at his desk finishing up business for the evening when the phone rang. Jim Reilly was again on the line and with the same excitement in his voice; this time, however, he exclaimed, "The dam just broke! You'd better get up there!" Stunned now and shaking his head in disbelief, Dennis, along with a visitor, Tom Sweeney, a friend who had stopped by after work and who would later become a noted local politician and ironically a next-door neighbor to the Moodys, quickly made his way to his car which was parked just outside on the street.

Not immediately understanding the consequences of the dam break or the logistics of the ensuing flood flow to the town, he headed down Broadway and turned left onto Main Street and then onto Franklin Square, unknowingly driving directly into the oncoming flow. Thinking initially that the best way to get to Mohegan Park and get a look at the dam would be to go up Franklin Street and then veer off on Boswell Avenue, he got to Centennial Square with the idea of heading north on Baltic Street. His thinking then was to go into the park from the southern side. Unbeknownst to him and, ultimately, being the beneficiary of extreme good fortune, Dennis would only escape the flood's initial battering by mere minutes.

Now as this main flow, unduly burdened with ice and rocks and trees, washed over Mohegan Park Road, completely ensconcing a large new concrete culvert built on the north side of the road just six years prior, it completely engulfed the baseball field where the present-day Mohegan apartment complex resides. This baseball field, owned by Salvatore Colonna, sat on what was previously Moore's ice pond and earlier, "Bates Pond" by the locals.

Colonna, who purchased this area in 1948, subsequently had it filled in and now sponsored the local Junior Major League baseball games that were held there. But because of its low-lying position and also due to the large natural brook that still flowed over, around, and under the field's north side, and because a downstream culvert was seemingly undersized, he was constantly having to deal with high water conditions and flooding and, therefore, became a constant nuisance to the city Public Works Department, demanding help in diverting this overflow away from his field.

The area to the immediate east of Colonna's field, also part of the original Bates property, was in the process, this day, of being landscaped, being cleared of trees and rocks. As a result, there were large mounds of dirt and mud all around, which added greatly to the downtown cleanup misery the next day. The twenty or so homes in and around here became instant flood victims as well, as cars were tossed about and damaged in this sudden onslaught.

Farther down, Richard Makowiecki of 14 North Street watched as his backyard became a swirling miasma of tree limbs, rocks, and large ice cakes. His backyard work shed was instantly smashed off of its foundation by the rushing mass of water and ice blocks, while his garden of small shrubs, which he had been raising for sale, was instantly swept away in the flow as well. The next day, he would be pictured in the *Norwich Bulletin*

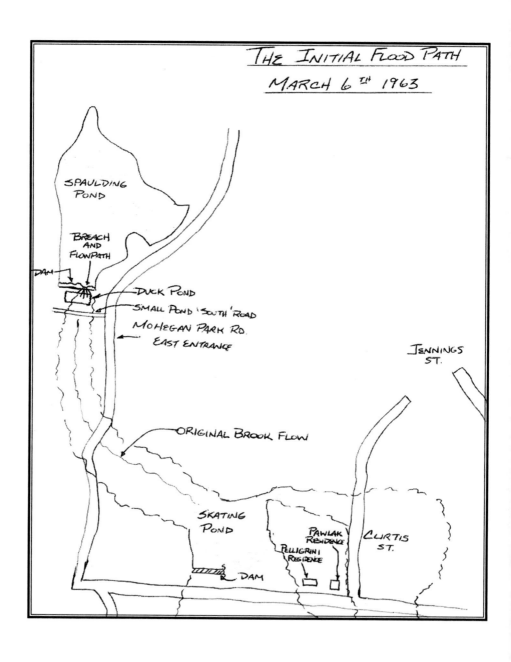

THE INITIAL FLOOD PATH

MARCH 6TH 1963

SPAULDING POND

BREACH AND FLOWPATH

DAM

DUCK POND

SMALL POND 'SOUTH' ROAD

MOHEGAN PARK RD.

EAST ENTRANCE

JENNINGS ST.

ORIGINAL BROOK FLOW

SKATING POND

PAWLAK RESIDENCE

PELLIGRINI RESIDENCE

CURTIS ST.

DAM

newspaper staring forlornly at the massive ruin in his backyard while standing on one of the left-behind ice chunks.

After carving large gullies in the manicured playing field and washing away any vestige of baseball ever being played there, Colonna's field was now a river of mud and muck. Flowing along to the land immediately south, the wave converged east of Baltic Street and headed down toward the Brook Street Public Works garage where Director Walz and the nightshift Public Works employees had been conducting last minute business.

Another culvert approximately 150 feet north off Hickory Street, situated almost evenly between Baltic and North Streets was now becoming completely inundated. Sized to handle merely mild rainwater overflow, the flood wave quickly overtook this rocked-in structure, popping its manhole covers off and eschewing raw sewage before the entire enterprise became one giant flush pipe while backing up the entire flow to East Baltic Street and North Street, causing immense flooding there.

As the flood crossed over Hickory Street, houses to the north and south of the road were immediately awash in the muddy onslaught. One man, stranded on his porch as the waters engulfed his house, yelled up in the direction of Baltic Street, which was still on dry ground "Stay there, honey. Don't try to get over here," he shouted out. At the same time, the woman, his daughter, was screaming, "Stay there, Daddy. They'll get to you!" In light of what was to occur next, it was miraculous that none of these homes were destroyed by the ice, tree limbs, and boulders that were now comprised in this flood flow and moving rapidly through the area as the homes here were essentially taking a direct hit.

Assaulting the city garage south of Brook Street (a plywood and aluminum makeshift structure that housed the offices of the department) with the immersed ice chunks and tree limbs acting like battering rams, the building, with its large facing surface area, became damaged instantly, and the equipment inside immediately saturated with the trucks and heavy gear in an adjacent garage suffering water inundation and exterior wreckage by the ice. Public Works director Walz, while still trying to coordinate his department's response, and three other workers who had stayed on station to the very last moment actually had to escape the engulfing flood flows through a window in the building, in a grim piece of irony, before it had become submerged with water.

Careening past the garage now and flowing southerly over Baltic Street and through the backyard of a small house at the corner of Baltic and Broad streets, the land contour forced the flow to take a modest turn southwesterly as it came upon Centennial Square. Here, this configuration allowed some of the water to diverge west where it attacked Broad Street and branched south to flow down Lake Street. This was the shin-deep flow that Ronnie and Honey Moody were experiencing as they were loading their children into the car. This small divergence, however, did little to mitigate the damaging effect of the main wave, as the Turner-Stanton Mill on the south side of Broad Street now stood directly in its deadly path.

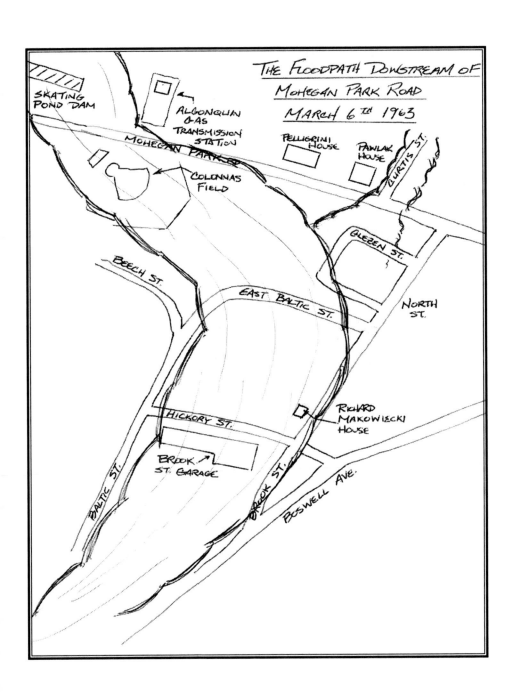

THE FLOODPATH DOWNSTREAM OF
MOHEGAN PARK ROAD
MARCH 6TH 1963

SKATING POND DAM

ALGONQUIN GAS TRANSMISSION STATION

MOHEGAN PARK RD

COLENNAS FIELD

PELLIGRINI HOUSE

PAWLAK HOUSE

CURTIS ST.

GLEZEN ST.

BEECH ST.

EAST BALTIC ST.

NORTH ST.

HICKORY ST.

BROOK ST. GARAGE

BALTIC ST.

BROOK ST.

RICHARD MAKOWIECKI HOUSE

BOSWELL AVE.

Built in 1888, the Turner-Stanton Mill Company was a producer of twine, string, yarn, and other textile materials largely serving the greater New England area. It employed approximately fifty people at this Broad Street plant of which eight had been assigned to run the evening shift (all of whom were at work this Wednesday evening).

Turner-Stanton was also one of the more-prosperous businesses in the downtown area in 1963 and one of the main contributors to the town's dwindling industrial sectors. The mill building itself was a large three-story red brick structure encompassing over three hundred thousand square feet with a substantial inventory of custom machinery and inventory. The structure was also notable physically as it was offset on its west side by a towering boiler smokestack that could be seen from many points around town and this, along with its somewhat gloomy outward appearance, gave the area a bleak and desolate industrial aesthetic that seemed to conflict with the congenial and communal surrounding area.

The front of the building, cordoned off by a chain-link fence topped with barbed wire, faced north onto Broad Street and was exposed directly to Centennial Square. The south side formed a precipitous drop-off downward onto the Lake Street playground.

With the abundance of thick ice blocks, large tree limbs, and boulders, all riding in an estimated twelve-foot-high water wave, the ground floor of the east side of the mill now took a direct hit as this watery mass smashed into it with a deadly force. It was 10:14 p.m., and its impact would be morbidly and forever recorded, as if frozen in time, by the employee punch clocks, which would be later dug out of the debris, stopped at that 10:14 p.m. timeframe when all electrical power in the facility had been instantly lost.

Torrents of the floodwater, meanwhile, were now encompassing Centennial Square and parts of Broad Street and Boswell Avenue. As the Turner Mill structure became surrounded by the water wave, all eight of its nightshift workers, upon hearing the unmistakable roar of the flood, raced to the third floor in massed chaotic confusion.

Once there and slowly realizing the desperation of their situation, they started calling out for help through the open windows as they saw the floodwaters engulf the structure. It soon became apparent however that

THOMAS MOODY, JR.

they would, in only the best of circumstances, be trapped inside for an indeterminately long period of time. Indeed, rescue for these folks now appeared beyond realistic as the engulfing water had made it impossible for anyone to reach them. "Had the workers gathered in another part of the building, as things developed, they might have escaped injury or death," an observer reported.

Benjamin Dubicki, who lived directly across from the mill on Broad Street, watched and listened as desperate cries went out to helpless observers. "It was awful, those people were yelling for help but there was nothing anyone could do for them. The people were yelling 'Help me! Save me!' but no one could get past that roaring stream of water."

Firemen and rescue workers soon arrived and attempted to approach the building, but even they could not get through the avalanche of water. Broad Street resident Mrs. Richard Celucci, who also lived across the street from the mill, observed in horror that "the lights went out . . . the building seemed to settle before collapsing." Her husband Richard: "You turned your head and the building was gone. The people in the building didn't know what hit them."

The mill, after seemingly withstanding the initial battering of ice, tree limbs and boulders, had, in fact and soon to be horribly realized by all in witness, been seriously damaged by the torrent of water as it now reached its menacing peak. "There just seemed to be smoke downstairs in the mill and then the building caved in."

This overwhelming flow appeared to be just too strong as the east side of the structure, horrifically, collapsed in sections under its own weight. As it fell, workers who had and those who had not made it to the third floor became victims to the sickening implosion.

Madlyne Atterbury, Alex Pobol, and Helen Roode, employees who had been fortunate enough to make it to the third floor, were nevertheless crushed and killed under the weight of the imploding structure, having ridden the collapsing assemblage to the basement. Their bodies, the next day, would take amazingly heroic efforts to extract as firemen and rescue volunteers had to navigate the still-formidable draining waters while balancing themselves on the increasingly unstable building debris.

Mrs. Atterbury at sixty-one years old, sadly, had been planning to retire from the mill in less than a month. "One part of the building just seemed to settle. All of a sudden, the lights and everything just seemed to go," reported Dubicki's father, Benjamin Sr. "People were hollering to be rescued. It was unbelievable." While sadly shaking his head, he sighed, "I never want to see anything like that again." Patrick Tedesco, a nearby resident also recounted, "I heard a loud boom. It looked like an ocean wave . . . foaming, bubbling water all over the place."

Theresa Moretti and Jean Bujnowski were second-shift workers who had also attempted to get to the third floor when the floodwaters hit. "Floors collapsed all around us before the building collapsed", Moretti exclaimed later. "We couldn't make it." By seemingly impossible luck, Moretti and Bujnowski were positioned in the building downfall such that as the walls started to disintegrate around them, "a shelter of boxes and girders formed a lein-to that saved our lives." Also saved, in this miraculous occurrence, was Mrs. Madeline Gordon.

These broken members formed a shelter for the three women, and though they suffered injuries, they were spared instant death. As the floodwaters increased in intensity, however, the three became at risk for drowning. "I was up to my chin in water," Mrs. Bujnowski explained. "I became delirious, talking to the water . . . please stay away, please stay away." Later when hope for survival was nearly lost "then all of a sudden just when we were frozen where we could feel nothing, we heard voices." After being taken to Backus Hospital, the water level was later determined to have risen to under her lower lip; another three inches, it was estimated, and she would have surely drowned.

After the east side of the building came down and as the full force of the flood now dispersed and headed south toward downtown, many who had survived the initial collapse were in shock over the incomprehensible devastation. "My friend! My friend! I kept calling to her! She didn't answer. I think she's dead" Theresa Moretti frantically cried out as she was extricated from the rubble after the water had receded somewhat: co-worker Anna Barrett was the friend Moretti was distraught over. Severely injured during the collapse, Mrs. Barrett was now helplessly trapped in the debris.

Having miraculously survived the initial trauma, Mrs. Barrett was later heroically rescued by an off-duty nurse, Richard Jaskiewcz. Mr.

Jaskiewcz, small and wiry in build and one of the many true heroes of this evening, managed to maneuver through the debris, feeling around for human limbs to attach rescue ropes to. Once out of the debris and loaded into an ambulance, Mrs. Barrett was nevertheless too severely injured and would unfortunately succumb to her injuries about four hours later at the emergency room in the Backus Hospital.

Her family, meanwhile, was certainly aware of the situation and obviously very worried. They lived on Burghardt Street which was just down Mohegan Park Road from the skating pond. Twelve-year-old Wendy Barrett, who was at home with her sisters Carole and Sandra, had heard the distinct sounds of the roaring floodwaters from their home. Knowing that her mother was working, Wendy suddenly felt a dire need to know that her mom was OK. "I kept waking up my father and saying it was time to get her at work. He kept saying 'It's too early.' Then he went and couldn't get through the floodwaters." It wasn't until early the next morning that the family would learn of Anna's death.

Hartford Times reporter Dennis Riley and Tom Sweeney, meanwhile, had just made it up Boswell Avenue and entered its intersection with Centennial Square when they both saw and heard the avalanche of water. Wave upon wave of floodwater seemingly came out of nowhere and looked completely misplaced here. Stopping his car, Dennis heard the screams of help from the Turner Mill employees and then quickly saw the east end of the building collapse. Using his reporter's instinct, he now realized that this was a story that would require his full attention, and he suddenly realized that he would become his paper's focal point for this disaster in the days ahead.

City firemen and police that were congregated in the square, meanwhile, struggled with what to do next; the water flow was still formidable, although the destructive leading edge now had now thankfully passed and was wreaking havoc further downtown. The residual flow was still engulfing Centennial Square, however, and making rescue operations tenuous. Many onlookers were also attempting to assist, yelling across the expanse of water from Broad Street to Boswell Avenue and back to alert would-be rescuers of the size and depth of the water surrounding them. Two men in particular were soon noticed wading into the vast pond that had quickly formed past their knees from the Boswell Avenue side while firemen on the Broad Street side yelled for them to stop.

One of them indeed thought better and stopped, but the other, with an intense and determined look on his face, kept going. Continuing to shout at the man, another fireman decided to wade in after him. As the first man closed in on the rubble, the rescuing fireman dove and tackled him in the hip-deep water: "My wife is in there. My god, my wife is in there," he exclaimed. The fireman, soaking wet now, was nevertheless successful in convincing him to get out of the water and onto dry land back on Boswell Avenue.

Later at about 3:00 a.m., a reporter who had witnessed this heartbreaking rescue attempt noticed the man still stumbling back and forth on the bank opposite the mill, muttering over and over, "My god, my wife is in there!"

Now as Centennial Square became increasingly crowded with onlookers, police and rescue workers, newspaper reporters from the surrounding areas were soon joined by their journalistic brethren from cities farther and farther away. By the next morning, the disaster would claim national attention as a team from the *New York Times* flew in overnight and were on the scene reporting for the next several days.

Outside the flooded area of the square, three young girls were suddenly noted pacing back and forth, almost willing the water to recede. When asked "Do you live here?" by a reporter, one of them replied with a worried "Yes" . . ." She's worried about her mother," her friend replied. "Her father and brothers are OK. They live on Hickory St. and she can see them." The reporter then asked the young twenty-year-old named Patricia, who had just returned to the area from playing bingo in Greenville, "Where's your mother?" "In the mill," she answered. "She works in the mill. I don't know if she got out or not."

Feeling a sense, now, of responsibility, the reporter hurried to a nearby fireman and asked if there was anybody still trapped in the mill debris. The fireman reported that all were out and accounted for. "Oh I hope so. I can't get near there," the girl replied when told of the fireman's response. The girl, Patricia Macomber Roode, was the daughter of Helen Roode, one of the workers who had been immediately killed in the initial collapse of the building. Patricia would only learn of her mother's death later at 4:30 a.m. "I just never expected to hear that the mill had gone down like it did. I was

THOMAS MOODY, JR.

more concerned about my father and my brothers, figuring it could cause more damage (at her home). I never figured the mill would go."

Ironically, it was young Patricia who had tried to convince her mother to stay at home this evening. Her four-year-old brother, Robert, had been sick with the flu, but Helen, nonetheless, felt that he would be in good hands with the boy's father and their twenty-year-old daughter. Upon hearing of the dam break though, and after she had returned from bingo, she went directly to the square to see for herself and it was here, with two of her friends, that the reporter first encountered her.

During this chaotic initial period of disaster and recovery, all of the mill night-shift workers (whether dead or alive) would ultimately be accounted for before dawn of the

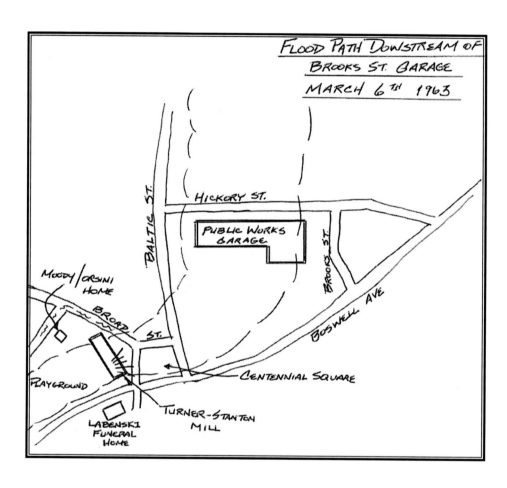

seventh, except for Mrs. Carol Mae Robidou, a night-shift worker who would remain missing, inexplicably and curiously, into the next day.

An examination of the building, meanwhile, noted that the section that had absorbed the initial blow had simply disappeared into a pile of debris as the structure had been, seemingly, surgically ripped right from its moorings. The back half of the east side had been separated from the front, causing a cavity of destruction that had allowed Mrs. Atterbury, Roode, and Mr. Pobol to fall to their deaths, and had crashed downward in a heap toward the steep drop-off into the Lake Street playground.

The destructive front end of the wave, meanwhile, roiling past the mill now and loaded with a profusion of new debris from the Turner Mill collapse, was once again unobstructed as it raced through the Lake Street playground. An area of approximately one hundred fifty yards by fifty yards, the playground now provided an area for the flood flow to expand and gain momentum as it headed toward the downtown area.

Roberta Delgado, a pretty eighteen-year-old senior at the Norwich Free Academy in 1963, resided at 76 Boswell Avenue, a house whose backyard overlooked the basketball courts of the Lake Street playground. The Delgados were a large Norwich family (seven siblings including Roberta) who lived on the ground floor of the building there. Roberta's younger brother Ronnie would go on to become a well-known basketball player at NFA in the mid-1970s while becoming an early sports hero to young Tommy who would listen to the broadcasts of his games on WICH radio and would, one Saturday morning, while himself playing in a local elementary school youth league game, suddenly run into Ronnie at NFA's Norton Gym and become starstruck at the young "super star."

This night however, Roberta was awakened by her older sister Delores who had excitedly proclaimed to "come and see the water!" Running to the back of the house, the girls witnessed the river of water as "indescribable." Where could this have come from? It was while they both were seemingly mesmerized at this phenomenon that Delores somehow slipped away from Roberta, apparently deciding to go upstairs to check on her friend Charlene without mentioning to Roberta where she was going.

Now as Roberta suddenly looked around, there wasn't a family member to be found. Panicking and thinking that the water would soon somehow engulf her, she darted back into the house and attempted to wake up her sisters Brenda and Laura and brother Ronnie, but to no avail. Not seeing her parents, she became even more terrified and went to their bedroom and immediately grabbed her five-and-a-half-month old baby sister Doreen.

Wrapping the baby in blankets, she quickly left the apartment via the living room, running up the stairs to the street level of Boswell Avenue, where she was determined to run down toward Franklin Street to seek help. This, of course, would have spelled disaster, as the flood was inundating Franklin Street at this time; fortunately, Roberta ran straight into her parents, Tony and Mary, who themselves were coming back down from the their upstairs neighbors, and it was then that they assured her that everything was OK. They also explained to her that the flood had flowed around their home and was headed down Franklin Street toward the Shetucket River and that they were in no actual danger.

Mrs. Barbara Lentine, who lived on lower Lake Street, reported that at 10:00 p.m., "I got a telephone call from my father-in-law, Michael Depolito of Broad Street, and he told me that the dam let go and water was coming. I looked outside on the street and water was gushing downhill. Everyone was running out of their homes to get there cars off the streets. Some were too late." Lentine also was a firsthand witness to the destruction at the Turner-Stanton Mill: "I heard screaming from the building" before witnessing the collapse. Lucy Rinaldi of 45 Lake Street also added that the street looked as if "a glacier had been released."

Farther up the hill, Mrs. Rose Waldn had just arrived home to her house on 47 Lake Street at almost the same time that the Moody family was loading their children into their car. "I heard this rushing noise, but I thought it was just a heavy rain. Then my son jumped and yelled 'Ma! A flood! A flood!'" Her son Arthur, seventeen years old, had impulsively decided to outrace the flood and ran now outside to his car along with his friend Humphrey Maintain; Mrs. Waldn, chastising Arthur for his irresponsibility but failing, as most parents do with teenagers, to convince him to remain, decided wisely to ignore her son's impetuousness and remain at her home.

Arthur and Humphrey, in their car now, were racing down Lake Street while leaning on the car horn as an alarm. Accelerating past lower Lake Street, they sped down Pond Street and onward to Franklin Street and downtown; a car just behind them by only a few seconds would not be so fortunate.

Later investigation proved that virtually all the homes on Lake Street would absorb minimal flooding and as it turned out, it was a prescient decision for the local residents to stay there.

As the wave now progressed through the playground and on toward downtown, a three-story house at the intersection of Lake Street and Pond Street had its bottom floor instantly immersed in the murky waters with four young sisters trapped on the upper floors.

The Demicos, as with virtually everyone else this evening, were completely unaware of the impending flood and surprised by the immediacy and destructive nature of its onslaught. As the water level in the playground area increased and plunged their first floor to the ceiling, they raced to the top floor, wondering when or if they would be rescued. Fortunate that they were not in the immediate path of the wave, the Demicos' home did not suffer the battering damage that had destroyed the mill just a few seconds earlier. Firemen later were able to make their way down to the home and rescue Jennie, Lena, Nicholette, and Carmela. "It was like a nightmare. We'll never forget it as long as we live. Thank god for the firemen."

CHAPTER 4

"Ronnie, She's Gone . . ."

A T THE SOUTH end of the playground, Lake Street underscores the park's termination in an east/west direction. To the immediate south of the road, in 1963 and even now (on the right-hand side if one were travelling west to east), there is an abrupt drop-off of about ten feet. At the time of the flood, this drop-off was made up of a rock wall structure ironically similar to that of the downstream face of the Spaulding Pond Dam. From the base of this rock wall, the terrain sloped approximately twenty-five feet downward toward the roof of a garage that Lamperell's car dealership used for auto repairs and storage.

This garage had, as its back wall, another, albeit larger, rock wall drop, this one of approximately twenty feet at its zenith and would connect to and make up its concrete floor. From here, the floor and terrain leveled out for another forty yards southward before sloping down again into the car lot and where the town elevation then stabilized at approximately ten feet above sea level.

This severe downward stair-step terrain (an estimated thirty-six feet in elevation) was compressed into an area of only thirty to thirty-five feet beginning at the south end of Lake Street to the floor of Lamperell's dealership giving gravity an indomitable waterfall effect for the dam failure flow as it left the playground. And now as the Moodys travelled along Lake Street in their west-to-east direction along the south end of the playground, tragic fate would suddenly intercede and alter their lives forever.

"RON!" Honey screamed as she was the first to see the cascade of water exit the south end of the playground and head directly for them. Realizing that they had gone too far and that there was now no going back, she and the rest of the adults quickly braced for what they imagined to be a violent impact. The swiftly rushing water flow, instead, simply floated their car off the road, upward into its swirling mass, and carried them toward the drop-off south of Lake Street. The car quickly met its violent termination though as it and the water both spilled down the ten-foot rock wall drop off with the automobile violently rolling over twice, and as it spun in the swirling flow, it somehow managed to land with its tail tilted upward, pointing frontward into its previous line of travel.

Young Tommy remembered having his eyes wide open during the rolling of the car and seeing the total blackness of the swirling water and debris. If there was a way to be instantly drenched and frozen to their core, the Moodys and Tony Orsini now experienced it as the car finally became stabilized in the onrushing waters against the garage roof abutment at the east end of the structure. And as it turned out, this shoddily constructed and poorly supported roof turned out to be only one of several territorial lifesavers for the Moody family and Orsini this evening.

With a manic survival instinct now taking hold, the adults, while struggling, managed to somehow reorient themselves while upside down. They got the front passenger-side door to open and while the onrushing flow cascaded through the smashed windows of the overturned car, Ronnie, Honey, and Tony all managed to locate the children and physically grasp them before the unthinkable could occur.

Noticing their proximity to the, for now, dry and stable roof and realizing that this was their only means of escape, Tony and Ronnie immediately started climbing out of the car and onto the roof while they themselves were still reeling physically from the impact of the crash. The fact that not one of the passengers in the car had been wearing seat belts was not even reflected upon until later in the investigation. In fact, it was concluded in the accident report and by the adult survivors themselves that by not wearing seat belts, although definitely incurring some bumps and bruises, it was an omission that actually saved their lives.

Tony, from the rear seat, was somehow able to get out first, carrying young Tommy with him and, after placing the youngster standing on the roof, now crouched down near the car to brace himself against the menacing flow. Ronnie, meanwhile, climbed out of the crushed car's front door and straddled the area between it and the roof. Honey, completely soaked and still in the car with the freezing floodwaters circulating around her while heroically having little regard for her own safety, now frantically surveyed the interior of the overturned car for her children.

Standing on the car's inverted roof, she grabbed Jimmy from the overturned front seat and handed him out to Ronnie who then passed him on to Tony who was maintaining his crouched position on the roof while the water flow now seemed to reach its crescendo around them. Honey then grabbed the baby Shawn who was floating in the car's interior waters and passed him up, and as Ronnie grabbed him and cradled the baby in his left arm, a sudden, violent, but momentary collapse of the garage roof suddenly changed the dynamic of the roof and the overturned car as it was wedged against it.

With everyone out of the car now except Honey, the weight change inside made the vehicle substantially lighter, and the water flow now caused it to naturally shift away from Ronnie at the very moment that he had grabbed her right hand with his. Losing his grip, as both their hands were wet and muddy and with the car continuing its flow induced turn, this transposing flood flow abruptly caused Honey to be quickly swept away and then under by the still-substantial force.[3]

---

[3] Up to this point, I'm somewhat confident of the facts and sequence as is spelled out here. What caused my mother to disappear under the water, however, is still only conjecture. Many extant explanations and theories have been deliberated on over the years but my father (before he died) nor Tony Orsini have been able to remember or come up with any tangible evidence that would lead me to any concrete conclusions as to the exact circumstances of her death.

The official autopsy addressed her cause of death as drowning, to which I certainly have no argument. But what caused her to become so incapacitated as to not to be able to fight off the effects of drowning remain to this day a frustrating mystery.

The area where her body was found, as we'll later see, did accumulate an abundance of fast-flowing and damaging debris, but, the overall water level at the time she disappeared could not have been more than waist high, and

With the continued roar of the flood still around him and the sudden

---

she was discovered a mere twenty feet northeast of the overturned car. If the flood flow, somehow, had forced her over the wall down to the floor elevation of the garage (an almost impossible physical occurrence given the fact that the garage roof, still intact at this point, provided no path large enough downward to the floor of this garage), this being the next twenty-foot drop, then my reasonable conclusion would have been that she had suffered a tumultuous and somewhat more-violent death.

But after much questioning, researching, and further connoting, the still not-altogether clear theory that I've developed is that as she was standing in the overturned car and as the weight inside became considerably less (true, most of the vehicle's weight was above her) with the adults and children out, it then shifted rather extremely in the flow (remember, the car doors facing the on-coming flow were still closed giving the water full resistance), while the roof that my father and we were standing on also settled somewhat due to the worsening structural damage, at virtually the same time. These competing forces, which had the now-visceral affect of her rapidly turning away from my father while the downturned front section of the car moved towards him, speculatively, was enough for her to lose her grip on his hand.

It's also been speculated, within my family, that something may have hit her when she attempted to grab my father's hand (she was ultimately found with a broken arm and leg, surmised later by the autopsy doctors to have occurred prior to her death); but this, in my estimation, is unlikely, since at this point she was still physically standing in the overturned car. This "something" would have had to be not only large enough to disrupt her equilibrium, offsetting the water flow at this point, but still small enough to penetrate the upside-down car's smashed window openings while maintaining an energy level high enough to knock over a young determined woman with an adrenalin flow and mother's survival instinct that had been kicked into ultra high gear.

The water flow rate was, admittedly, very high at this time; so in all probability, what occurred was a combination of the sudden turning of the car along with the collapse of the garage roof that caused her to fall and where the dynamic of the water flow captured her. This then presented a completely different and dangerous picture of potential harm.

and staggering realization that he was now helpless to his wife, Ronnie, who was still standing on the unsteady garage roof, was momentarily at a loss as to what to do next. Should he forsake the clear but rapidly degrading safety of the roof and dive in after his wife to see if he could somehow rescue her? How could he do this and risk his life while his young children were standing there freezing alongside of him?

These, at their core moments, are the truly seminal and life-changing circumstances that determine people's character and what their lives ultimately turn out to be and, based on these immediate decisions, allow no going back. A hard choice, right now, had to be made, usually with instinct alone as its guide, and it is one in which the decision maker forever shapes the lives of not only himself but also of others. Ronnie Moody, clearly not realizing nor wanting to have reached such a transcendent and life-altering moment, had to now make this split-second decision, and it was one that would clearly formulate the rest of his and his children's lives.

———————————

Now as she was suddenly under the water, out of the car and struggling to get back to the surface, I speculate that she somehow lost consciousness, maybe by either being hit in the head by some of the larger debris flowing down from the mill or, worse, becoming entangled in something that would not allow her to get back to the surface (the multitudinous yarn and string that was now caught up in the flow from the mill).

Also, as one notices the exact location of the car in relation to the roof and drop-off, the upper portion of the concrete wall that made up the next drop-off protruded upwards approximately one foot and was directly in the flow path; it is entirely conceivable that she could have hit her head on this abutment after going under. It was also at this time that she could have somehow suffered the blows that broke her arm and leg.

Regardless, while constantly rehashing these details in my mind even after fifty years, I can only hope that, as potentially insensitive as it may sound, that my mom was very soon rendered unconscious and that it was an extremely rapid experience, as expeditiously unharrowing, unpainful, and unfrightful for her as is possible, and it has been a long held and heartfelt hope that she suffered little or not at all.

THOMAS MOODY, JR.

Instinctively, he was bitterly certain that Honey was gone . . . he had seen the way she'd fallen and had been witness to the still-turbulent flow of the flood. He also knew that he was, at least for the immediate future, the responsible agent for his children. All of them on this roof were still in severe danger, and he realized that with Tony's help, he needed to get them out of danger, and it had to happen right now.

Tony, meanwhile, with these same thoughts on his mind and saddened by what he had witnessed, noticed Ronnie's momentary hesitation and grabbed him quickly, saying, "Ronnie, she's gone." Now, with both adults feeling the imminent collapse of the roof, Ronnie and Tony, necessarily, turned their entire focus to saving the children. Spying a tree at the west end of the roof (another natural area lifesaver), they, with the children, being carefully brought along with them, eased their way ("duckwalking") over the remaining seventy feet of roof area toward it.

Upon reaching the tree, whose branches fortuitously hung out over the east end of the garage roof and made for easy access, Ronnie and Tony breathlessly lifted first Tommy and then Jimmy up onto the prevailing low branches where they were told to grab onto and hold tightly. Ronnie and Tony, with the baby Shawn still under Tony's jacket, then wearily climbed up onto higher branches that extended out and over the opposite far west side of the roof. Tony, being as careful as he could be under the extreme circumstances, was attentive not to expose the baby to any more of the elements than he had suffered already.

Now for the moment safe in the tree while the floodwaters rushed by and thankful for the turn of events that made the roof and then this tree available to them, the Moodys and Tony watched incredulously as the garage roof, their brief sanctuary, now gave way under the still-murderous flood flow, violently collapsing southward toward the car dealership. Realizing that had they stayed there just another few moments, they would have been swept away, Ronnie and Tony, for the first time since being hit by the floodwaters, had a moment to collect their thoughts and comprehend that they had indeed made the correct decision, as painful as it was, and that they had gotten off of the roof and up into the accommodating tree right in the nick of time.

Young Tommy, meanwhile, still shaken over the rapid recent events and shivering in the extreme cold in his drenched clothing, now looked out upon the city from his tree branch with a sort of detached excitement that only a very young child could muster in the wake of such a tragedy. Spellbound by the floodwaters now engulfing Franklin Street and with the city lights shining off the water in the late evening skyline, for a four-year-old, this spelled adventure, and he ventured that this was something exceedingly beyond his imagination while becoming, momentarily, excited and transfixed with the enchantment of it all.

Initially not contemplating "what got me here" but more "Wow, this is serious, but I'm still OK, and this is cool and something that I'll probably never see again," Tommy's mind now raced with an enthusiasm and intensity he'd not experienced before.

As he suddenly noticed seemingly every detail surrounding him, the massive water flow picked up and carried large pieces of "stuff" down below him at Lamperell's and on down as it curved leftward toward Franklin Street, like a river to the curious four-year-old.

The sensationally loud and roaring sound of water flowing past him below the tree was a danger, he knew, but still intriguing as long as he was up here above it. After a few more minutes though, some seriously mixed emotions started to overtake him—Dad, he remembered now, hadn't really been right; he had been somewhat disheveled, soaking wet, not calm at all, and looking completely unhinged; I've never seen him look this way before. Maybe this is worse than I thought.[4]

Now as he looked away from the floodwaters to the tree branch opposite him that was supporting his younger brother Jimmy, it was then that his mind was suddenly forced to fully refocus on the stark reality of the crisis and what it meant as he now saw his younger brother crying violently while still steadfastly holding on to the tree. Tommy, instantly forgetting about the fascination of the flood spectacle, now felt an immediate and overwhelming need to help him, but while himself holding intently onto

---

[4]   Certainly not a four-year-old's exact words but those that, after fifty years of contemplation, most adequately describe the memory)

the tree branch, realized sadly that there was really nothing he could do for him.

As Ronnie and Tony, meanwhile, clung to their side of the tree, they were now forced to face what had occurred in the last fifteen minutes. Looking out now on the damage caused by the flowing waters from their tree top vantage point and as if magnetically drawn, as young Tommy had been moments ago, they watched as empty cars were being strewn about while strange-looking large black cylindrical tanks floated in the water.

These tanks, which had been stored on the grounds of Lamperell's dealership and were the property of the plumbing business under the same name, were large empty fuel tanks, designed to be buried underground, but were now floating atop the flood flow, ramming up against buildings on the opposite side of the street, smashing the outer walls and causing structural damage before, while still being caught up in the river of water, flowing onward down Franklin Street.

Ronnie, still up in the tree, meanwhile, was, not surprisingly, feeling a deep devastation at having watched Honey disappear in the flood flow. Even in the miserably cold night air and while being thoroughly soaked and still realizing that they were in a precarious position, he was, nonetheless, hard pressed to forget something that he, ultimately, had no control over—if only he had had a few extra seconds before that garage roof violently shifted after getting everyone out. If only he had been able to get a firm grip on her hand, they would all have made it and would now be safe in the tree. Ronnie, recalling her go down, realized that if he could not find her, he would never forget the last images of his wife—How unfair it was for such a wonderful wife and mother to suddenly be gone.

As he continued to agonize over her, he also thought about what life would be like without her. If she was truly gone, what would happen to him and his boys? He still had to work after all, so what would he do to ensure that they would be raised competently while remaining together and with proper upbringing? He could not imagine what the near term would be like nor, for that matter, could he envision living the rest of his life without her.

And as it turned out, given the events of the ensuing days and years, Ronnie would, regrettably, never fully recover.

His nature, since becoming married and having children, was to be that of the conscientious provider and the immutable presence in his children's upbringing, which he would certainly continue to succeed at but, without her, would also become a severely different and flawed person that would have emerged had Honey stayed alive.

His deep and overriding motivation for continuing would turn out to be based entirely on his children's lives, and he lived for and supported them as best he could while, at the same time, clearly missing and tacitly crying out for an important and stabilizing component to his still-maturing personality. This loss of emotional compass became a subtending trait, not easily recognized by those who weren't closely associated with him; but to those who were familiar, he had clearly suffered a loss of something far deeper than anyone could imagine, and, subsequently, given his other emotional instabilities, it was a loss that rocketed him on a path of personal and emotional undoing that no one could have stopped.

While grasping the tree for what seemed like an eternity and shivering violently in the cold, Ronnie and Tony suddenly noticed two people exiting the upper floor of the nearby Longo's Funeral Home, a longtime establishment facing Franklin Street which was itself experiencing serious flood damage. A white two-story structure, the tree that they were in was actually part of its backyard property and was located just a few feet southwest of where the Moodys now clung. The funeral home proper was located on the ground floor of the building with the owners living on the second level. These owners, Katherine and William Longo, were now tentatively hazarding a look outside to check on a loud noise that they had heard while they were quietly settling in for the night.

Only a few moments earlier, the Longos had been sitting comfortably, watching television, when a sudden and loud banging noise came from the rear of their house. This crashing sound was significant enough to not only startle them but also to cause them to venture outside, notwithstanding the cold and miserably wet night. Now standing on their second-story porch in the rear of the house, they saw that the large black fuel tanks, which were normally stored passively behind their house were now, incredibly, floating down and crashing into and past their house. It was then that they saw the protagonist for all this unsettling activity—a huge river of water with large ice cakes floating aloft was pouring down from Lake Street and into

Lamperell's auto lot, immediately engulfing their first-floor funeral home and floating their black Mercury automobile from behind their house out onto the lot and down into Franklin Street.

Where in the hell was this water coming from? Bill Longo thought. There was certainly no water source this large anywhere near this part of town—something, perhaps a water tank or pipeline maybe, must have ruptured? As he and his wife continued to stand on their second-floor backyard porch, the destructive flow continued to surround the lower level of their home. After a few more moments, Bill heard the surprising and, if at all true, deeply disturbing intonation of what sounded like human "moaning." Asking Katherine if she had heard it as well, he thought that it "must be some sort of sound effect of the water flow" as Katherine said that she'd heard nothing.

While absorbing the shock of this massive and completely surprising flood, Bill became increasingly panicked as he now watched a large piece of ice in the flood flow slam into one of the wooden beams supporting the porch that he and his wife were standing on. This of course caused him to mentally prepare for subsequent ice blocks flowing into and potentially snapping the wooden supports off their moorings in the cement foundation below. If this were to occur, the porch and possibly the entire house would crumble, and he now realized that he needed to formulate a quick escape plan that would get him and his wife to safety as quickly as possible.

Meanwhile, still up in the tree, Ronnie and Tony started shouting out to the Longos, calling at first and then screaming at the top of their voices, all with no effect. Again and again they cried out, but to no avail as the torrent of the still-substantial flood flow drowned out their voices. Ultimately, as the minutes seemed like hours and as the flow and roar of the water subsided somewhat, a period that would total over an hour, the Longos finally heard their pleas and then made hurried efforts to rescue them.

Bill Longo, initially grateful that his porch had held under the battering flow, was still uncertain about continuing downstairs to the first level, though. But while still on the upstairs porch, he went to the south side of his home and, there, seeing many onlookers on upper Franklin Street, who were standing just beyond the flood's reach on McKinley Avenue, he called out for help. "Hey", he said, "I need help in rescuing some people from a tree in my back yard."

This myriad group of onlookers, whose names are unfortunately lost to history, would turn out to be of enormous assistance that night. Calling back up that, yes, they would certainly help, they then grimly, in the wake of the flood's intrusive damage, trudged their way back through the mud and debris to the Longos' backyard while Bill and Katherine, themselves, descended from the upper floor of their home.

The Longos, with the volunteers now amassing in their backyard, found a way to maneuver to the tree and helped to first get the children down. Upon initial examination, it was clear that their condition mandated immediate transport to the Backus Hospital. As the group of rescuers next concentrated on getting Ronnie and Tony down, these wonderful helpers not only took on the responsibility of transporting the hypothermic children to the hospital but also concentrated on rescuing the adults. Loading Tommy and Jimmy into separate cars, they quickly sped up McKinley Avenue and onto the Backus emergency room.

Meanwhile, as Tony Orsini was brought down from the tree, with the baby Shawn still under his jacket for protection, he noticed that the floodwaters had dramatically receded and that city fire and rescue workers had gathered both below him on Franklin Street and atop the Lake Street drop-off at the spot where the wave had initially hit them. Without thinking and certainly still traumatized from the crash, he started walking up the steep drop-off (instead of down to Longos where he would have been immediately transported to the hospital), through still ankle-deep water and mud, to Lake Street where he found a rescue worker and to whom he handed the baby Shawn off.

This surprised rescue worker then handed Shawn off to an onlooker, Mrs. Charles Trask who lived nearby on Lake Street. "Take care of the baby" were the somewhat hurried words, and Mrs. Trask, without a second thought, grabbed the child without even knowing whose baby it was. "He was so blue and cold and covered with mud," Mrs. Trask said afterward. "We took off the old clothes, wrapped it in warm blankets, and then took it to the hospital," she said. She also later testified to the terror that the Moody family, along with Tony Orsini, was experiencing: "We could hear the screams for help from the rest of the Moody family over the roar of the water . . . We were petrified and terrified."[5]

After handing the baby off and having seen the other two children and Ronnie being rescued, Tony remained at this lower Lake Street location for a short while, seemingly invisible while blindly surveying the chaos. Feeling helpless and not knowing what else he should do, he now decided to walk the short distance back up to his home. Trudging despondently up the slope of Lake Street amid the chaos of rescue people, neighbors, and onlookers, he reached the house where, only a short time ago he had agreed to help his struggling-downstairs neighbors escape with their children. Now, in seemingly mere moments, the young family's mother was dead, the father was in shock and the children were in transport to the hospital, and Tony could only shake his head at the unfairness and rapidity that fate seemed to alter lives.

Approaching his house now at the top of the hill, he saw his father Pasquale standing at the top of the stairway to his second-story home. Rapidly asking about what had happened, Pasquale was at once happy to see Tony still alive but also angry that he had taken such a risk. Tony explained to him all of the explicit details of the car rolling over, Honey going down, and the rest of them making it to the tree, all of which made Pasquale further incensed, "I told you to stay here!" he exclaimed.

Tony, still in shock and also still extremely saddened, decided that the best thing for him to do on this tragic evening was to go back to bed. It wasn't until later that rescue workers learned of his heroics and came up to his house to check on him that they would convince him to finally go to the hospital to get treatment.

Ronnie, meanwhile, having also been helped down from the tree by the Longos and the crowd of helpers, was a study in shock and confusion. After convincing him that his children were safe and in transit to the hospital,

---

[5]   Mrs. Trask is clearly another of these "unsung" heroes of the immediate flood aftermath and is truly held in esteem by the Moody family . . . not just for caring for an unknown baby but for going the extra mile and transporting him to the hospital. She is a hero to my family for saving my brother Shawn's life. Alas, an attempt to locate her after all these years has proven fruitless.)

these helpers watched him immediately leave and go to the shattered remains of the garage roof and begin a frenetic search for his wife.

Intently struggling past the debris and water flow, Ronnie made his way to the east end of Lamperell's dealership where he suspected Honey had fallen, but with the rubble and still rapidly surging water, ice, darkness, and the collapsed roof hindering his effort, he could not quite get to where he thought she was. Compounding his effort, the freezing cold night air made his soaked-through clothing soon unbearable, and he realized that it was a virtual impossibility to conduct a thorough search under these conditions.

Sadly realizing now that he wasn't going to find her this evening, he made his way back over to the Longos' home, where the rescue people again noted his extreme condition, and urged him into the house where they quickly stripped him of his soggy clothing and drew a hot bath for him. Hypothermia was the foremost affliction of all who had been exposed to the flood this night, and Ronnie had now certainly reached a critical state.

While preparing the bath and assuring him, again, that his children were being cared for at Backus, the Longos had become still another miracle for the Moodys that evening. While still shivering from the lengthy exposure to the cold and clearly in shock, Ronnie slowly recovered in the hot bath water and, after about thirty minutes donned dry clothing, thanked his saviors again and made haste to the hospital to check on his children.

He was sped to Backus by another of the efficacious but anonymous onlookers and, as he arrived, rushed into the emergency room. He was told by the ER doctors that, although the children had suffered from thermal shock, ingestion of muddy, polluted water, and that pneumonia could not be ruled out, their diagnosis was not immediately life threatening, and a full recovery was expected. Grateful for this encouraging assessment and still in an overall dazed and despondent condition, he was now told to wait on a nearby gurney for an available doctor to examine him.

While seated, Ronnie now saw Honey's mother, Nana, rushing into the emergency room. Seeing the desperation on her face, he quickly went to her and explained that Honey had been washed away and was probably dead, "She's gone, Ma . . .". Nana, also clearly in shock over the whole proceedings, refused to believe it as she assured Ronnie that Honey "was an excellent swimmer." Ronnie countered sadly with an explanation of his aborted search for her, but Nana was nevertheless undeterred in her faith in Honey's survival.

In the seemingly interminable time frame between getting the initial phone call from Honey telling her that "a dam" had apparently broken and that she, Ronnie, and the kids were coming over to her house and now finding herself at the hospital, Nana, throughout the night, had become more and more apprehensive as she had heard no further word from anyone.

The initial call came moments after 10:00 p.m., and it would be near midnight, as the real panic set in, that she started asking herself, "Where could they be?" At her small rented home on Elizabeth Street, which was directly behind the house that she had raised Honey and her other six children and where her eldest son William "Bud" Shea now lived with his family (wife Jean and children Mark, Ellen, and Nora) she was virtually inconsolable.

Listening to reports of the flood coming in as she listened to the radio, she heard that a family was trapped downtown near Lamperell's Dealership. Immediately imagining the worst and becoming somewhat frantic, she started calling around before finally reaching her son Jerry who lived on Tetreault Avenue on the extreme northeast side of town. She asked Jerry if he had heard any news of the dam break and if he wouldn't mind going out and looking for anything that might alleviate her concern.

Jeremiah Shea was Nana's third child, born in Norwich in 1929, and it was he who would ultimately outlive all of his siblings. A remarkably enlightened and intelligent man, Jerry at this point was thirty-four years old and had been married to Rita Deroshiers for fifteen years. Having one daughter, Catherine, who had been born in 1950 (and would later become "the cool grown-up teenage cousin" to young Tommy), Jerry and Rita would later adopt a daughter, Bernadette, who was Tommy's age, and would also have a son, Jeremiah Jr., born in the early 1970s.

A fixture in local business while also having a strong political leaning, Jerry would become a Connecticut state selectman in 1972 while also following his father's influence by owning a profitable meat-packing business in Norwich for many years.

This night, however, after receiving Nana's frantic call, Jerry decided that his first stop would be at the Backus Hospital to see if anyone had been admitted—assuredly, the doctors and nurses there would have the latest information on the injured and stricken flood victims.

Driving to the hospital from his home and arriving there in approximately fifteen minutes, he was surprised to learn that the Moody children as well as his brother-in-law Ronnie had been admitted. Extracting as many details of their condition as he could from the intransigent nurses on duty (who had been ordered not to give out information to anyone but immediate family members), Jerry left the hospital and went directly to his mother's house on Elizabeth Street to tell her about Ronnie and the children. Loading Nana into his car now, he brought her back to Backus where it was then that she rushed in to meet with Ronnie.

Jerry then hurried to the downtown area to see if there was anything he could do to assist the search for his sister. Arriving there amid total chaos as fire, police, and rescue workers were seemingly on station in every direction, Jerry, intuitively, decided to start his nomadic search at the Lake Street area. After finally finding a parking place he worked his way on foot to the south end of the playground where, looking down, he now saw the Moody car horribly overturned on the first drop-off. Climbing past the chaotic scene of onlookers and rescue helpers, he made his way down through the mud and puddles of water. With the soaking debris and still dribbling water everywhere and with little light to help him, he searched here, nevertheless, on this slope for what seemed like hours.

While walking back and forth throughout this area, he looked down to the next drop-off and saw that the upper Franklin Street area had been so overrun by floodwaters and debris that any recognizance or logistics, on his part, of this area would be near impossible. The legion of rescue workers, police, and firemen here, as it had been on lower Lake Street, was only offset by the steady stream of onlookers from the surrounding area, and Jerry was thankful that he would not have to maneuver through that throng as he intended to stay up here on this debris-lain slope where the Moody car was.

THOMAS MOODY, JR.

Encountering similar obstacles that Ronnie had in his aborted search a couple of hours earlier, those being the dark and freezing conditions, Jerry nevertheless remained here, searching and questioning anyone who would talk with him, until about 2:00 a.m. when he reluctantly decided to go home for some rest with the objective of coming back at dawn, where he was sure daylight would provide a different and far more agreeable perspective, to continue.

The Moody children, meanwhile at the hospital, were all being wrapped in blankets after being divested of their drenched and muddy clothing. After being placed in criblike beds, they were surrounded with hot water bottles to help relieve the hypothermia. Young Tommy would remember awakening in one of these hospital beds with numerous nurses, doctors, and interns surrounding him and looking down upon him. Being abundantly agitated from the aggressive medical treatment, which had cleared his nose and throat of the mud and muck, he started immediately crying out in discomfort.

Undoubtedly needing his mother for comfort, Tommy, along with his brothers Jimmy and Shawn, would now start the long and emotionally trying process of learning to endure life without her. Indeed, many of the young nurses and interns would later recount stories of heartbreakingly providing motherly comfort to the young boys, which imparted in them a palpable and deep lesson in adult life, as most of these secondary caregivers were barely into their twenties.

Pictures, later, of the nurses with the children show a clear and devoted motherly affection, and although no record remains of their thoughts, these nurses were undoubtedly filled with a mixture of sorrow and empathy while caring for them and certainly became sad and hopeful upon their release.

Young Tommy and his brothers had all been diagnosed with severe thermal shock and hypothermia along with ingestion of muddy and potentially contaminated floodwater, but, of all of them, the baby Shawn was admitted with, by far, the worst condition. Being an infant and thus most susceptible to the exceedingly cold and wet conditions, he would come the closest to dying as pneumonia soon overtook him, and he was the child who would ultimately spend the longest time in the hospital.

Tommy and Jimmy were in comparatively better shape, with a regime of robust antibiotics and rest being their cure, but this trauma would bring out latent health issues for all of the children that no one could possibly foresee, and these health issues would manifest themselves in forms uniquely singular and specific that would require some unusual diagnosis later in their lives.

THOMAS MOODY, JR.

CHAPTER 5

" . . . A Shambles of Mud and Debris."

NOW AFTER TRAGICALLY afflicting the Moody family, the wall of water swept onto Franklin Street where its punishing effect of ice and accumulated damaging debris lost some of the intensity that it had gained at the outlet of the playground. Expanding outward from Lamperell's and into the open area of upper Franklin Street, the floodwaters now had ample area to spread out.

Flooding, as opposed to intense battering destruction as felt at the Turner-Stanton Mill, would become the major catalyst for damage, as the downtown area was unfortunately rife with opportunities. As the water surged out of Lamperell's, cars, tires, and assorted other automobile parts and accessories became accumulated in its crest. The wave flow through here was rapid and intense while debilitating street erosion would occur throughout due to this severe flow, with chunks of the Franklin Street road surface along with the muddy sand underneath it being joined now in the flood flow.

The garage roof that had been crucial for the Moody family and Tony Orsini's survival had crashed onto an untold number of cars in the dealership parking lot, thus making them instantly scrap. All told, nineteen new and twenty used cars that had been for sale at Lamperell's were ruined, along with an untold number of other cars that were in the garage awaiting service. Most of these were later found either overturned or on their sides, toppled by the intense water flow. Fortunately, for the dealership owners, all the vehicles in their possession were covered by insurance, but the offices and main showroom (which had seven or eight new cars inside), owned by the Fatone Realty Company were not. These offices "had been awash from the twelve foot wall of water" and had sustained substantial damage

Next to the auto dealership, Lamperell's also owned a plumbing supply business, and the curious-looking large black fuel tanks observed by the Moodys while stranded in the tree and by Bill Longo on his second-story porch were now engulfed in the water flow and

THOMAS MOODY, JR.

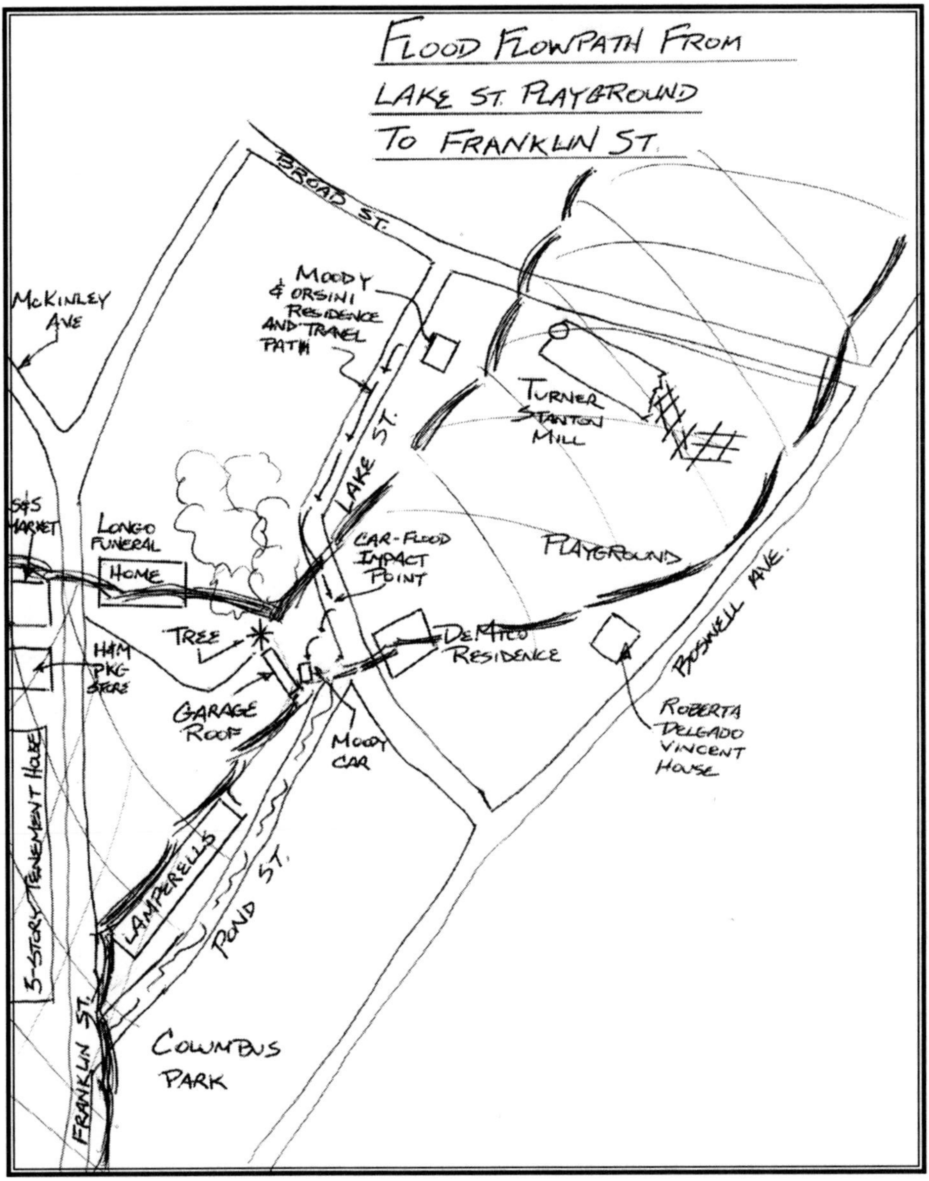
FLOOD FLOWPATH FROM
LAKE ST. PLAYGROUND
TO FRANKLIN ST.
BROAD ST.
McKINLEY AVE
MOODY & ORSINI RESIDENCE AND TRAVEL PATH
LAKE ST.
TURNER STANTON MILL
PLAYGROUND
S&S MARKET
LONGO FUNERAL HOME
CAR-FLOOD IMPACT POINT
TREE
DeMICO RESIDENCE
H&M PKG STORE
GARAGE ROOF
MOODY CAR
ROSWELL AVE.
ROBERTA DELGADO VINCENT HOUSE
3-STORY TENEMENT HOUSE
LAMPERELLS
POND ST.
FRANKLIN ST.
COLUMBUS PARK

were being spread out onto Franklin Street. Two of these weighty tanks in particular crashed with the force of the flood flow into the front entrance of the S & S Supermarket, which was directly across Franklin Street from the dealership and which caused major structural damage. Water now inundated this store and lay waste to virtually all that was inside.

Stanley Stadniki, who was the proprietor of the business and also owner of a group of tenement houses just south of the store, said that he "was ruined." The flood rushed through the store and the apartment houses leaving them "a shambles of mud and debris." Stadniki also stated that most of his stock, the "basement and all it stored was a total loss." The next day, many of these large, odd-looking black cylindrical tanks, which had done immeasurable damage in the upper sections of Franklin Street, amazingly, would be found nearly a mile away, awash in the flow toward downtown

Many other businesses in this area would now also feel the inundating effect of the water wave. Still carrying the large ice blocks, tree limbs, and boulders from its two-mile traverse from Spaulding Pond, the surge hit the H & M Package Store, the three story tenement building owned by Stadniki, the Speedwash Laundromat, and the Troy Laundry, seemingly all at once as it escaped Lamperell's parking lot.

The H & M Package store, in particular, had a white Edsel automobile rapidly float from Lamperell's, across the street and smash into its front door. Mrs. Philip Greenwood, meanwhile, who lived in the tenement building across Franklin Street and had just awakened her husband who was asleep after working a second shift job, testified: "I heard a rumbling like tumbling stones. I looked out and the water was pouring through Longo's Funeral Home across the street."

William Zeitz, who was seven years old and living in the direct path of the wave across from Lamperell's on the third floor of the tenement apartments, was awakened by his brother at about 10:15 p.m. to look out the window at the onrushing floodwaters. Zeitz watched in amazement as the wave engulfed Longo's and then rushed into the lower floor of his building. Being the beneficiary of living on the third floor and, mercifully, not having it collapse, Zeitz continued watching, awestruck, throughout the night as the flood seemed to ricochet off his building and race downtown.

Then, as it receded and while still awake into the early morning hours, he then watched as the firemen and police took over, searching the debris for Honey Moody while starting the long and arduous cleanup process.

Now as the wave proceeded further down Franklin Street, it was joined by a significant tributary that joined it from Pond Street. Moments earlier, as the main flood flow exploded out of the Lake Street playground, most of its force centered on the slope at southern end of Lake Street where it hit the Moodys car head on. Just in front of them as they were driving, however, was the escape that they'd so narrowly missed, the downward slope of Pond Street. This small road veered directly down to Franklin Street to the east of the playground, and because of its narrow girth and high leveled buildings on both sides, it became a bottleneck of sorts for the water and thus water pressure to build up and immediately expand as if exploding from a pressure hose as it hit Franklin Street. The result was a huge eroded hole at the south end of the tenement houses on Franklin Street where city road repair, along with similar repair on Pond Street, took the longest to accomplish. This tributary flow now merged with the main flow as it carved its destructive path down Franklin Street.

At the Troy Laundry a little farther southward on Franklin Street, a popular business that washed, dry-cleaned and provided laundry services, the water wave, as it crashed into the structure, caused severe damage to the main lower floor where the washers and dryers were. Some of them became unhinged from their floor supports and floated up to and crashed against the far south wall. At the same time, the flooding also damaged one of the boilers in the basement, completely immersing it in the filthy, polluted water.

These businesses on the upper west side of Franklin Street, which were all in the direct path of this engulfing flow, saw possibly the most damaging effect of the dam break as the wave now pounded up against them while breeching each of their structures before turning southward. In most cases, this destructive flow would eventually wipe out their entire inventory while also devastating their future business prospects, as all of them had no flood insurance to help with reconstruction.

The water level in all these buildings reached a menacing four feet in height and, in most cases, took a significantly long time to recede, leaving inches-deep mud and muck and wreaking cleanup havoc for days thereafter. The recovery for these businesses and the surrounding area would require much local and state assistance, and reopening for them would be delayed the longest in comparison to the majority of their downtown counterparts.

Expanding further now, the flood seemed to take a two-pronged approach as it still attempted to regain its long ago subjugated path to the Shetucket River. The urban modified portion of upper Franklin Street shifted the flood flow somewhat to the west. Just past the tenement houses where William Zeitz had watched the lower floor of his apartment become ruined by the water, Chestnut Avenue turned west onto Chestnut Street. The floodwaters here proceeded in a general southerly direction and, due to the natural concavity of the terrain, became a focused and straightforward concentrated force within the structures between Franklin Street and Chestnut Street. On Chestnut Street in particular, all the businesses became instant victims to these damaging effects.

At 103 Chestnut Street, the Connecticut Beverage Company, a leading distributor of liquor and beer for the New England area, now experienced major damage structurally when the lower door of the main building was demolished by some of the large ice slabs. One glacial piece in particular, estimated to weigh over a ton, literally smashed through the office door, allowing water to pour in and flood the building to over eight feet in depth. The stock room and boiler room were immediately ruined, and the entire inventory of beer, domestic and imported wines and liquors were later condemned by the City Health Department.

The Franklin Press, established in 1890 and located on the bottom floor of a three-story brick structure on 77 Chestnut Street and just down the road from the Connecticut Beverage Company, was next to face the inundating effects of the ravaging floodwaters. One huge ice chunk, still predominant in the flow and estimated to be as big as an office desk, was in the middle of the administration office, discovered the next day while others, albeit smaller, were found on top of printing presses that had been toppled over in the surge.

In the pressroom, and unique in their disparity with the surrounding equipment, were two overstuffed living room chairs lodged between two printing presses that had somehow been washed away from an apartment building upstream (likely the Franklin Street tenement house) by the torrent. An 1,800-pound safe was overturned by the flow and had subsequently slammed against other equipment, giving stark reality to the force of the water wave. Thousands of print orders that were in progress (catalogues, labels, etc.), were ruined by the water, or, later by the inches-deep mud, all resulting in an enormous monetary loss.

Next door, the Lord Manufacturing Company was also severely crippled. A small business that specialized in decorative products, its machinery was custom built for these processes and, as a result, would cost much to replace. The store was established in the mid-1930's and produced Christmas tinsel and other holiday-related products. A toy fair was scheduled in mid-March and now, as a result of the flood, Lord's was destined to miss this major advertising event, as it had nothing left to show. And as if all the interior damage weren't enough, a truck from the Lambert Aluminum Products Company on Franklin Street, opposite to the store to the east, smashed through the rear of the building, causing irreparable structural damage; this vehicle was found the next day parked inside the machine shop. "We think we are 100 per cent wiped out . . . ," reported owner Bennett Berman three days later.

Lord's would later reopen with the help of funds raised by a group of Norwich volunteers (discussed later) but would last only until September 1963 before closing for good; the flood having wreaked a disproportionate amount of damage both physically and economically.

To the east and farther down Franklin Street, meanwhile, amid numerous misplaced cars and debris floating in the stream, D'Elia's Bakery would now experience its share of extreme flood damage, having its baking ovens overrun with water and all its food inventory lost. Workers in the store that evening, having watched incredulously as the torrent and rushing water increased outside their window, narrowly escaped the onslaught by opening a window behind the serving counter and climbing out to a higher elevation to the building beside it.

The next day, their entire inventory would also be condemned by the City Health Department and it would be a testament to the owner's resilience that the store would, by reopening the following week, prosper in the ensuing years. In fact, it became, for the most part, the only business on Franklin Street (not counting the *Norwich Bulletin* necessarily as a "business") to survive the flood and it would continue on into the twenty-first century and is today still serving "grinders" and making their own unique brand of bread products while still inhabiting the very same building. Also, amazingly, the basement of D'Elia's today still has a small symbol of the flood—a fuse box that was flooded that evening still shows the sand and dirt reminders of that tragic night.

Miss Pauline Leone, who lived in an apartment house a short distance south on Franklin Street from the bakery, said that "It was like a tidal wave. In seconds we were surrounded by water." People living in this area reported kitchen stoves, fuel tanks, chairs and luggage all drifting by in the water flow. Another woman who lived in this area told news reporters later how she had learned of the raging floodwaters: "I'd fallen asleep while watching television. A noise woke me. I opened the door and an oil or garbage can hit me in the knees. At the same time I saw the water. I thought I'd never get the door closed in time."

Many of these residents of upper Franklin Street, having endured the initial tidal wave and all the anxiety that it had wrought, were alarmed again later as a gas main near the intersection of Pond and Franklin Street, the site of the aforementioned severe street erosion, ruptured causing all of them to be evacuated again, adding further to the incommodious nature of this night.

Approximately three hundred yards south of D'Elia's, the J.B. Martin Company of 132 Franklin Street, a major New England corporation and producer of velvet and other textiles, employer of about 135 people and an industrial giant in the city, was next to become victim to the floodwaters. Encompassing a huge factory building with many smaller structures at the corner of Franklin and Willow Street, the damage ultimately done to the interior of these buildings and to the business infrastructure was severe. This business too was able to restart but soon became a victim of economic forces and was forced to reluctantly, relocate to South Carolina, integrating itself with the new plant there, in 1969—this after spending over sixty years in the same downtown Norwich location. There, in Leesville, the J.B. Martin Company still prospers to this day.

But now as the floodwaters bore down on the Martin structures, the outside north of the main factory building, which held the electrical distribution for the plant, became instantly covered with four feet of water. Transformers, breakers, and other distribution panels and electrical equipment immediately lost power, which subsequently tripped the boilers off, paralyzing the buildings.

Pouring through large open windows on the north side of the main structure, the flood spread out onto the lower factory floors, causing immense and indescribable damage; in fact, a terrified night watchman became almost trapped as the floodwaters nearly engulfed him inside the main building. "He told us the place was being flooded. We told him to get out of there as quick as possible. He did, but his car was washed away," owner Roger Charbin reported the next day.

The ice chunks, imbued throughout the flood flow, did their predictable damage here as well since "every room was left with these huge pieces mixed in with the sodden cloth, broken benches and other debris. One huge chunk measured four feet long, three feet wide and almost two feet thick and found a final resting place in one corner of the boiler room."

The departments that made up the lower floors now bore the brunt of the onslaught. The machine shop, dye shop, boiler room, and grey room, which had two to three thousand pieces of grey goods, were ruined instantly while the entire basement floor saw water level rise to beyond four feet. Dye stuffs, motors and delicate electrical control instrumentation also suffered as the floodwaters engulfed them and then departed, seemingly as quickly as it had come, through the equally large south side windows, where the curious sight of grey goods and cloth, unraveling in the flow made for long, sodden and odd-looking debris the next day.

Farther down Chestnut Street and across from the Martin Company, the Norwich Fire Department was also experiencing its share of the flooding. Three feet of water "sloshed into the building and had to be flushed out the front doors." The aftereffects to the building of the mud and muck were later mitigated as the firemen used their extensive hosing to spray down the interior. By this time luckily, all of the trucks were out on call, thus avoiding damage, but additional resources such as William LeFleur were needed and subsequently called in; LeFleur specifically manned the fire station switchboard, which had received hundreds of calls by this time for assistance, and it was here that he would stay throughout the night.

Across Chestnut Street from the firehouse, Goldberg's Appliances also received its share of damage and destruction. Refrigerators, washing machines, and untold other appliances on the ground floor were ruined and it would be many days before this now-useless inventory could be hauled off.

Back along Franklin Street towards downtown, there were, however, a few "miraculous" stories of only marginally damaged businesses—one of them included a store and a man who would become a unique friend with the Moody children only a short time later. The United Package Store was a small "drop in" business on Franklin Street about one hundred yards from the Square and was an establishment later frequented by Ronnie for many years. Usually bringing the children along when he was out running errands, he often stopped in while the owner, Louis Zeirler, a small outspoken, loud, and exceedingly gregarious man, would affably greet them as they entered: "Hey! Tom, Dick, and Harry . . . Pete and Larry!" , causing the youngsters to be at first confused but ultimately embracing and indeed looking forward to these convivial encounters from the avuncular Zeirler.

Ronnie for his part also enjoyed talking with "Louie," as Zeirler was a man who had taken on, seemingly as a mission, all the gossip and goings-on of the downtown scene while being an outspoken and vehement critic of said happenings. Zeirler's store was mostly spared flood damage on this night of seemingly random destruction (minor water damage on the main floor with a small loss of inventory), and he was able to return to business within the next few days and continue for many years thereafter.

Most other small businesses here, however, weren't as fortunate and saw instant destruction by the floodwaters as they continued to race down Franklin Street. Stavrou's Soda Shop, Vasington's Liquor Store, Columbus Park Tavern, Sabby and Jim's Barber Shop and Cedrone's Bakery were but a few of the many establishments in this middle Franklin Street area to see their life's work essentially disappear in a few dreadful minutes.

THOMAS MOODY, JR.

CHAPTER 6

The Franklin Square Story

T HE *NORWICH BULLETIN* newspaper had never failed to publish a daily edition in its storied 172-year history. Now, though, that record was in serious jeopardy as the torrent of floodwater continued its ravaging path through downtown toward the Shetucket River. The *Bulletin* newspaper offices sat right in the middle of Franklin Street along with many of the smaller businesses similarly destroyed by the flood. A two-story structure, the *Bulletin* building employed a staff that would be severely tested this night in its ability to churn out its next day's newspaper and would see this crisis ultimately push them, in the middle of a rampaging flood, to come up with new and innovative solutions to printing it.

The newspaper, an accepted and revered mainstay in the town's culture, had, through a complex and far-ranging history, its origin all the way back to 1791 when it was initially printed and distributed as the *Norwich Weekly Register*. This name was subsequently changed in 1796 to the *Chelsea Courier* to more identify itself with the then small but self-pronounced popular downtown scene, which felt itself worthy of its own news publication; Chelsea being the societal designation of the downtown area near the confluence of the three rivers that make up the town. The *Courier* then merged with another smaller local newspaper called the *Norwich Morning Bulletin* in 1860 and was soon published daily using that name. This version now also included a Saturday edition called the *Norwich Weekly Courier*. In 1873 the Bulletin Company was formed and the name of the newspaper was formally changed to the currently recognized *Norwich Bulletin*.

Another competitor to the *Bulletin* would spring up in 1888 during a time of immense growth and expansion in the town—the overriding, if perhaps haughty, opinion being that the area had ample room and readership for two newspapers. But as with all journalistic competition, this new paper, the *Norwich Evening Record* was clearly looking to monopolize the area news distribution for itself and, with limited funds, did an otherwise admirable job, managing to last until 1927 where it finally succumbed to greater economic forces and was ultimately absorbed by the larger Norwich Bulletin Company.

The first Sunday edition of the *Bulletin* was published in 1930 and was called the *Norwich Sunday Record*. This was changed to the *Norwich Bulletin Sunday Edition* in 1960 and finally the *Sunday Bulletin* in 1981.

It was at this time, in 1981, that the *Bulletin* ceased being a "small town" newspaper when the local owners sold its interests to the nationally owned Gannet News Service who then sold it, in 2007, to Gatehouse Media, which runs and publishes the daily and Sunday editions to this day.

But on this evening, the 6th of March, 1963, the *Bulletin* staff was only about halfway through the process of publishing its next day's newspaper when the dam break was confirmed at their Franklin Street offices. Within minutes, floodwaters as not seen in this part of downtown Norwich since the 1938 hurricane[6] were racing through Franklin Street towards them, which meant, sadly, that their normal business routine would not become ordinary again for many days hence.

Antiquated by today's standards, the process of publishing a daily newspaper in 1963 took on many disparate processes and numerous manual efforts that today are handled much more transparently with high-tech equipment in a fraction of the time, eliminating much of the human element. This art, in 1963, involved engraving and large printing presses that took up considerable floor space while also involving a significant human investment. Today, an advanced technological process called "offset printing" which is predictably computer driven, is the industry standard.

---

[6]   The great 1938 New England Hurricane whipped across Long Island in September of that year before its epicenter made landfall near the Bridgeport/ New Haven area. The storm surge in Long Island Sound however raised water levels to menacing heights which propagated up the Thames River and into the downtown regions of Norwich, flooding the area and becoming, ultimately, the comparison for the 1963 flood.

THOMAS MOODY, JR.

Just prior to the flood warning that night, the staff had ten of the thirty-two pages already engraved and ready for print. The floodwaters then came pouring into the building, instantly engulfing the basement area where large rolls of newsprint were stored. Immediately, the upper floor pressroom section raced into action, attempting to remove as many of these basement newsprint rolls as possible. The water, however, came in too hard and too fast, pouring into the cellar and washing all the supplies up against the outer walls and making all these consumables now useless.

The staff unfortunately was only able to save eight of the 175 rolls that were down there. Sensing that this potent force of the water would not subside soon, the building heating system was immediately shut down by the managers, fearing that electrical shock or, worse yet, explosion would occur. Employees not engaged in saving what supplies they could, initially raced outside to the parking lot to move their cars to higher ground where, as on Lake Street, some were successful and others weren't.

The water at this point was approximately five feet in depth in the basement and lapping now at the ground floor of the main offices. Downstairs and also completely submerged were the engraving and photographic areas. All of these Bulletin assets would become overwhelmed, ultimately, as would the print presses and the unsaved newsprint paper.

Amid this chaos though, the newspaper management team that was on hand that evening soon realized that publishing the next day's newspaper from these inundated offices would be an impossible task. Fortunately, pre-thought-out contingencies for a similar sort of disaster had already been developed. True, these actions had been built largely upon electrical outages, and certainly they did not think about a natural disaster devastating them in such a manner as this, they nonetheless implemented the plan that they had conceived.

The details of this process, as laid out, involved contacting the *New London Day* newspaper offices, twelve miles to the south, and to use that company's assets to assist in publishing an issue of the *Bulletin* newspaper. This contingency also called for short-term usage of the *Day's* delivery services; and as it turned out, the *Bulletin* would require help from The *Day's* offices for the next three days. It would be a testament then to the "brotherhood" of newspaper publishers that the *Bulletin* ultimately achieved success this evening and in the days to come despite this seemingly insurmountable obstacle thrown before them.

A serious competitor for the area's newspaper readership, the *New London Day*, would now gratefully reciprocate for the use of the *Bulletin's* offices and facilities that they themselves had needed back in 1954 when a fire at the nearby New London Williams Street electrical station knocked out power to their plant and, even earlier, in 1938, when "the great hurricane" struck and the downtown area of New London became particularly untenable. The *Day* staff later all reported that they were more than glad to be of assistance to their brethren to the north in this disastrous period.

Donald Oat, the *Bulletin's* assistant general manager and Harrison Noyes, assistant treasurer, were the senior management team on hand that evening and it was they who would have to immediately implement and oversee these contingencies while trying to control the chaos that was erupting in the street-level newsroom. The *Day*, when contacted, first summoned its press and stereotyping crews from home as well as members of its composing room staff. All of them then gathered at the New London offices to await further word from Norwich on subsequent resources to call in.

Meanwhile, the *Bulletin's* Circulation Department under the management of Bob Sampson ordered his mail room and mail delivery staff into emergency transportation duty; the previously completed portion of the next day's (Thursday's) paper had to now be transported rapidly to New London. At the *Day's* printing offices, meanwhile, problems with atypical printing presses and styles became apparent immediately as the two newspaper printing presses were noted to be markedly different. This became the first of many obstacles to be overcome; the *Bulletin* was an eight-column newspaper while the *Day* was a nine-column.

To make this work, it was decided to make matrices of page type (essentially a large wooden block framing the metal print press letters of the Bulletin's type) in Norwich and transport them quickly to New London to be cast into metal for placement into the Day's unique presses. Also, since the story was still being played out, the front page, the most telling, and on this day, the most important in terms of sales, would subsequently be changed three times in a matter of hours. This required still more coordination between the two offices, as part of the page-one type had to be set in Norwich and then quickly transported down to New London.

As press time neared, a decision by the *Bulletin* management staff, now on site at the *Day's* New London offices, was made to leave the *Day's* printer press required ninth column blank to match the other completed pages in the paper. Also, the early pictures of the tragedy became problematic as well, as the *Bulletin* and the *Day* used completely different processes and formats to print pictures. Because of this and the time pressure inherent in publishing the next day's paper, some early editions of the *Bulletin* would have different pictures of the tragedy than later editions.

For the *Bulletin* reporters however, getting from their flooded office building to the scene of the disaster would become a logistical bind that thankfully was alleviated, incredibly, by something as insignificant as a small dinghy owned by one Marco Altamura of nearby School Street. Ferrying reporters back and forth over the flooded parking lot was actually performed throughout the night by Altamura and, as they hurriedly disembarked and went to the scene or entered the flooded *Bulletin* building to file their reports, the reporters became able to efficiently report on the disaster real time, making Altamura another unseen but nevertheless key component of this long night of makeshift operations attempting to get the March 7 newspaper published.

Also, at this time, a crude communications network was being formed inside the flooded building, involving numerous new and rigged telephone connections, which would ultimately be capable of sending the latest updates to the New London offices. With all of this provisional effort in place, finally at 3:30 a.m., the front page was declared finalized, to the extent possible for such a rapidly moving story, and the printing presses went to work.

By 6:00 a.m. the paper had been printed and the drivers, who'd driven frantically to New London to get the operation started, were now driving back to Norwich with equal zeal such that the first paper to hit the streets was only one hour late—an amazing accomplishment and testament to the teamwork and management that the staff at both newspapers would hold proudest of their memories of this awful night.

On the scene reporting of the disaster was also, in and of itself, a story of heroic proportions. When word of the dam break was received initially at the *Bulletin* offices, city editor Tom Winters dispatched reporters Ed Popham and Pete Fox to initiate the coverage. Jumping into a *Bulletin* company vehicle, the pair, presciently, proceeded up Broadway (away from the oncoming floodwaters) and to Reynolds Road and into the park, coming down to the dam area from the west side. "There was no special reason for taking that route but it could have proven fatal for the *Bulletin* duo if they had taken a route involving Boswell Avenue and Mohegan Park Road. As they later learned, the floodwaters had reached the downtown area even before they reached the dam. Presumably, the two would have driven smack into the cascading torrents"; it was reported two days later in the same *Norwich Bulletin* for which the two were now risking their lives.

Upon arrival at the park, the pair encountered the erstwhile Charles Phoenix, the Public Works employee who was still at the dam site radioing reports to the Public Works Garage. Having witnessed the dam break, Phoenix, with eyes still wide and with a voice still filled with excitement, exclaimed, "It's gone! It just blew!" to the now equally amazed reporters. Looking down in the nighttime darkness at the remnants of the dam, Popham and Fox saw and then heard water still roaring menacingly through the yawning breech while the screeching of geese and ducks, undoubtedly perturbed at the uncommon commotion that the evening's activities had caused, provided an eerie backdrop to the scene.

Orienting themselves and trying to visualize the path that the flood took, the pair sped off in pursuit of the rushing waters, hoping to come upon anything that would enhance their story. Having to backtrack and go completely around the quickly emptying pond, the pair now raced toward Mohegan Park Road from the east side of the dam, where they encountered an area of road washout. This area was where the initial volume of water had raced over, and careened toward the skating pond. Miraculously, the two reporters were still somehow able to cross over the still-significantly flowing water and reach Judd Road, which was on the immediate south side of the flood path and onto significantly higher ground.

Continuing their chase while rushing down Judd Road past the Rose Garden (an area of arches, fountains, and rose arbors beautifully maintained by the park and the site of numerous spring and summer weddings) they then turned up Rockwell Street and down Beech Street to a point where they now saw the torrent flowing through the East Baltic Street area. "They saw waters race unhindered over Colonna Field and watched the city's Brook St. garage doors crumble under the tremendous force," the next day's story reported.

"They saw city trucks go crashing through the intersection of Brook and Hickory Streets. There was a Ford Falcon lodged between a tree and a city pickup truck. Searchlights played a macabre trick on the eye as it looked like there was a body slumped over the wheel."

Upon seeing this vast river of water flowing toward Centennial Square, the reporters quickly determined that trying to go forward toward downtown from this point would now be impossible, so Popham and Fox were forced to again backtrack, this time down Rockwell Street and, while trying to avoid the manic traffic suddenly on the roads heading toward the city, eventually ended up at a blocked-off section of Broad Street east of Platt Street. Here they encountered yet another of the many ungodly traffic snarls that had erupted this evening such that the pair decided to just abandon their car and venture out on foot.

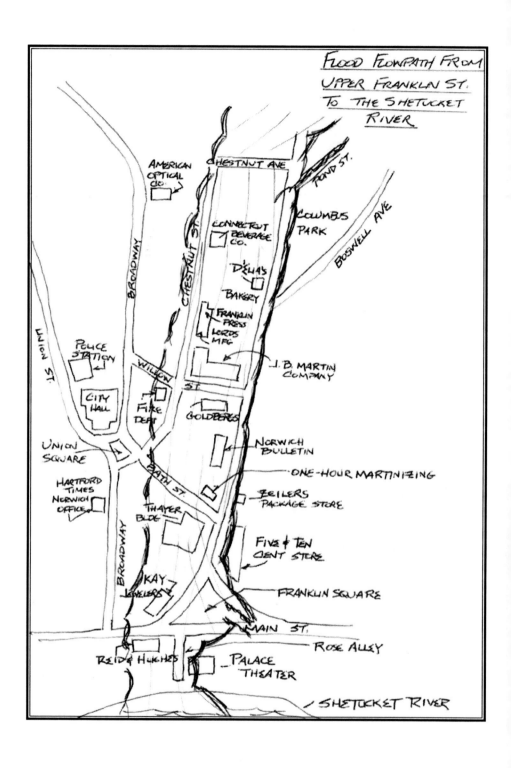

FLOOD FLOWPATH FROM UPPER FRANKLIN ST. TO THE SHETUCKET RIVER

As they trudged eastward, they noticed fellow *Bulletin* pressman Joe Strouse beyond a police blockade and much farther down Broad Street. Calling out for his attention, they saw that he was, curiously, standing near the Turner-Stanton Mill along with a large crowd of people. "The Mill! The Mill! It's going," Strouse shouted back to his associates and then suddenly, along with his many onlookers, turned to watch helplessly as the east side of the building simply disintegrated.

Rushing through the blockade and trampling through the crowd now to get to the Mill and, once there, staring incredulously at the ruins and shaking their heads at the unimaginable turn of events that this evening had cast along with the imagined terror that those poor people who had been trapped in the Mill must have gone through, Popham and Fox decided that this was clearly a story that now needed immediate and priority journalistic attention. Agreeing on strategy, they decided that Popham would stay here at the scene, gathering eyewitness testimony, while Fox would go back down to the *Bulletin* offices (unbeknownst to him, these offices were, at this point, being abandoned for the *New London Day* printing effort) and start writing the story. Later, they agreed that they would somehow reconnect, in this pre cell phone era, and finalize this incredible story.

As Fox now attempted to return to the *Bulletin* offices, he quickly realized, in this night of sudden destruction, that driving logistics would again be the key to arriving at any downtown location. Doing a quick city layout review in his head, he surmised that if water was present on Broad Street and flowing such that the Turner Mill had become devastated, then Franklin Street, at least the upper portion of it, would surely now be seeing a large portion of the flow and would, assuredly, not be available as a viable driving route.

Deciding instead to approach downtown from Union Street, he thought that this would take him close to the *Bulletin* building (the rear of which could be seen from Union Square) and, perhaps, he could then somehow get to his office from the rear entry and file this incredible story.

Fox, at this point, was still unaware that the *Bulletin* folks were themselves, in dire straits and in the middle of salvaging what little they could from their office. Driving down Union Street and entering Union Square, Fox now saw firsthand the destruction and devastation to the downtown area as the *Bulletin* building and parking lot were almost completely submerged with water. Almost laughing at the incongruity of the night's events, he also noticed his personal car and that of his fellow reporter Popham bobbing around in the floodwaters behind the building.

Realizing that he probably would not be able to reach his office tonight (he was unaware of the Altamura ferrying services), he, instead, sought assistance at the nearby Norwich police station, which appeared to be the only city run facility still in service this evening. As he entered though, he was immediately faced with unmitigated chaos as the building was jammed with people who were, themselves, in dire need of help. After making his way through the throng of helpless flood victims and finally finding an officer that would help him, Fox was ultimately able to relay his fractured storyline to the newspaper (which still maintained a skeleton crew in the Norwich building) by teletype through a phone line to an affiliate in New Haven, some seventy miles away.

Popham, meanwhile, still on the scene at the Turner Mill site, spoke with, among many of his interviewees that evening, a Mr. Bujnowski, whose wife had been among the many injured in the Turner-Stanton collapse. Popham, critically, was also able to recall the names of all of the co-workers of Mr. Bujnowski's wife, which, when relayed to the Mill owners and the police, proved crucial in assisting in the reconstruction of the story of the tragedy and identification of all of the mill workers that night.

It was Popham who had also first interviewed Benjamin Dubicki, the man who witnessed the collapse of the Mill from Broad Street and who was expansive with reporters afterward. Several times Mr. Dubicki broke off his interview to serve as a rescue stretcher bearer. Ultimately, Dubicki told Popham that "at least ten persons" rushed up to the third-floor doorway of the structure, screaming for assistance, before the crushing floodwaters slammed into the building and permanently silenced their plea for help.

Pete Fox, meanwhile, after his struggle at the police station with establishing a firm and reliable connection to his offices, now made his way back to the Turner Mill site. Navigating his way through the crush of cars and onlookers, he came upon the ravaged building where his fellow reporter Ed Popham was still stationed.

As Fox reconnected with Popham, both newsmen now noted the absolutely surreal conditions surrounding them. Ruin, it seemed, was everywhere—water was still flowing abundantly down through the crumbled east end of the mill. Fire trucks and rescue workers were now here in en masse and configured all along the outskirts of Centennial Square, their number being exceeded only by the throngs of onlookers and cars that were either afloat in the waters, still pooled in the square area, or abandoned altogether by people trying to get through to their homes.

Amid the crushed timbers, bricks and tangled metal of the destroyed Turner-Stanton Mill, a woman's scream was suddenly and clearly heard. Onlookers, also hearing this searing plea for help, and heartened by the fact that here at last was a reassuring sign of life, started shouting for rescuers to "come and do something!" Rushing through the still-deep waters and the myriad debris of the building collapse to the location of the screams, firemen and rescue volunteers clamored over the building rubble and balanced themselves on splintered timbers while calling out for rescue ropes and harnesses. They "yanked, pushed, tore and heaved until the woman was worked free," Fox reported. This woman, Mrs. Theresa Moretti, was the victim who had exclaimed "My friend!" over and over while she was being extracted from the debris. It was Fox, in fact, who had decided to ride with her in the ambulance and follow this story angle as far as it would go.

Upon arrival at the Backus Hospital with Mrs. Moretti, Fox observed, with great admiration, that the doctors and nurses on duty this evening were a uniquely prepared team, trained to quickly respond in an emergency while being extremely compassionate with treatment for these battered victims. Noting that Mrs. Moretti was attended to by "student nurses, RNs, doctors, and orderlies working in speedy silence," he was struck with the precision-like manner that was taken in her care and the confidence that they all seemed to exude.

While still at the hospital, Fox contacted the *Bulletin* offices, again through his New Haven affiliate, to update the story. After reporting the heroic actions of the rescuers at the Mill and the subsequent expert care given here by the hospital staff, he now left the hospital and returned once again to the city, where he reconnected with Popham. There it was that these two intrepid reporters continued to stay throughout the night, relaying events as they occurred to the skeleton staff that remained in the darkened *Bulletin* offices.

The bulk of the Bulletin reporting staff, meanwhile, was now in New London and, as Fox, Popham and others continued their coverage, they forwarded their updates mostly from the alienated and darkened Norwich office on to their disaffected annex in New London, through the modest communications network, where they, in turn, were now rapidly set up to convert these late breaking stories onto the disjointed Day printing presses and ultimately onto the front page of the March 7th Norwich Bulletin.

As the *Norwich Bulletin* worked its publishing miracle, the floodwaters, meanwhile, continued past the middle Franklin Street area onward toward its short path now to the river, inundating Franklin Square with up to four feet in water. To see the center of downtown Norwich now was to witness a vast expanse of seemingly unmoving water with the unnervingly abstract observation of buildings and structures peeking upward through its looming domain.

The contour of Franklin Square was such that the floodwaters had nowhere else to go but to pool into the center of it, at the intersection of Franklin and Main Streets, giving the alarming late-night impression of a large lake with menacingly sinful lights shining off of its surface. The only place for this massive inventory to drain was down a diminutive, seemingly unnoticed passageway to the south called Rose Alley, a small road that sloped downward and away from the square center and which terminated into the Shetucket River.

Because of the relatively limited size of this street and its inherent inability to pass large amounts of water, it would take many hours for the entire pond in the square to bottleneck its way through this street and empty into the Shetucket.

Franklin Square, although not really an "official" city sobriquet, was nonetheless the symbolic location of the center of Norwich's business hub. Many small and assorted stores and attractions were arranged around this oblique circle, and the area was, at this time before the onslaught of suburban malls and superstores, critical to the town's survival and local industry.

Many a Christmas season from those long forgotten 1960s celebrations were typified by the large Rockefeller Center-style tree in it's middle, giving a charm and coziness to the downtown area that's long since been replaced by a rather cold and despondent traffic circle. Clothing stores, bakeries, discount stores and many smaller family-owned businesses, arrayed around and facing into the interior square, now, in this night of terror, saw their structures and stock overwhelmed with floodwaters ice, tree limbs, and instant destruction.

Just to the south of the *Norwich Bulletin* office building, on the corner of Franklin and Bath sreets, in an area contemporaneously absent any structures and used as a small parking lot for the very same *Norwich Bulletin*, the popular dry-cleaning business One Hour Martinizing was then housed in a small corner building. The store, which had been a fixture at this corner for many years, now saw its first floor flooded and its finished dry-cleaning and inventory ruined.

Across Bath Street at Longo's Fruit Stand, perhaps the most ignominious and extreme symbol of this night's lunacy occurred when the store's entire basement stock of peanuts was unceremoniously floated up and onto Franklin Square, providing the macabre sight of thousands of peanut shells riding along the crest of the floodwaters and then settling onto the square area the next day when the waters finally receded.

Also across from Bath Street, the Thayer Building, which housed Longo's Fruit Stand and many other prosperous businesses in its four-story structure, was, arguably, the highest symbol of entrepreneurism in this immediate downtown area. On the ground floor, facing Franklin Street, many stores were walk-in types which made it a popular shopping and gathering place for both city inhabitants and suburbanites. Young Tommy Moody would in fact spend considerable time here in this downtown hub in the mid-1970s, purchasing and adding to his growing record collection at Gaffney's Records, which was housed on the ground floor, and where he would inevitably run into high-school friends outside the popular record store and share the latest music news and his purchases with them.

On this night, however, the street level of the building, which housed Gaffney's, Longo's, and other popular businesses, was immediately awash in the engulfing flood. "There was extensive damage to the Thayer Building along with all of the stores on the ground floor of the building," it was reported by the *Bulletin*. "Isadore Berkman, speaking for Berkman Realty Company, owners of the building, stated that the water rose three feet above the ground floor. As a result the heating system was knocked out completely as was the elevator service and power to the occupants of the building. Water and mud caused additional damage to the hallway of the building."

In the rear (west) of the building and similar to the *Bulletin* parking lot upstream, all of the cars parked here would become afloat in the floodwater. One of these in particular, a 1961 Buick Imperial belonging to lawyer Milton Jacobson, a person who would play a prominent role in the inevitable litigation following this disaster, careened into the back door of Strick's Bakery where it was discovered, completely sodden, the next day.

Some of these ground-floor businesses, which were severely stricken but were inevitably able to return to service several days later, were Strick's Bakery, Franklin Hardware, Debuteen Shoppe, Fortin's Diner, and Lavassuer's Barber Shop. At the Franklin Hardware store, a large supply of seed, electrical fixtures, wallpaper, and other household items that had been stored in the basement were now completely ruined by the flood. The upstairs portion of the store was also so severely affected that it would be days before an assessment of reopening could be given.

At Fortin's Diner, the entire interior succumbed to the flood with tables, chairs, and other equipment afloat in the three-foot water level. The ovens and food stores were ruined as well, but, as was the case with D'Elia's Grinder Shop farther up Franklin Street, it was a testament to the fortitude of the owners and employees, who had worked around the clock in cleanup operations in the ensuing days, that the business was ready to open Monday morning awaiting the City Health Department OK.

Bill Stanley, in 1963, was a young thirty-four year old investments broker employed at the Cooley & Company, a top investment firm for the town and local area. In later years, Stanley would become a vocal advocate and locally renowned figure for his memories and storytelling ability, publishing numerous articles and books on the history of Norwich before passing away in 2010. This night, however, he was at home preparing to go to bed when he heard over the radio that a tremendous flood had suddenly engulfed the downtown area and that most businesses there were ruined. Racing to the downtown area, he made it as far as Union Square, where he then encountered the same barracades that later thwarted *Bulletin* reporter Peter Fox.

From Union Square, the large downtown intersection point where six city streets converge in front of the large and ornate city hall building, one could look downward toward the city at Franklin Street. The city hall building, at Union Square's center was on significantly higher ground than the central downtown area and the viewer could see clearly that the contour of the land sloped downward, and note immediately how water would pool in its center. Stanley, looking out now upon the area from the city hall building, saw that "Bath St. was like a big pond and water almost covered the cars left in the parking lots." His first thought, as it was with all who came upon the flooded downtown this evening, was "Where did this water come from?" While not learning of the dam break until later the next day, Stanley, like all others who were anxious to check their businesses, was nevertheless resigned to wait until the water receded, and, frustratingly, so he now did.

At his office in the Thayer Building, meanwhile, "water was desk high," later leaving a three-foot-high mark on the walls, with all of its expensive furniture in the lobby and waiting areas being floated about by the murky waters. This office area was at the northern corner of the Thayer Building and took the brunt of the flood force. Moreover, a road duct opening from Bath Street that drained water into the piped underground brook was now overflowing and this additional water volume and force seized the floor area inside the Cooley offices, such that a whole new floor and supporting structure would have to be added later at great additional cost.

The unique and sensitive equipment used by the firm to update and analyze stocks, again dated by today's online standards, was also destroyed; a Dow Jones teletype machine, New York Stock Exchange machines, and a Western Union Trans-Lux stock tape machine were among the battered and muddy leftovers in the office ruins the next day. All of the office handwritten records and memo paper investment records were also destroyed, but duplicate records were, fortunately, on hand in the firm's corporate home office in Hartford. To replace these, however, would take a mighty and time-consuming effort of copying by many of the firm's administrative employees, again an example of the technological atrophy of this era as their format prevented rapid reproduction.

Stanley also recalled how, when he was able to access his office the next day, he watched as the City Health and Fire department personnel quickly rushed in and proceeded to smash up and tear apart all the equipment, furniture, and consumables with a ferocity and abandon that symbolized the seriousness of that evening's disaster, while also giving notice to the potential for toxicity and the spreading of germs and disease. This destruction was quickly followed by a cleanup crew that rapidly dispensed with the now manageable size of the potentially contaminated ruins.

Just down from the Thayer Building, Kay Jewelers suffered not only interior damage but also saw its cement foundation seize as well from the pounding and saturation of the force of water. In subsequent days, the store would require help from not only the downtown cleanup crews but also from civil engineers as they were needed to help shore up the foundation so that a reasonably early reopening date could be contemplated.

Another prominent downtown business, and one that gave Franklin Square a share of its unique quality and 1960s charm, was the Woolworth Store across Franklin Street from the Thayer Building. Commonly called "the Five-and-Ten Store," Woolworths was possibly the most popular of shopping points in this area.

The store, this night, did absorb severe basement damage, but because of its orientation in relation to Franklin Street, missed much of the main wave and which undoubtedly allowed it to escape more-extensive damage. The floodwater expanded, instead, out beyond its front doors with the highest water level being reached more toward the center of the square, such that the main floor of the business got very little water intrusion, and the owners faced no more than minor cleanup before they could reopen.

Other businesses in and around the Franklin Square area now faced grave ruin brought on by the floodwaters, while some, miraculously, saw little to no damage. The sheer randomness of the destructive force left most owners scratching their heads and, for the fortunate, thanking whatever Divine Intervention that interceded to keep them from financial ruin. Logic seemed to play little part as the inner square became literally a huge pond with all of the businesses witnessing the same water level reaching their front doors. Some of the lucky businesses were Perkin's Candy Shop, Nadik's Kiddie Clothes, Carroll Cut-Rate Stores, Brine Jewelers, the Cranston Store and Spencer Shoes.

At the popular Reid & Hughes clothing store on the south side of the square, there was, illogically, no damage even though the store was in the direct path of the flood. "We are really happy, we didn't get a drop of water damage in any part of the building," store manager Stearns Martin reported. The store was ready to open the next day, Thursday afternoon, after City Health Department concurrence, but saw understandably light business.

Next door, however, at the Lincoln Store, again seeing the same engulfing floodwaters that Reid & Hughes experienced, inexorable damage was wrought as the building was "rather badly hit." The basement of this structure was completely flooded and all inventory lost. Store manager Robert Wentworth, the next day, was unable to provide an estimate of monetary damage or a re-opening time frame as he also was completely at the mercy of cleanup crews and the City Health Department.

Perhaps the most absurd and illogical business survivor story and certainly the most intriguing of the evening was that of the Palace Theater on Rose Alley. Upon receiving word of the dam break and the potential for flooding, Norwich police officer Frank Vallarelli, making the rounds of notification in the area, immediately informed theater owner Leslie Barrett of the threat. Barrett, who was in the middle of the late evening showings for that day's movie schedule, was forced to evacuate the entire building and then watch frantically as the floodwaters raced by his glass front door, covering cars outside his theater while pouring up against the outer windows, on its way to the nearby Shetucket River.

Inside, amazingly, nary a drop of water invaded the entrance lobby, nor was there any substantial damage to his establishment (there was, however, some very minor water damage in the basement), but not a showing in subsequent days was missed, truly an amazingly fortunate occurrence.

As the initial onslaught of floodwater neared its end down Rose Alley and into, finally, the Shetucket, the long and devastating path that the bombarding wave took from Mohegan Park through downtown was now, thankfully, past. It would still be many hours, though, before water levels receded enough to make any assessment of the damage that this tragedy had brought; indeed, pictures showing a still-sizable body of water in the Franklin Square area were taken as late as 3:00 a.m. with what seems to be a still-significant pool of water present in the square.

But, again, the damaging initial flow buttressed with the huge ice chunks, tree limbs, and boulders had now gratefully gone past the downtown area and into the river. By most estimates and observations, the water had receded enough later that morning to walk about Franklin Street and the Square, although many small pockets of still rather deep water remained with these small "ponds" still pervasively finding their way to the many basements and interiors of the numerous buildings along its path.

Now, just after midnight, in the denuded flood's path, lay unbelievable destruction and ruin. On Franklin Street small rivulets of water still flowed while numerous left-behind ice chunks, tree limbs, and large rocks were strewn about in un-patterned and disassociated arrangements. On upper Franklin Street, the water level near D'Elia's Grinder Shop was still nearly two-feet deep, being harnessed there by the narrowing of the road as it passed by Columbus Park.

As neighbors and onlookers braved the nighttime air and migrated to the safety of this elevated park slope to look firsthand at the devastation, fish, amazingly, could be clearly seen swimming in the still-abundant flowing river. Almost impossibly, it was realized that these fish had flowed with the Spaulding Pond water and made the nearly two-mile trek as it had escaped the dam, and they were now collecting here before moving on. Curiously, most of the talk here became whether the fish would actually make it all the way down to the Shetucket River.

Near Lamperell's auto dealership, crowds of people, still in the nighttime freezing cold temperatures now migrated in and around the scattered fuel tanks and water-strewn automobiles to witness firsthand the destruction, or to just solemnly pray for the injured and the dead. On top of the rock wall that only moments ago provided support for the garage roof above the dealership and at the bottom of the small hill that sloped down from Lake Street lay the overturned Moody's 1957 blue Ford Fairlane, hideously upside down, brazenly smashed with windows fractured and crumpled passenger-side front door wide open, eerily shining in the now moonlit night, a spectral symbol of death and suffering.

Farther up, past the mangled, mud-and sand-strewn terrain of the Lake Street playground, the magnitude of the disaster was never more strikingly evident than at the ruins of the Turner-Stanton Mill. Rescuers, firemen and the multitudes of volunteers and onlookers picked over the ruins, careful not to become casualties themselves in the still-dangerous dynamic of the caved-in structure.

Perhaps the most incongruous of all scenes this late evening, though, was at the now-devastated Spaulding Pond Dam sight. The dam break, having upset the indigenous ducks and geese and their customary domesticity, caused them to be now randomly swimming and flying about, clearly confused, throughout the small puddles of pond water that still abounded around the gaping trenches and gullies that the floodwaters had carved out, all of them having, it seemed, demeanors of animosity, as they now massed, squawking fervently for the return of their small pond.

CHAPTER 7

Aftermath . . . the First Few Days

I T WAS THE worst disaster to hit Norwich since the famous hurricane of 1938. In that seminal moment of New England history, Franklin Square became exceedingly flooded by the Long Island Sound storm surge. But now, as the morning of Thursday, March 7 shed its peeked daylight on the frozen surroundings, downtown Norwich was again awakening to receded floodwaters as the area was, in '38, mired in inches-deep mud, muck, and destruction. But this time, the damaging flow had come from inland, not from the coast.

Damage estimates from the Spaulding Pond Dam break would ultimately run into the millions of dollars. Norwich Police Chief Clarence Simpson had declared a local state of emergency at 3:30 a.m. and closed the immediate downtown area to all automobile traffic. Foot traffic would be the only method this morning of gaining access to the area, and dozens now came from the outskirts of town and surroundings to view the tragedy firsthand. The overriding and undeniable feeling of all who made it to Franklin Street and into the Franklin Square area this morning was a numbed, unbelieving shock—nobody seemed to understand where this massive flood had come from. When the unimaginable truth finally spread and that this disaster started at Mohegan Park, residents and onlookers again were dumbfounded—how did water all the way up there cause such damage all the way down here?

The image of the Spaulding Pond Dam breaking and causing all this destruction, led to the next inevitable question: "Why weren't we warned?" Many of the more curious minded and unbelieving would, in fact, wait for the affected areas to be cleared before embarking out on foot to see for themselves, and it was only then, after understanding the contours of the land and the existing brooks and flow paths, that their inquisitiveness would be abetted and the logic of it would sink in. The water did in fact flow from that pond unbelievably all the way downtown!

This path and the areas in and around it, as traced from Mohegan Park to downtown, was, this day, in various states of destruction and ruin. As the early March 7 daylight increased, this carnage and devastation became even more palpable to the local masses, with the true impact showing itself in shocking and graphic detail.

Flood control experts later estimated that Spaulding Pond took as little as thirty minutes to empty after the dam collapse; other experts thought a little longer. Regardless, a devastating amount of water moved rapidly in a short period of time and over a comparatively short area. Engineers, later being asked to put the effect of the water's destruction into laymen's terms, would characterize the flow as being close to the velocity of a large river as it approaches a steep waterfall. Some would put it in terms of speed: forty miles per hour at its fastest would be a number used time and again.

Now, looking over the devastation, the imagined force of last night's destruction was clearly on display as area after area in the two-mile path had its own peculiar and unique story to tell.

At the park, the immediate area surrounding the dam now resembled nothing like the previous terrain. A large V-shaped gash, as if carved by a knife, supplanted the dam structure on its east side while the earthen support material was now hideously diffused downstream; the eastern rock wall base, what little of it was left, was strewn outward into the immediate downstream expanse while boulders from the earthen wall were also scattered both to the east and to the west, with the mud, stone, and trees that had inhabited that portion of the southern dam face now all spread haphazardly downstream. Timbers and other remnants of the rose arbor structure that had adorned the top of the dam causeway were now ridiculously hanging over both ends of the gash; a strong wind would have undoubtedly disengaged them from the rest of the arbor structures and the ruined framework would have fallen hideously and unrestrained to the bottom of the breech.

The small duck pond at the south end became the first victim to the dam break and had simply vanished. Instead, a cavernous trench had been carved out of the existing landscape by the rapidly escaping floodwaters. Farther down, one could easily follow the destructive path simply by viewing the wash out—trees had been uprooted and ripped away; mud was everywhere. On the dam's east side entry on Mohegan Park Road, where *Bulletin* reporters Fox and Popham had taken their major risk to cross over on their way to chase the flood the previous evening, the road was now completely washed away, leaving behind a gash of sand and mud.

The steep area surrounding the brook, immediately southeast of the dam, which directed the flow toward the skating pond, looked as if a large tornado had set down and dragged its tail along this path. The ample tree population here was devastated, boulders had been tossed about, and everything here in the flood's path had been either gathered up into its battering flow or tossed violently aside.

Farther down and again, if one imagined a vantage point standing south of the duck pond, on the surprisingly still-intact small dam looking north, the view would look devastatingly different than it had twenty-four hours earlier. A huge gap in the woods leading from Spaulding Pond down to the skating pond was the first thing the viewer would notice. Simply gone was a large section of trees that gave this area the semiprivacy enjoyed by park visitors who would walk out into this area. The skating pond itself was now a huge semi-filled expanse with washout and devastation surrounding it. Large ice chunks still abstractly littered the terrain throughout the area, and a destructive flow path could now clearly be seen eastward where a branch of the flood had diverted towards Curtis Street.

The image of trees torn away on this easterly tree line was only exceeded in devastation by the large amount of ice still trapped among the remaining woods. Down on Curtis Street, the Norwich police cruiser #2 of Officer Richard Paradis sat forlornly on the upper part of the road, abandoned. Left here the night before when the inundating waters made it impossible for him to drive out, he left it and took out on foot, all after doing a heroic job of warning people in the area.

Where the main flood flow crashed through the skating pond and then crossed over Mohegan Park Road, the devastation was immense and surreal. The small dam south of the skating pond and the under-road drainage system were all now a garbled mix of rocks, ice, trees, pipes, and large trenches sliced into the road and land. Indeed this portion of Mohegan Park Road suffered severe erosion and it would be many days before it would be repaired.

Across and south of Mohegan Park Road, the area that had comprised Colonna's baseball field along with the Bate's property east that had been under development with the huge dirt piles was now just a vast expanse of gullies and water-filled trenches. Debris, huge puddles, trees, and ice were again the prevalent leftover of the ravaging floodwaters; it was here that the wave most likely had its first opportunity to expand and gain the intense velocity and momentum it later exhibited in its destructive force downtown, as this terrain was somewhat level before it sloped downward again toward Hickory Street.

As the flood engulfed Colonna's field, another huge destructive path was carved out of the landscape, this time into the residential areas around Baltic St. This part of the landscape was contoured such that most homes, on the slightly higher ground east and west, saw only minor flood damage, but their backyards, which sloped prominently downward into the open area between East Baltic Street and North Street, was now reminiscent of a raging riverbed gone dry. Left behind was a virtual valley of ruin with uprooted trees and the ubiquitous ice chunks seemingly littered about the entire area.

Farther south, the damage to Hickory Street was astonishing as well. This road dipped in its virtual center about one hundred yards from its western entry at Baltic Street and was now completely washed out over a fifty-yard section with cars and trucks arrayed in all unimaginable angles and configurations. Again, how any of these homes structurally survived the initial onslaught of ice, boulders, and trees is still a mystery.

The Brook Street garage of the Norwich Public Works Department, where Director Walz had made his initial frantic calls to the police the previous evening, was now a tattered shell of its former self. Barely standing or recognizable, with doors crumbled and windows smashed, it resembled instead a bombed-out war bunker. City trucks and other smaller vehicles were scattered about the yard, most facing, at a minimum, minor repair time with one pickup truck in particular being crippled beyond repair (all told thirty-three Public Works vehicles would be damaged in the flood, while thirty-five to forty new tires and other assorted vehicle supplies had floated away), the area was a complete washout.

These city trucks would now become a valuable commodity, as all, or as many of them that could be put into service, would be urgently needed in the cleanup effort to follow. The radio systems and other sensitive electronics inside the garage had been immediately destroyed by the water while the small office area also absorbed a large share of damage with the crushing ice chunks and tree limbs smashing the desks and dispersing supplies all over the floor.

It was here, however, at the city garage, that an amazingly rapid and coordinated effort of repair and cleanup was held: by the afternoon of the seventh, most trucks that could run were out and engaged in transporting the trashy remains from downtown. The office, meanwhile, had been rudimentarily reconstructed such that basic radio communications had been reestablished. The garage, early on this Thursday, was thus able to carry on with coordination and cleanup efforts while, roughly at first, radio communications with the troubled areas of the town were established.

Farther down, Centennial Square was, predictably, a quagmire. Sand, which had been stored in the parking areas outside the city garage as supply for the trucks and plows when the winter snow and ice would overwhelm the city, had flowed with the floodwaters down to the square and now added to the devastation, as inches deep of it, along with the mud, now coated the sidewalks and outer roads.

Water was also still fairly deep here, as observed in the early morning light, segregated into giant puddles while drainage continued to pour downward toward the Lake Street playground through the destroyed east side of the Turner-Stanton Mill. Most of the city rescue resources and volunteers were still congregated here, since an enormous amount of help was still needed to comb through the ruins and assist with any potential survivors.

This initial assistance work had been gratefully accomplished by the many volunteers, policemen, firemen, and any other able-bodied persons who were experienced in rescue operations or in the medical field, who had quickly responded to the tragedy. The first obstacle to overcome for these rescuers and firemen, who'd arrived on the scene seemingly minutes after the building collapsed, however, was lighting. Volunteers from the Coast Guard Academy, stationed in New London, along with many from the adjoining Naval Submarine Base in Groton, worked diligently throughout the night, establishing temporary lighting, bringing strings of it with them. These folks were also later prominent in rescue and volunteer duties, working wherever resources were directed or needed.

Richard Jaskiewicz, the off-duty Backus Hospital nurse who had displayed uncommon bravery in assisting with rescue operations, wasn't alone in his heroic actions in Centennial Square this evening. In his mind, it was the police and firemen who deserved the credit. As Jaskiewicz, at great personal risk, went to the bottom of the ruined mill, he employed his small and wiry physique to crawl between fallen girders, lumber, and bricks in an attempt to reach the potentially surviving mill workers.

Connecticut state trooper Patrick Hedge and two volunteer firemen, Bill Murphy and John Hawkins, meanwhile, were atop the rubble trying desperately to remove what debris they could. Jaskiewicz squeezed through a small tunnel-like opening at what would have been the ground-floor section of the Mill. "It was dark and I just reached, I felt a leg. I felt another. And then I felt another. Then above me I felt a hand. There were three tangled bodies in this one spot.

"Trooper Hedge was above me. He is a real man. He risked his life for those people. He pulled the bodies up over mine after passing down ropes. I just tied the ropes and he pulled them up. He was great.

"The firemen were the first ones out on the pile. They didn't have to go there. They got little hand saws and started making passageways to take out the bodies. Edwin Savitsky of Fitchville was another in there first." It was Savitsky, in fact, who was the rescuer responsible for pulling out Mrs. Teresa Moretti, the woman who would cry "My friend! My friend!" over and over again. "She was a woman about 40 to 45 and she was in shock. But, she told us she wanted to try to get out herself." As he continued with the extraction of the other mill workers, Jaskiewicz observed that they "were lightly clothed. One, however, had on a drenched coat and another, a sweater."

To the immediate east, on Boswell Avenue, the road traverses north and south, perpendicular to Centennial Square, and slopes rapidly upward, making it instantaneous high ground. It was here that Labensky's Funeral Home became the defacto central headquarters for the many disparate organizations and newsmen gathered in the square covering the unfolding tragedy. As small children, misplaced from their parents when their homes on Broad Street became inaccessible, ran up and down the front stairway of the funeral home, Mrs. Labensky would become, suddenly, "room mother" to these many disaffected who sought relief from the cold, all while staying busy throughout the evening and into the early morning preparing sustenance for the throngs that would camp out here.

Out on the street, in front of the funeral home, were fire trucks and emergency vehicles so numerous that the road could not now be seen from the house. "Have you been outside?" she was asked. "Not much. I'm rather busy." "Any wakes here now?" she was asked jokingly. "No, thank god." A girl in a housecoat and pajamas passed her on the stairs, and Mrs. Labensky looked at the reporters, "Excuse me, I have to get more milk." As a young woman now came in carrying a toddler, an onlooker quipped, "It looks more like an orphanage than a funeral home." Seeing the young woman and child, Mrs. Labensky sighed again, "I have to get more milk."

A young fireman, meanwhile, was conspicuously standing alone on the outer reaches of the flooded square. Looking across to the battered mill where rescue operations had hesitantly started earlier while the flood was still carving its murderous path toward downtown, the young man suddenly exclaimed, "I just came in here. I was one of the first ones in. We need a power saw! We need a crane! We could go in there if we had power equipment!" Crying profusely now as he had witnessed the extraction of the wounded and the dead, the scene reminded him of a battlefield.

His co-worker, trying to calm him, said, "We just fought a year for a fire engine. There's no way that they'd pay for power equipment." "I can't stand it over there," the first man said. "I can't do anything. I can't move anything. Some of that machinery weighs ten tons." He was still muttering as he returned to the square and, while clinging to a rope thrown across the swirling waters, returned to his grim task. Then, as if providential, a crane, at about 3:00 a.m., suddenly rumbled into the area to assist with the ongoing rescue operations.

All but one person employed at the mill that night had been accounted for by morning. Mrs. Carol Mae Robidou, strangely, could not be found even after a thorough search and subsequent re-search of the ruins had been performed. This revelation, by 3:00 a.m., led to an even more intense and

THOMAS MOODY, JR.

even further investigation into the morning light as the fire/rescue workers risked life and limb in extended efforts to pull apart and clear the rubble.

Also, a small controversy concerning a boiler explosion at the Mill was now being denounced as Fire Chief William Confrey confirmed that none of the numerous boilers at the Mill had exploded as was assumed by witnesses to the cave in. This was also confirmed later in the day when State Labor Department consultant Thomas Carroll personally inspected all the boilers at the wrecked facility. "There was no damage to the low pressure boiler at all. The other high-pressure boilers in the stricken areas were not damaged with the exception of one which had its casing blown off. So in summary, the boiler did not explode. The roar heard by the people in the area probably was the tremendous force of the building collapsing." Further, it was speculated that the smoke seen by onlookers when the mill collapsed was that of the main boiler tripping offline.

Compounding the rescue effort and causing dangerous distractions, however, were the still abundant onlookers and passersby, out by early morning in the freezing weather to get an initial look at the damage. These sightseers, as reported by rescue officials later, ventured much too close to the ruins to be safe and, as a result, caused Police Chief Clarence Simpson to be called upon to quell this dangerous curiosity. To completely ensure the safety of the rescuers, and the onlookers themselves, he, reluctantly, now had to divert officers, badly needed in other areas, to stand guard around the damaged zone strictly to keep people out.

Extolling a common theme among all downtown business owners, Turner Mill president Edward Hall, when asked at the scene about disaster preparedness, exhibited a controlled fury. "If we had been notified of the weakened condition of the Mohegan Park Dam, several lives and hundreds of thousands of dollars worth of goods could have been saved.

"We had an unusual amount of inventory on hand and planned to move three-quarters of it to a warehouse today on the other side of town." As Hall now surveyed the scene, his initial assessment was that the building was now clearly beyond use and that a new one would have to be found. Shaking his head, he realized that there was, however, much to do before a new location and reopening could be realized.

At 6:00 a.m., Thursday, Jerry Shea awoke at his Tetreault Avenue home with a start. Getting only a couple of hours of sleep after spending most of the night searching for his sister, he now awoke with a strong resolve to go back downtown and, with daylight as his ally, find some evidence, some object, anything that would give him and his family an answer. Jerry's mother Nana had stayed at the hospital with her grandsons until Ronnie, still somewhat in shock, was examined by the ER doctors and subsequently released in the early morning hours.

Ronnie, absolutely adamant about going back to the terrible scene of last night's events to look for his wife, took Nana and left the hospital, knowing that the children were in good hands. In Nana's car (someone [nobody in the Shea or Moody family that is still alive is sure who] had brought Nana's car to the hospital that evening after her son Jerry dropped her off), they drove to Ronnie's sister, Virginia's, house on Union Street where he met with his brothers and regrouped before going out on the grim task.

At his sister's, Ronnie not only spoke with his brothers Bill and Andy, but also answered questions for Dennis Riley, who was still documenting the story for the *Hartford Times* newspaper after spending all night covering the tragedy. Ronnie recounted the previous evening's events, with Nana, meanwhile, in the background still distraught over Honey's whereabouts. "She was my baby . . . Oh, what's happened to her?"

Meanwhile Jerry now drove toward downtown; and as he got close, he noticed that the police had blocked off all access to Franklin Street and the surrounding flood-damaged roads. Parking as close as he could, he again approached Lake Street from its intersection with Broad Street and took out on foot down the road past the Moody home to the bottom where the playground intersected with it. Here he once again descended onto the drop-off area and realized immediately that daylight added a whole new and welcome perspective to his search. As he looked out upon Franklin Street below, he now saw that the whole downtown area was amassed with police, firefighters, and trucks of varying kinds along with the multitudinous onlooker traffic—people were seemingly everywhere.

Explaining to the police that he was Honey's brother and that he wished, indeed needed to assist in the search effort, Jerry made his way over to the area where the Moody car was still sitting, hideously upside down in the early morning light. The debris from the flood flow over this drop-off was extensive and Jerry quickly realized that any success in his search would involve digging through this vast array of waste. Proceeding over to the area in and around where the car was, he searched for maybe fifteen minutes when he saw it . . . it was 7:15 a.m. and unmistakably, there was the corner of a brown housecoat that he recognized instantly as his sister's. Climbing in closer, he now saw her fingers sticking out barely from the rubble, her wedding ring glistening ghastly in the early morning light, and it was at this point, and as his heart sank, he knew. Finally, she had been found and, grievously, it was the worst of everyone's conclusions.

With his heart beating rapidly now, Jerry looked up and saw, to his astonishment, that he was, suddenly, completely alone. In great desperation he looked for someone to help him. Moving away, still along the drop-off area, he saw a police officer atop Lake Street and hurried toward him. Exclaiming that he'd found his sister and that he needed assistance, the policeman immediately called others, and together the group hurried back down to the site of the Moody's car.

Pointing to where he had found her, Jerry then backed away so that the officers could climb in to make an assessment. "It was horrible . . . just four of her fingers were exposed from beneath the water and a pile of rubble resulting from the upheaval of the pavement," Police Chief Clarence Simpson reported. The others in the group who would assist in extracting Honey from the pile were policemen Joseph Grillo, Philip Mondor, and Sergeant John Sisco, and all would later relate similar, unfeigned feelings.

While they dug through the rubble and extracted Honey's lifeless body, one of the officers now went to contact the coroner. Jerry, meanwhile, went in search of a telephone as he suddenly felt an overriding need to contact the rectory at St. Patrick's Cathedral on Broadway to get funeral arrangements started. Chief Simpson, meanwhile, sought out Ronnie Moody from the area, learning from Jerry that he was nearby and also engaged in the search for his wife, to relate the sorrowful discovery and that it was, alas, the worst of all outcomes.

Ronnie, upon hearing confirmation of what he had intuitively known all along, started to walk away after hearing Simpson's details. Making his way through the barrage of police cars and road barriers, he walked, somewhat dazed but yet eerily calm, as if a great weight had now been lifted, up McKinley Avenue. He got as far as the old Armory building, a giant pre-World War II structure that housed, among other things, many military jeeps and trucks, Norwich's contributions to the Cold War effort, before a moment of great grief and contemplation overcame him. Sitting down now on the street curb outside the Armory, chin on top of folded hands, he thought to himself over and over again, "What am I going to do now?"

Jerry, now also equally distraught over his discovery, knew that, next, he needed to inform Nana, and he needed to do it immediately. Quickly heading back up Lake Street and jumping into his car, he made the long drive home to Tetreault Avenue, where he called Nana as soon as he entered the house. Almost surprisingly, she seemed to accept it, indeed expect it; for her now it was closure. In Nana's mind, perhaps she had somehow already accepted that Honey was gone but was still holding out the briefest of hopes that a miracle would happen. Faced now with this stark reality, she shifted her concentration immediately to Honey's children. Remembering that prescient disclosure at young Tommy's birthday, Nana was now determined to raise Honey's sons as she obviously wanted.

After calling his mother and recounting his finding to his wife Rita, Jerry now realized how truly exhausted he was. Soon, however, the phone rang, and it was the Dougherty Brothers Funeral Home on West Main Street. Unable to reach Ronnie, they had received Honey's body and were doing the initial preparations for the funeral but they needed clothes for her—would he mind bringing funeral attire down there and talking with them. While there, they said, and if he desired, he could also see his sister for one final time.

Now in another long drive to the city, this time to the west side of town where the funeral home was, Jerry arrived and spoke with the directors. Upon viewing his sister, however, he realized that he'd made a big mistake—not nearly prepared yet for viewing, she was still covered in dirt and mud, along with contusions and the myriad afflictions one would associate with such a violent death, and Jerry quickly turned away. Again plunged into shock and dismay, he could not believe that the last twelve hours had resulted in this.

Absent the Turner-Stanton Mill and possibly the J.B. Martin Company, the downtown area with the most visible destruction was the region in and around the Lamperell's auto dealership parking lot. Water, road surface, and cement erosion along with damaged cars and those numerous large black fuel tanks were scattered about a scene of marked desolation. The bulk of the new and used-car inventory at the dealership had been destroyed. Car parts and other disparate auto-related supplies were now arbitrarily strewn throughout the area while the large garage roof in the rear of the lot, now laying in a hideous pile of ruin, had demolished all of the cars that were parked beneath it; it was here that those cars that were in the shop for service and repair had been parked and were now crushed virtually beyond any repair.

Patti Pellegrini, in addition to the trauma that she'd been through the previous evening, would ironically lose her car at this lot also; it had been parked beside this garage structure for repair. A white Pontiac station wagon, it had been mysteriously losing power while Patti was, typically, driving her children to and from events. During the flood, it somehow escaped the roof collapse but had nevertheless been washed away with the other cars while sustaining serious water damage. Insurance adjusters attempted to convince her to repair it, but Patti, typical of her practical outlook, saw it as a total loss.

The sight, Thursday, of these mangled garage roof remnants and cars that had been floated away only added to the overall perception of devastation as cleanup operations here would go on for a relatively long time.

One of the multifaceted services provided by this auto dealership was a full service gas station situated right in the middle of the parking lot. The service pumps, however, had been severely affected by the floodwaters as they had all been ripped off of their stanchions by the water and would obviously need replacement. Fortunately, the large underground storage tanks had been refilled on Tuesday and "served as ballast which prevented them from being forced from the ground," reported Donald Hafner the Lamperell gas service representative. Had these tanks been empty, they would have undoubtedly broken through the surface concrete, causing immense and additional terrain damage to the area.

At the nearby Longo's Funeral Home, meanwhile, the devastation and destruction to the lower floor had been quickly assessed by the City Health Department to be beyond repair and, as such, was condemned. As owner Bill Longo and his brothers ventured down to the first floor this next day, they bleakly discovered ruin even beyond their imagination. The water and oversized cylindrical fuel tanks had destroyed the doorway entrance from the north side, smashing windows, while the opposite-side doors had been ripped off of their supporting structure; this damage was so extensive, it was later surmised, that it was miraculous the entire house didn't collapse.

The water intrusion also caused the flooring of the ground floor to cave in and collapse downward into the basement while tossing much of the furniture and fixtures either down into this new expanse or smashed up against the far southern wall.

At about 3:00 p.m. this Thursday, as they continued to survey the damage, possibly the most gruesome occurrence borne of this disaster was discovered. While Bill and his brothers were uncovering shattered flooring and broken floor boards, they suddenly found a human body strewn downward through the battered flooring toward the basement. Aghast at what they'd found, Bill and his brothers now looked at each other incredulously. "We need to tell someone about this."

Immediately noticing the firemen and policemen out in the parking lot connecting their funeral home with Lamperell's, Bill quickly exited the damaged lower floor of the home and spoke with one of the nearby police officers. While relaying the events that led to their tragic discovery, he was appalled when the policeman refused to believe that a human body was trapped in his house. Almost belligerently, the officer told him that everyone had been accounted for.

Now though, and with a bit of forceful language, Bill convinced him to come inside and look for himself. Overhearing this confrontation, meanwhile, was a contingent of city and state officials, including Connecticut governor John Dempsey. With the police officer, Police Chief Clarence Simpson and the governor all following, Longo went back into the battered first floor of his funeral home . . . and there, clearly, was the woman's body, distorted, still soaked, muddy, and apparently drowned in the destruction. With somber looks, they all asked themselves the inevitable question—where could she have come from?

It was then that Bill Longo suddenly recalled those mysterious moaning sounds from the previous evening. Quickly realizing that this woman must have been the source of those sounds, he now also came to the horrible conclusion that she was, incomprehensibly, still alive at that point and struggling against the onslaught of the raging torrent while trying to get into his home.

Apparently, she had found herself at Longo's bottom floor and then battled the still raging torrent while trying to open the door. Struggling against the immense pressure of the flood flow and after finally getting it open, the force, in all likelihood, slammed her inside. Speculating now, a violent struggle ensued that had her fighting against the swirling flow that was quickly filling the first floor of the building, while careening against furniture and demolishing floorboards, making it impossible for her to get back out.

In her undoubtedly weakened condition, she may have passed out or been struck by the swirling debris; the thought of this struggle and what she went through is both eerie and heroic and makes her brave plight for survival even more heartbreaking as she ultimately and horribly lost her battle for survival.

The police, conferring now with nearby rescue workers and officials on the scene, quickly determined that this was the body of Mrs. Carol Robidou, who had been reported as one of the missing Turner Mill workers the previous night, and who the police were still frantically in search of. As this ghastly discovery now sank in, it became apparent to all that the most horrific part of this scene was the realization that Mrs. Robidou had somehow survived the Mill collapse only to be washed away in the floodwaters, surviving the swirling water wave as she was being swept over the Lake Street playground and drop-off (some 150 yards), finally ending up violently smashed against the Longo's Funeral Home. There, still somehow alive and undoubtedly using all of her remaining strength, she miraculously made it inside the building only to succumb to the careening debris and the caving in of the floor.

Mrs. Robidou's story, as it was later pieced together, was further evidence of the horror and destruction that the flood had wrought that evening and one that profoundly affected people associated with rescue operations all over town. Later, it was somehow mistaken that her ordeal was that of Honey Moody; many news stories would, in fact, erroneously state that it was Honey who was found in Bill Longo's basement, and not Carol Robidou. Obliquely, both women would now be, in a sense, martyred for their bravery and would be, notwithstanding the differences in their deaths, journalistically linked throughout the following days and months.

At Pond Street, a short distance south and east of the playground, onlookers gaped at another area of massive devastation. This was the road that had channeled a portion of the main flood flow as it had escaped the Lake Street playground, causing the severe erosion seen at its bottom as it intersected Franklin Street. After the water receded, alarmingly, this channeling effect had caused such erosion that a huge cavernous chamber now existed which previously had been simply a section of road and hill that sloped upwards toward Boswell Avenue.

Unbelievably, this entire area of elevated road and its underneath supporting groundwork had now just disappeared. In its wake was a huge cavelike formation cut into the ground, up to a depth of twelve feet in some places. Water pipelines and gas mains were exposed and dangling in the air, grotesquely, like octopus tentacles all along the entrance to this short street while cars that had been parked in driveways or on the street were now either teetering on these pipes or laying decimated downward into the crevices.

The Albert Lawton's of 19 Pond Street were symbolic of these malevolent proceedings. Their family car was in ruins, having been slammed up against a utility pole. To get to a point where they and the other victims on this street could walk to the downtown area, it now required them to "jump the ditch" across this cavern of washout. Road repair here would be extensive, time consuming, and complicated as not only fill-in and repaving would be required, but also restabilization of the water and gas pipelines would require much engineering and add to the already complex rework. These efforts would ultimately take many months to complete and as a result, Pond Street would not be open for normal traffic until October.

At the S & S Supermarket across from Lamperell's, the discovery of huge ice chunks in the basement and in the nearby tenement house was reported by a somewhat overwrought Stanley Studnickie, owner of both establishments. After pumping out these basements, which was a service now being supplied by the Public Works Department and other volunteers, Studnickie would, nevertheless and frustratingly, find himself having to call them back when the enormous ice cakes melted, causing minor enough flooding to warrant this repumping.

Also in this early Thursday morning light, many intrepid automobile owners who had parked their cars along upper Franklin Street the previous evening were now engaged in a sort of somnolent search for their vehicles. Over twenty cars alone had amassed at the southern end of Lamperell's, most of them from the dealership, all having been deposited after swirling around in the changing current of the flood flow, as it'd turned southward, down Franklin Street. Some of the more-fortunate car owners would find their autos strewn close by on upper Franklin Street. Others found their vehicles floated farther downtown; most of the fortunate cars were only in need of minor repair, albeit with waterlines nearly as high as the side windows.

Some of these owners, however, discovered that their cars had been an unfortunate and unmistakable part of the structural damage in the city, as they were found smashed into buildings, destroying doorways and large window fronts, while the cars themselves suffered irreparable damage. These unfortunate "accidents", in most cases, not only damaged the structures they had floated into, but also provided an unwelcome path for even more water to pour through, causing additional devastation to their victims' interior infrastructure.

All of the local store and business owners, both on Franklin and Chestnut streets, who had ventured downtown this day to assess damage, even though somewhat prepared for it, walked into overwhelming devastation and surreal surroundings. Their businesses were severely water damaged, commodities strewn, and smashed about, freezing cold (as most buildings' boilers were either destroyed or knocked out of commission by the flood), and dark. The common theme among all was one of "How are we going to recover from this?"

Franklin Square, as with most of downtown, also became symbolic of the devastation as up to a foot of mud in places, sand, and left-behind debris completely littered the area. Adding to the almost lurid scene of destruction were the yards of cloth, velvet, and grey goods from the J.B. Martin Co. strewn haphazardly throughout the area. Rolls of this material had been caught up in the flow and became subsequently unrolled, as it was entangled ghoulishly around stop signs and lampposts. The next day, the disquieting effect of streams of this material, hideously misplaced, wrapped around poles like sails and streamers in a bygone breeze, cluttering the area, added to the surreal perception of desolation and destruction in the lower Franklin Square area.

On Rose Alley, meanwhile the street that had served as the final funnel for the flood flow to the Shetucket, untold debris was now scattered on, around, and to the side with much of it emblematic of the water's source. Most of the aforementioned material from the Martin Company joined twine and sodden yarn from the Turner Mill as all of it had floated with the flood and become morbidly settled here. Much of this elongated cloth and string had also wrapped around the signs and lampposts on this street, similar to the cloth and velvet from the J.B. Martin Company. Many of the Franklin Street traffic signs, broken off and captured in the ravaging flow, now became deposited here as well, sticking out of the mountain of trash as a forlorn reminder of just how far this flood had traveled.

Hideously stacked up against fences and road curbs at the street's outlet, it was almost impossible now to see over this mountain of garbage to catch even a glimpse of the river. Once past this, however, the river eerily resembled last evening's flood, as it had swelled to enormous proportions with its rain and flood-induced flow carrying what trees, ice, and assorted other debris that had made it into its distended path toward the Thames.

Cleanup efforts this day would be focused mainly on returning the downtown area to a useful assemblage of businesses and of clearing the roads and sidewalks in and around them. These operations, with the first visible signs beginning with the activation of the local Army Corps of Engineers (who were seen gathering about the downtown area as early as 2:00 a.m.) were started in earnest by 6:00 a.m. By then, these soldiers were out in full force, with their heavy earth-moving machinery, literally plowing the inches-deep mud off the streets, and pushing it into the Franklin Square area and on into the river through the trash at Rose Alley. Right behind them, firemen and fire trucks from the city (and with much-needed assistance from many of the neighboring towns) used their collective high-pressure hoses to spray down the roads and outside walls of all the downtown buildings, pushing the muck and grit also on into the Shetucket.

Another huge obstacle for all the affected downtown businesses would be the delay in the return of building heat. Reestablishing boiler operations, as most of these old buildings had been built before the pervasive use of electricity, would be tantamount to reopening. Most of these old boilers, however, were now in need of repair, as all had suffered, in one respect or another, significant water damage. The buildings and businesses that were fortunate enough to get their boilers going were the first, generally, to be able to ask the City Health Department for reopening inspections.

State and federal assistance, predictably, was soon on the scene. Connecticut governor John Dempsey arrived first, getting into town shortly before noon on this Thursday after cancelling his regular schedule. His first act was to quickly alert all state departments to be available for the downtown cleanup effort after a short briefing at city hall with city council members and acting city manager Carashick. Large highway earth-moving equipment and associated manpower were brought in immediately and Dempsey assigned State Highway Department engineer Roland Brown to coordinate any additional needs with the town and surrounding areas.

Dempsey, a citizen of Putnam (a town in the far northeast corner of the state), announced that "Norwich came to the aid of my town in 1955 . . . I am here to be of assistance in any way possible," referring to large floods that had left that town in ruins in 1955 while he was mayor. Now, as he toured Norwich's devastation firsthand, he stopped initially at the Turner Mill where he expressed condolences to the families of the victims who were on hand. He then proceeded on to Mohegan Park to view the devastated dam in full daylight, and his tour then ended back in town where he and his contingent happened to be in the parking lot at Lamperell's, observing cleanup operations, when the distraught Bill Longo came out of his funeral home with the discovery news of Carol Robidou.

On Friday, US Senator Thomas Dodd, a native of the town and one who had, as a young child himself, swam in the Spaulding Pond waters, arrived around noon to view the damage. Observing that the area had suffered "a great tragedy," Dodd's self-imposed first priority would be to somehow acquire federal funding specifically for Norwich's disaster relief.

In these seemingly halcyon days of the early 1960s, the requirement for acquiring federal funding for disaster relief was nevertheless still bureaucratically complex and was predicated on an official (Dodd entourage guest Albert O'Conner, regional director of emergency planning would be this official) declaring the area a major Federal disaster area. Dodd, along with O'Conner, was required to view the devastation firsthand before concluding that this warranted a federal declaration. Without making this declaration initially, Dodd did, however, state that all federal agencies were at the ready to help, in any fashion, with cleanup operations or manpower.

Taking essentially the same tour route that Governor Dempsey took, Dodd and State Civil Defense director William Shatzman took this opportunity to warn the council and cleanup workers against standing water and debris being unattended, as these were antecedents of or could be obvious harbingers to disease. Responding to this was City Health Department representative Alfred McNerney who indicated that his group was still shorthanded despite the volunteering of twelve qualified helpers from the State Health Department. Both McNerney and Dodd indicated that federal assistance was available and could be obtained for this effort.

Along the route, Dodd reminisced and recounted stories of his youth, pointing out various landmarks of his deep area family history, and he would be pictured in the *Bulletin* the next day stopped at these indelible points. One picture in particular attested to the devastation as Dodd et al, were walking along the southern Lake Street lower rock wall that had formally held the garage roof at Lamperell's. Although the collapsed roof itself had been largely removed, the mud, large remnants of roof debris, and, eerily, the Moody car, still upside down and seemingly dangling over this rock wall, were all evident in the background. The shocked and sorrowful look on Dodd's face is markedly conspicuous.

Saturday, US Congressman William St. Onge, whose constituents encompassed the district that included Norwich, arrived for a similar tour. St. Onge, although, in the end, struggling harder than he'd ever imagined, indicated that he would work with Senator Dodd's office to garner flood insurance, in emergency measures, from federal legislation. "My first impression was of shock and grief at the loss of life brought about by this tragic event . . . Norwich officials, the public works, police and fire departments are to be congratulated on the quick recovery."

An unfortunate affliction associated with this type of mass flooding and the one that Senator Dodd and City Health Department spokesman McNerny warned of was the potential for typhoid. A disease known to proliferate when uncontrolled water dissemination occurs and mixes with raw human or animal waste, the typhus bacteria is cultivated in the waste and carried along with the water flow and can infect all that it comes in contact with, requiring inoculations for humans and disinfectant to control and prevent its spread.

The city health office at city hall recognized early this Thursday morning that inoculations for all who had been or would become exposed to the potentially infected floodwater would be required. As a result, they opened at first light on Thursday with Winifred Egan, the supervising nurse of the Norwich Health Department, along with a myriad of volunteer nurses, doling out over nine-hundred shots, largely to residents and police/firemen, with four-hundred more administered on Friday.

While giving these inoculations, the City Health Department also proved very proactive in disclosing and disseminating information on the proper method of disinfecting basements and other structures saturated with this potentially infected water. Dr. Lewis Sears, city director of public health, released a directive from the State Health Department that explained in great detail the mixtures of chlorine, lime, and water to use for the cleanup. For all who would spend time in the downtown area this day, "flood workers should be cautioned to guard against infection. They should not get their hands near their mouths after handling polluted surfaces or polluted water until their hands have been washed with soap and clean water. They should also not handle food without clean hands."

Now while the politicians were lending their support to the disaster and the health department was specifically directing disinfection operations, other cleanup activities had commenced and were well in progress, all with the profound and greatly appreciated assistance of numerous outside sources. Offers of help from these surrounding areas would come in abundance this early morning of the seventh.

Connecticut State Police from neighboring Groton, Colchester, and Danielson made themselves available (about thirty troopers in all) and were immediately stationed downtown to help with traffic and onlooker control. The New London Police Department also offered fifteen officers for assistance, while the previously mentioned Coast Guard Academy sent between fifty to one hundred cadets along with numerous ambulances to the scene. Norwich police captain Cascy, meanwhile, had to assign additional Norwich officers just to assist with telephone requests, as the call volume overwhelmed the three policemen initially assigned to this task.

At the Backus Hospital, now, twelve doctors had been sent from the Norwich State Hospital to assist, with a promise of additional help if needed. The giant Norwich State Armory on McKinley Avenue, just north of the flood zone and the site where Ronnie Moody sat on the curb contemplating the direction of his life after learning of the death of his wife, offered to shelter any citizen affected by the flood.

The Norwich Salvation Army opened its office on Broadway late Wednesday evening with Lt. Donald Spencer heading up the operation on Broad Street near the Turner Mill while volunteers soon populated the downtown area, many working over forty-eight hours without sleep, supplying coffee and food to firemen, rescuers, and police officers. All told, a total of ninety-three hours were given to the emergency call. The Southern New England Telephone Company, inundated themselves with pole repair, line outages, etc., offered to provide emergency service, sacrificing all other operations, to the Norwich Police Department if needed.

Crews of experienced city maintenance workers, volunteers from the Groton Submarine Base (arriving almost ceremoniously in large military busses, carrying twenty-eight Navy "nukes" and tons of equipment), and inexperienced volunteers alike were soon assembled with cleanup plans formulated and strategies set to most efficiently collect trash, pump remaining water from basements, and disinfect all affected buildings. The scope of this effort was so large, and the undertaking so resource heavy that inquests were sent out (with ads in all the local newspapers and

THOMAS MOODY, JR.

publications) for help. City council president Henry Lucas[7] solicited an "army of workers to complete the cleaning of every single piece of property hit by the flood."

The city also, magnanimously, undertook an effort to "help anybody who was involved in the disaster." This need would become so dire that by the next day, high-school-aged volunteers from the Norwich Free Academy were amassed and sent out to assist in any manner possible. The want for paid workers, however, was still so distinct that days later, wages were raised above the minimum (a whopping $1.75 per hour in 1963) to lure townspeople and other locals to work. Ultimately, through hiring and volunteering, enough help was assembled to get the job done.

In parallel with all the initial cleaning and recovery operations, however, was an overriding and urgent need to start raising funds for a focused citywide "return to business." Although both Senator Dodd and Congressman St. Onge indicated that federal assistance would be forthcoming, the wait for the federal bureaucracy to decide on and approve a plan for funding would have, undoubtedly, carried into the following weeks, if not months. Serious money was needed and needed immediately. Most, if not all, businesses in the downtown location had zero flood insurance, and the cost of recouping inventory and infrastructure lost in the flood, while restoring order was needed now and would run into towering amounts, sums clearly beyond the means of these small businesses and their owners.

Recognizing this, the city council quickly introduced a resolution to appropriate $50,000 from the town's Civil Defense budget to help initiate cleanup operations at a quickly coordinated Friday night council meeting. With the confusion and bewilderment of Wednesday's tragedy still very apparent in the council's comportment, an attempt to organize and set in motion a plan for recovery became their highest priority.

City alderman Stanley Israelite presented a three-point program that would serve as the basis for recovery operations: first in his plan was to report in full to the people of the community the details of the catastrophe,

---

[7]   Norwich had deviated from a mayoral central governing system many years earlier, forming a body, a city council, to administer the city governing system while electing a council president as executive oversight.

its cause and effect. This report would be generated by the council and would be seen as their duty and responsibility. Second, to demand a report from each of the city department heads as to what was done during the emergency and what was not done. Clearly, said Israelite, the city was not prepared for the exigencies that arose during the flood. No visible evidence was available as to the organization or direction of city leadership, and this was something that needed to be fully understood and realigned into a process. Third, he indicated that they needed to unite in a combined community-effort and attempt to tackle the problems arising from the flood on a local level prior to calling on state or federal agencies for help. "The city cannot sit back and demand to be bailed out by outside agencies . . . community effort can only be augmented by state and federal help; it cannot be replaced by it," Israelite said in closing.

Also at this impromptu meeting were the owners of the Martin Company and the Turner Mill. Both officials were still disturbed at the suddenness of the flash flood and baffled as to how this could have happened without any warning. Roger Charbin, owner of the Martin Company was particularly pointed in his comments to the council. If he had only one-to-two hours of warning, he said, he could have moved equipment and supplies to a higher floor, thus avoiding a half-million dollars in damages. L. Downer Johnson of the Mill staff reiterated this concern—people and materials could have been saved had they even the slightest warning.

Council president Henry Lucas assured both that a full report would be issued that would analyze the weaknesses in the city's warning system and that plans to improve it would be included, in a few days. Lucas went on to say that he was also aware of innuendo and rumor that Public Works director Walz was ultimately responsible, and he wanted to clarify that now. "Director Walz is a competent city servant who has the backing of the council and the city."

While the quickly appropriated $50,000 would go largely toward physical cleaning of the flood zone, one of the first administrative initiatives voted on by the council (an initiative so important that it would not be until Monday the 11th that a vote could be had such that the proper personae would be assured of being there and processes could be set up) was the establishment of a committee to undertake a large fund-raising campaign to assist local businesses in their recovery efforts. This task force, while performing some seemingly overlapping operations with other local and government agencies, would be given a purposely wide berth by the council in terms of means and avenues adopted to garner money.

The Norwich Businessmen's Rehabilitation Fund was overwhelmingly voted into service with Bill Stanley, the young stock broker at Cooley & Company, as its chairman. Along with Stanley, other city elite named to the committee were Walter LaFontaine (treasurer); Milton Jacobson, the attorney whose automobile had floated into the rear of Strick's Bakery during the height of the crisis; city alderman Martin Rutchik, Kenneth Johnson, Joseph Conner, and Shepard Palmer, a young city engineer.

This group assembled for its initial meeting on Tuesday the twelfth, to establish a charter of operations, all the while quickly establishing a schedule of meetings for the following Tuesday and Wednesday with the affected downtown businessmen to hear and then assess damage costs. The idea was to start quickly beseeching and soliciting as much donation money as could be achieved. All monies, as per the charter, would then be distributed to the affected businesses, "in the form of a gift," as needed for recovery "with no strings attached."

Sensitive to stepping over their bounds, the committee was careful to stipulate that "the fund will not conflict with the efforts of the Red Cross, the official disaster agency for the city, since that organization offers help mostly to private families." The first donation the committee received was an omen of what was to come—$1,000 donated by the local S & H green stamps company (a service that many older, native Norwich-ers will undoubtedly fondly remember; these green stamps were given out at local supermarkets with the amount of stamps dispensed based on the amount of groceries purchased. These stamps would be then glued into a "stamp book," and "valuable merchandise" was then traded for a predetermined amount of stamp books).

The swiftness with which this group was able to not only promote the need for emergency funding but also to then get it, and in a timely manner, was really a testament to Stanley and his cohorts. They advertised effectively not only in the state but also nationwide—the *New York Times*, Christian Science Monitor, and even John Cameron Swayze's *Camel Caravan* (an

NBC national radio news program) were but a few of the more famous enterprises to describe the disaster and solicit funds.

The committee's charter also determined that the funds would be dispersed on a priority bases. The most dire of circumstances would, obviously, receive attention first. Clearly, the Turner-Stanton Mill and J.B. Martin Company, being the most devastated, were set up to get most of the initial monies. Also, any business that could show that, without immediate funding, they would have to declare bankruptcy was also moved to the front of the line.

In the end, over $26,000 would be raised by the fund, and this effort, singularly, would be the most responsive and responsible for thirty-six of the thirty-seven downtown businesses returning to service. Bill Stanley, as leader of this group, would go on to be a sort of "cult" figure later on, writing with passion about his memories and the history of this town that he clearly loved, but it was this sole effort that made him and the members of the rehabilitation fund initially memorable and heroic.

While the Businessmen's Rehabilitation Fund was gaining momentum, other emergency assistance organizations were also on the scene and equally eager to help. The US Small Business Administration, headed by acting branch manager Thomas Higgins, set up temporary offices at the police station on Union Street and started the process of establishing loans to all affected businesses and nonbusinessmen alike. Declaring the area a disaster area (a SBA disaster area, not a federal disaster area), the SBA was now, with this declaration, empowered to establish loans to all who were affected.

These loans could then be distributed to any who needed them, business or individual, and would supplement the federal assistance that Norwich would ultimately come to realize. As with the Business Rehabilitation Fund Committee, the amount of money available was contingent upon damages, so the worst would get the highest priority. These loans would be processed at a secured 3 percent interest rate and could be financed for up to twenty years.

One of the main components of disaster relief throughout the country in the early 1960s was the National Civil Defense Organization. A formation that was symbolic of the Cold War, its primary purpose, in

1963, was the militarization of citizens for the defense of the country in case of nuclear attack. A secondary function, and one that would prove important here, was disaster relief. The head of Norwich's Civil Defense Agency was William Confrey, who was also the area fire chief and which, in the best of times, was a full-time, plus overtime, job.

As a result of this seeming conflict, the CD was predictably disorganized as a needed force and subsequently nowhere to be found the evening of the sixth when its demand was at its most desperate. State CD director William Shatzman, upon review of his department's lack of effort that evening, criticized Norwich's CD organization and promised changes for the better.

The official city manager John Fitzgerald, who, at the height of the flood, was a patient at the Backus Hospital recovering from a broken arm, leaving Orrin Carashick as acting head, would now have to bring order into a city government that was being routinely accused of disorganization and confusion by various agencies, as damaging information about the dam break and flood was slowly surfacing.

Silvio Zanni, area commander of the State Civil Defense Organization was one of the more vocal. Zanni had attended two postflood city council meetings and afterwards stated that "I never saw a city in all my life that had so many people working at cross-purposes." Noting immediately that Fire Chief Confrey was overwhelmed with his Fire Department duties on top of his CD job, he stated that Confrey's "first duty is to the fire department . . . and as a result, Civil Defense suffers."

Recommending that Confrey step down from his CD duties, city alderman Stanley Israelite then stepped up to volunteer for the role. Accepting no salary increase, his stated purpose for accepting this assignment was to "beef up Norwich's Civil Defense setup to a point where it could work effectively."

In the final analysis, the large outpouring of help and philanthropic effort to the town was one of the many amazing success stories in the immediate aftermath of the disaster. Many who would become involved in the solicitation of money and even those who would go out to collect it would report that they witnessed, they believed, the true "New England spirit," and their observations were simply that most people (re: New Englanders), at their base, were helpful, caring, sympathetic, and above all, empathetic to the adversity of the victims. Moreover, they felt that this recovery effort could, in the long term, prove to be a study and true lesson in humanitarianism.

Meanwhile, as this Thursday now passed into the early afternoon hours and as the downtown roads became increasingly passable, all of the useable city trucks from the Public Works Department garage on Brook Street, had the unenviable task of loading the trashy remains of the varied cleanup efforts for transfer to the city dump. Public Works employee Frank Majewski, having been awakened by his mother the previous evening at about eleven o'clock to inform him of the flood, was now driving the only large city truck that had escaped damage by the floodwaters and had been assigned cleanup duty on Chestnut Street. This day he had the dubious distinction of loading 160 kegs of seemingly undamaged beer from the washed-out Connecticut Beverage Company onto his truck that the City Health Department had that morning condemned.

Young Ned Carlson of Norwich, a sixteen-year-old sophomore at NFA and a volunteer helping with cleanup efforts, was witness to the vehement arguments between the City Health Department and the owners of the Connecticut Beverage Company over what constituted "contaminated" consumables. "These bottles only got wet!" the owners argued, but the health officials were adamant in their rulings—if it was contacted by the floodwaters, it was potentially infected. Dumping them later at Hollyhock Island, a small island in the Yantic River, which served as the site of the city dump, Majewski and his crew wearily admitted later that they had mixed feelings about destroying this "trash."

The first thing that most of the Franklin Street business owners would do on this Thursday would be to gather volunteers, typically their own employees, to engage in cleanup efforts. Once the basements of these structures had been pumped out, the foul, potentially disease-ridden left-behind debris was seemingly everywhere. Workers, using gloves and face masks and layers of dense clothing for protection, then carted this sodden trash out of their buildings and began building up huge piles on the curb that the Public Works folks would then pick up.

This effort, although in no way unnoticed, was, at its base, the unglamorous and unpleasant but, at its core, the true cleanup of the town and would go on for many days thereafter. The young volunteers from the Norwich Free Academy, some 150 of them, were also prominent here as the largely physical effort of carting dirty trash out to the curb suited these energetic young men and women. Working for the Public Works Department, three groups of these high-school helpers were dispatched around the town.

The first busload of teens went to Hollyhock Island where assistance was needed in organizing and dispatching the loads of city trash that subsequently came in. The second busload arrived at the Brooks Street garage area where they were deployed and would play an important role in the return to operations of that facility. Finally, the third busload became spread out from upper Franklin Street down to Franklin Square. These young men and women also played a pivotal role in the quick cleanup of this area and later all were commended by Public Works director Walz: "They did a good job and we certainly want to express our appreciation for their helping out at this time."

As pile after pile of this sodden, muddy trash was loaded onto the sidewalks, the City Health Department now became the single focal point for recovery operations. Setting a strict department policy prior to allowing anyone to return to business, city health inspectors became the responsible agents for going door to door and inspecting to these criteria. Most of these inspections involved removal of the potentially disease-ridden trash and a full disinfection campaign. To facilitate this, a huge barrel of disinfectant, mixed to the proper level of lime, water and chlorine was provided at the lower end of Bath Street in the parking lot area between the *Norwich Bulletin* and the Thayer Building.

Using this, structure owners were required to scrub floors and walls completely, with health department officials on hand, who then took quick swipe samples to determine if the residue contained bacteria. The cleanup was so intense and supported so well that this barrel was virtually empty by the following Monday morning, the eleventh and most businesses would have health department clearance by the next day.

Governor Dempsey, having toured the disaster area on Thursday, returned again on Tuesday the twelfth. Impressed by recovery operations thus far, the governor made it a point to see the areas that he had bypassed in Thursday. "I am amazed at the recovery that has been made. Disasters bring many problems and the way the victims of this most recent disaster have met the problems which it created is a tribute to their courage. My hat is off to them."

Arriving at about 5:30 p.m., Dempsey met briefly with city council members again before setting out on his tour. Stopping first at the still-crippled J.B. Martin Company, the governor met with Roger Charbin, the VP of the Martin Company and together they went into the basement of the plant, the hardest hit by the floodwaters. "Although considerable progress had been made in cleaning up the grey room and dye house, the governor had a chance to see some of the damage and got a first hand briefing on the extent of the damage, the progress made and prospects for the near future", it was reported by the Bulletin the next day.

"We started the weaving department Monday, the finishing department Tuesday, the shearing department will start today and with good luck and some steam we will probably start this dye house Thursday or Friday," Charbin told the governor. Upon completing the tour of the facility, one that was losing $6,000 a day by being offline, Dempsey commended Charbin and his staff for significant progress. "Mr. Charbin, this shows a great deal of courage of the type shown by all Norwich flood victims. There are some ways where we can help and we will not let a manufacturing business like this down." Charbin replied, "We have been here for sixty-four years . . . and we want you here for another sixty-four," the governor replied. Continuing on, Dempsey saw the cleanup progress made at Lamperell's, Longo's Funeral Home and the Turner-Stanton Mill—all areas having made significant headway from his last trip here. He stopped and conversed with workers and extolled similar encouragement before returning to Hartford.

Also on Tuesday, Congressman St. Onge reported that the federal government had finally passed a $248,688 grant for the town after reconsideration of a previously defeated bill. The congressman had headed legislation earlier in November 1962 that sought to compile federal funding for state-mandated repair to the eternal downtown sewerage drainage problem that the town had been experiencing. Now with the flood further damaging the sewer system and with the onus of this "damaged" system capable of spreading disease, the government body relented and quickly passed the grant. St. Onge was informed of this change directly from the Kennedy White House who'd remained "deeply concerned over the disaster." He also stated that "it will be a big help to getting Norwich back to normal life and aid restoration of the financial position of the community."

One of the many ongoing consequences of this tragedy and one that continued to be problematic was the unrelenting surge of sightseers and onlookers to the area. Sunday the tenth saw an exorbitant amount of traffic to the city and to Mohegan Park; travelers from Rhode Island, Massachusetts, and New York along with both downtown and suburban gawkers, made traffic control a continual and growing problem for an already exhausted and overworked police staff.

Fortunately, an affiliate of the Norwich police department, called, unpretentiously, the "auxiliary police", was already engaged with Capt. George Armstrong in command, and it was he who had recognized that the traffic flow would be a problem the day before on Saturday the ninth. Calling his counterparts in Griswold and Montville, Armstrong literally begged for officers to come and help with the traffic problem and the untold other issues that the mass sightseers would bring.

The Griswold auxiliary police civilian director Leo Baulanger brought in twelve men, ostensibly, to help in cleanup operations, but they were soon put to work covering the gaps that the Norwich police could not support. Chief Adam Taylor of Montville also responded with twelve of his own men, and this combined force proved to be both effective and essential in controlling and rerouting onlooker traffic away from the downtown area as well as the park where this huge throng hoped to see the destroyed dam. And as Sunday turned into Monday, the crowds that were drawn to the scene were as plentiful as the day before. In fact, this "battlefield mentality" which is typical of people racing to see a disaster area would continue for most of the coming week, adding additional time and burden for these already overused outside officers.

Now, as cleanup operations were in full swing and the promise, vague as it seemed early in the week, that money would be available as an aid for business and home recovery, the binding question on everyone's mind became . . . What happened? Why did this happen? Why was there no warning? If there was a leak, had it been leaking for a substantial period of time?

Public Works director Walz was clearly the focus of much of this query and it would be on him clearly to submit a plausible explanation of the events leading up to and through the night of the sixth.

Harold Walz, though, was clearly a man up to this task; a short, trim man in his fifties, Walz was known throughout the town government as an extremely hard worker and honest broker. If his department was at fault, he would get to the bottom of it and fix the problem.

Inspecting the washed out dam on Friday the eighth, Walz realized that there'd been a clear and inescapable gap in his and his department's understanding of the dynamics of their earthen structure. Inquiring with state authorities on Thursday the seventh, he learned that timely inspections had not only been lacking, but that the state inspection office, the "officials" responsible for carrying out these inspections, was severely undermanned.

Further preliminary research by Walz found that not only was there inadequate monitoring evident but follow-up actions taken on clear symptoms of degradation went unheeded. Learning also of the basic design requirement for saturation instrumentation and understanding now that this dam had none, he was of course compelled to ask why. The dam was over one-hundred years old he'd learned; he wondered now why hadn't any preventative maintenance program been established to warn of ensuing problems? Why hadn't the town or, at a minimum, his department been briefed on potential flood paths and/or the potential for disaster to the entire downtown that a break of this magnitude could bring?

Clearly, a negligence investigation, the size and sort that had never been undertaken in this town before, was forthcoming. But first, the pressure to provide the particulars of what had occurred on that afternoon and evening, in detail, was clearly needed as a means to explain his department and the town's actions that evening.

So with this urgency in the forefront, twelve days following the flood, on March 18 Walz and Carashick, while realizing that many unanswered questions still remained, submitted to the city council their preliminary report. Therein, it told of Walz's personal and his department's official actions leading up to the dam break. The report, as written, clearly shows a lack of understanding of what the true condition of the dam was prior to the break and how complacency was seemingly commonplace (re: Public Works foremen Patsy Ferra's understated assessment of the leak; Walz's own uninformed inspection of the dam, etc.) in the department's attitude toward it.

Establishing a timeline for that evening, Walz and Carashick are candid in the report stating the facts as they had occurred, offering little analysis or, admittedly, drawing any conclusions. They seemed to realize, intuitively, that later litigation and a thorough and complete investigation would get to the bottom of what had happened and that this litigation would be the vehicle that would provide the detailed chronology of the event, and that this report was simply a first step. The council at that point would have to deal with those consequences as they arose.

The report as submitted:

CITY OF NORWICH
OFFICE OF THE CORPORATION COUNCIL
MARCH 18, 1963

TO THE HONORABLE PRESIDENT AND
ALDERMAN OF THE CITY OF NORWICH

REPORT ON THE BREAK IN THE DAM
AT SPAULDING POND IN MOHEGAN PARK

The following is a factual report of events leading up to the break in the Spaulding Pond (dam) at Mohegan (Park) which occurred on the evening of March 6, 1963 and which resulted in the flooding of an area of the City of Norwich and caused the loss of life and considerable property damage.

The facts set forth herein are those available at this time. As our investigation continues, it is probable that further facts will become available, particularly as to the cause of the break in the dam. We believe that this matter must be determined by expert engineering opinion and evaluation and not by the conjecture or guesswork of laymen.

Furthermore, in view of the continuing nature of our investigation no attempt will be made to draw any conclusions from the facts presently available and set forth herein.

Spaulding Pond is located in Mohegan Park in the northern part of the City of Norwich. It covers an area of approximately 13 acres and when at full level impounds an estimated 45,000,000 gallons of water. The water in the pond comes mostly from springs and such surface water as may flow from higher elevations. The pond is used mostly for boating and swimming during the summer season.

The dam which broke on the evening of March 6th is located at the southerly end of the pond near the recreational area of Mohegan Park.

The dam is what is known as an earthen dam and is approximately 40 feet wide at the base and 12 feet wide at the top and is about 220 feet long. The northern side of the dam which faces the pond is covered with stone rip-rap, while the southerly side of the dam is earthen except for a stone wall which measures approximately 8 feet in height from the base of the dam. A small duck pond is located adjacent to and southerly of the dam. A road which runs in a general east and west direction from the recreational area to the part of the pond used for swimming is adjacent to and southerly of the duck pond and runs parallel to the dam.

It began raining late in the afternoon on Tuesday March 5th and heavy rains continued through the night and during the morning and afternoon of Wednesday March 6th. It stopped raining about 4 p.m. on Wednesday. In all about 1.7 inches of rain fell during such period and as a result there was a great deal of flooding in the low area of the city.

On Wednesday, the Director of Public Works attended a meeting of public works officials in Hamden, Connecticut. He returned to the city shortly before 6:00 p.m.

THOMAS MOODY, JR.

Shortly after his arrival he was informed that commencing at about 4:00 p.m. water was seeping out of the Spaulding Pond dam.

He drove to Mohegan Park and observed the dam from the easterly end of the road which runs near the duck pond. He observed that the southerly side of the dam was covered with snow and that water was slowly seeping out at a point about two thirds of the way up from the base, which point was also about 4 or 5 feet above the top of the wall.

By reason of the fact that some seepage had occurred from time to time in previous years he was not alarmed by the seepage he observed at this time.

At that time the outlet (the valve at the bottom of the dam) was fully open and water from the pond was running onto the road (through the duck pond and onto the road south of it) and flooding it.

Employees who had been observing the seepage reported that there had been no change from 4:30 to 6:00 p.m. Mr. Walz further observed that there was no scouring or erosion on the face of the dam.

From the park he went home to have dinner. Approximately at 8:15 p.m. he left his home in his own car, accompanied by his son-in-law for the purpose of inspecting various sections of the city that were flooded as a result of the heavy rains.

At 7:30 p.m. he called the office of the Norwich Bulletin and advised them that water was seeping out of the Spaulding Pond dam.

At 8:30 p.m. Mr. Walz while driving down Williams St. met Orrin Carashick, Acting City Manager, who was turning from Oneco St. into Williams St. Both cars stopped in the street and upon inquiry from Mr. Carashick as to extent of flood conditions, Mr. Walz described several of the areas in which flooding had occurred. He did not mention Mohegan Park or Spaulding Pond.

Mr. Walz then turned into Oneco St. to observe flood conditions on Zepher St. and Clinic Drive. He then proceeded via Harland Road and Ox Hill Road to Mohegan Park and Spaulding Pond.

He arrived at Spaulding Pond shortly after 9:00 p.m. and observed that water was gushing out of the dam just above the wall on the southerly side of the dam.

Since his personal car was not equipped with a radio transmitter he drove to the Brook St. Barn of the Public Works Department and called the police department. The time was approximately 9:20 p.m. and the call was received by Capt. Casey of the Police Department.

The substance of the call was to the effect that water was gushing out of the Spaulding Pond dam and that there was the danger of a possible break in the dam, and that people living in the Curtis-Baltic Street areas should be alerted.

Capt. Casey immediately called several people on Curtis St. whom he personally knew and asked them to notify people in the neighborhood. He also alerted Cruiser No. 2 being operated by Officer Paradis to notify people of the danger over his loud speaker, and to warn them to remain in their house. When the loud speaker failed he ordered the cruiser to make passes on Mohegan Park Road with the siren wide open.

Immediately thereafter at about 9:25-9:30 Capt. Casey called radio station WICH and requested that an alert be broadcast.

This could not be done immediately since only one engineer was operating the station.

At about 9:35 p.m. Mr. Edward Leonard, New Director of WICH called the police station from his home in Montville to get the details so he could broadcast the alert over the phone from his phone.

While Capt. Casey was talking to Mr. Leonard, Mr. Walz called the police station and reported that the dam at Spaulding Park (pond) had just broken. It was then about 9:37 p.m.

In the course of his travels to inspect flood conditions, Mr. Walz had noticed lights in the City Manager's Office. After notifying Capt. Casey he called the City Managers Office to report the danger. The call was taken by Alderman Rutchik, who with Alderman McWilliams and Israelite were attending a meeting of the Purchasing Committee of the Council. The time was about 9:25 p.m.

The break in the dam occurred a little to the right of the center of the dam and was approximately 28 feet in width at the base and 62 feet in width at the top.

As the water left the dam it travelled in a general southerly direction. When it reached the Mohegan Park Skating Pond it broke up the ice covering the pond and carried along cakes of ice. An examination of Spaulding Pond on Thursday March 7th revealed that the pond still was covered with a crust of ice indicating that the cakes of ice strewn on streets and yards came from the skating pond and not Spaulding Pond.

Spaulding Pond was constructed over one hundred years ago by the owners of the land comprising Mohegan Park. Mr. Walz informs us that since he became Director of Public Works no changes were made in the dam. Nor do the records of the department indicate that there have been any changes since the dam was originally constructed (since refuted). He further informs us that neither during his term or prior thereto is there any record of the dam causing any trouble.

Signed,
Orrin Cartashick
Corporation Counsel

This preliminary report, in its pre-investigation form and as submitted to the council, however, seemed to be enough to exonerate Walz and the Public Works Department of blame, even though later, facts would surface to refute portions of it. "A general feeling among councilmen was that there was no negligence or blame in what happened," it was reported in the *Bulletin*.

Councilman Stanley Israelite, the self-nominated official to take over the Norwich Civil Defense, offered, "Who could ever think anything like this could happen to the dam?" Acting city manager Carashick, when asked if there was "any laxity in notifying persons in the wake of the flood to evacuate," stated "I would say there wasn't at the present time, pending further investigation." Slowly, a feeling of dismissal and denial pervaded the council and all involved. It would not be until almost three years later, during a detailed investigation for the damages and libel trial, that the true story of the dam's maintenance and inspection processes was fully disclosed.

Meanwhile, later in the week following the flood and early into the following week, the deceased were now being memorialized and laid to rest. The existing photographs are faded and hazy now, but they nevertheless depict a group of disparate, seemingly hardworking and conventionally ordinary people.

Alex Pobol was forty-three years old when he died and left behind a wife Anna. His picture shows a still young man who has a seemingly easy smile and sense of humor. A round face with a prominent double chin, he appears to possess a stout eastern European descent, and his photo is further enhanced by his immaculate suit with a vivid corsage—perhaps a wedding picture or some other celebratory event. Alex served with the Army Airborne division during World War II and received a veteran's funeral at Saint Nicholas Russian Orthodox Church at 10:00 a.m. on Saturday and a burial at St. Joseph's Cemetery with full military honors. In a bit of irony, his burial location would be only two spots to the right (looking down) from Honey Moody's and would be the object of much curiosity among her many visitors as his headstone portrayed the same date of death as hers.

Anna Barrett, forty-five years old stares at the camera with a sort of whimsical "hurry up and take this picture, I've got things to do" affectation. Wearing breezy summer clothing and a smiling tilt of the head, Mrs. Barrett seems to be the epitome of a woman loving life and looking forward to raising her kids. She was married to Edward Barrett and left behind three young daughters—which therein lay possibly the most heart wrenching of this tragedy; the young now having to mature suddenly without a caring parent. Mrs. Barrett's funeral was at 8:15 a.m., Saturday the ninth and she was buried at the Maplewood Cemetery in town.

Helen Roode was also young, only forty-four years old when she died, but she, in contrast, appeared more staid and sophisticated than her co-workers

Alex and Anna. Her picture also depicts her undoubtedly attending some formal event, wearing an ostentatious white hat with immense flowering surrounding the brim and a formal white dress while also appearing to be holding a bouquet of flowers. A happy and satisfied look, albeit a little forced, is on her face, a face that gives one the impression of a firm and disciplined New Englander. She was married to Charles Roode and left behind a daughter, Patricia, twenty and son Robert, four years old. Her funeral was also at 10:00 a.m., Saturday, at St. Mary's Church and she too was buried at St. Joseph's Cemetery.

Mrs. Carol Mae Robidou is also named Mae Caroline Robidou in the published record; nevertheless, a picture of her escapes the published accounts of the funerals, but a description of her that survives is that she was fifty years old at the time of her bizarre and horrifying death. Emoting untold sadness, perhaps even more so than her co-workers because of the circumstances of her passing, Mrs. Robidou's funeral was also on Saturday, the ninth, at eleven o'clock, at the Church and Allen Funeral Home. Mrs. Robidou left behind two daughters, a Mrs. Dorothy Foley who lived in Mystic, Connecticut, and a Mrs. Caroline Murphy, along with a brother and five grandchildren. Also, the newspaper records do not indicate any mention of a husband, all adding a measure of intrigue and mystery to a death of a fascinating nature. Mrs. Robidou was buried at the Yantic Cemetery.

Mrs. Madlyn Atterbury was sixty-one years old, the eldest of those who died, and, as mentioned earlier, was sadly less than a month away from retirement. A seemingly vigorous woman with still-dark hair and a steady countenance, Mrs. Atterbury wore the dark, horned-rimmed glasses that were the style of the day, and her picture shows a sturdy woman who undoubtedly was looking forward to her retirement. Her funeral wasn't until Monday, the eleventh, at 10:00, at St. Patrick's Cathedral, and she, among the others, was buried at St. Joseph's Cemetery in Taftville.

As with all of the Turner Mill workers, as sad and as seemingly unnecessary as their deaths were, the funeral for Honey Moody would become a watershed for family sorrow and a fixation on the absurdity and misguided meaning of all these deaths. The young (and not so young) who'd died as a result of this catastrophe, with important and profound family obligations and a deep immersion in life that was abruptly and shamelessly gone, clearly passed on an undeniable passion for living while also, regrettably, passing on unanswerable questions about the meaning of their deaths, making this period unbearably sorrowful and unnecessarily traumatic for their survivors and closest companions.

Both the Shea side and Ronnie Moody decided to wait until Monday the eleventh to hold Honey's funeral. Mary Shea Martell was Honey's older sister, a short, marvelously laconic woman who amazingly resembled her father, William B. Shea, and was married to Patrick Martell, a lifetime navy enlistee, and a resident of Key West, Florida; and it would take her some time to coordinate a sudden trip north to Connecticut. As it turned out, unfortunately, Mary was unable to make the trip; but since the plans had already been finalized, the funeral went ahead on Monday, nevertheless.

Viewings for Honey were held at the Dougherty Brothers Funeral Home on Saturday and Sunday, the ninth and tenth, and brought out many of Honey's closest friends and intimates who expressed both shock and disbelief. The circumstances and fate of her passing were almost too surreal to comprehend, and it was with a bitter reality that these patrons to her final resting were required to accept that she was truly gone. Ronnie and Nana, along with Honey's brothers, were still too much in shock to consider losing their composure at the funeral home, and regardless, none of them would really consider themselves fully comprehensible of what was happening to fully care about their outward emotional appearance.

Riding to the catholic mass at St. Patrick's Cathedral following the funeral at Dougherty's early Monday morning, Nana, Rita Shea (Jerry Shea's wife), Margie Shea (who was Honey's brother Joe's wife) and Jackie Shea all shared the same funeral limo. Stunned silence prevailed, which was only broken by the occasional slight weeping by Jackie, the youngest and closest to Honey. Most were stoically quiet, especially Nana who would hold up amazingly well considering her age and the emotional circumstances. At the church, a large crowd gathered to listen to the requiem high mass, and a subsequent long line of cars made the many-mile drive up to the chosen plot site at St. Joseph's Cemetery.

Adding to the overall sadness of the day was the notable absence of Honey's three boys who were still in the hospital recovering from the ingestion of the cold, muddy floodwaters and onset of pneumonia. In fact, it would be many years before young Tommy would be brought to see his mother's headstone at the cemetery. Honey would be buried a short distance from her father, William B. Shea in a section purchased by the Shea family for their children and relatives. Her headstone reads simply:

MARGARET SHEA

WIFE OF

THOMAS R.MOODY

JUNE 26, 1938 MARCH 6, 1963

For the rest of his life, on her birthday, all Mother's Days, and on each Memorial Day, Ronnie would make it a priority to make the trek up to Taftville. Turning into St. Joseph's Cemetery off the main road, he would slowly take the first right-hand turn, past the grave marker for William B. Shea, his father-in-law, and proceed about fifty yards down the small road before stopping and parking his car to the side. Getting out, he would carry his flower arrangement with him to the left of the road, walking into the grass approximately twenty yards where he would come upon Honey's flat headstone. Placing the flowers at the top of the stone, he would stare at the stone for a period and then, sadly and always with a measure of melancholy, say a private prayer for her.

The old Spaulding Pond Dam prior to the breach

The dam following the breach. Note the concentrated area of break and how much of the old dam that remained.

A picture of the southern face of the old dam showing the unchecked shrub and tree outgrowth that experts later determined caused severe structural failure.

'The East Side Crest.' This area of the dam clearly seen here curving toward the left of the picture was the area of the breech and where experts surmised took on the added pressure when modifications were done on the dam's spillway.

This photo of the left behind 1962 trench, taken after the break, clearly shows water buildup and spoil. Also note the large rocks that were removed during the digging.

The dam break looking at the east side. Clearly a very smooth break meaning the major portion of the dam here moved as one massive unit.

The dam break from the west side shows a totally different story. Massive ripping and tearing of the earthen content along with the clear flowing of the interior rip-rap shows that the flow out of the dam was massive and rapid.

The original Skating Pond looking from its original dam. Much larger than today's, this pond was completely frozen with a layer of ice over a foot thick. When the flood waters came crashing out of the distant woods, the ice blanket became obliterated, its now smaller chunks becoming battering rams in the ensuing flow.

The original Skating Pond Dam viewed from the west. Note the concrete interior of the structure (the dam's left side in this picture) with its age old cracks. The downstream side was earthen and only 4 to six feet in height. The flood waters had no problem overcoming this 'obstacle.'

The Skating Pond Dam viewed from the south. The dam's spillway is prominent on the left side of the picture.

The Skating Pond today. Much smaller and more confined, it still serves the same Spaulding Pond spillway outflow and flood protection that it did in 1963 but today has an intricate and more robust dam structure and spill area such that if the Spaulding Pond dam were to break, a flood similar to 1963 would be largely absorbed here.

Mohegan Park Road looking from the west following the flood. Note the massive road washout and fallen trees. The skating pond is to the left and Colonna's Field (not seen here) is to the right. The Algonquin Gas Company station that narrowly escaped major damage and potential explosion is the first 'house-like' structure seen on the left.

Stark photo of firemen and rescue workers removing a body from the still tenuous ruins of the Turner Stanton Mill.

Mill worker Alex Pobol.

Mill worker Madeline Atterbury.

Mill worker Helen Roode.

Mill worker Anna Barrett.

A good representation of the size of the ice chunks that became battering weapons in the flood flow. This photo shows the flood on Broad St., I believe, before draining down to the Lake St. playground.

An eerie picture of the ruin at the Turner Stanton Mill. The employee time clock frozen at 10:14 p.m. when the electrical power went out.

The revealing aerial photo taken the day following the flood. The damage can easily be traced from the top center and becomes sobering as it raced through the Lake St. playground in the center. Following that directly to the bottom, a clear depiction of the Lake St. drop off and the Lamperell's garage roof is evident. A more magnified look reveals the Moody overturned car. An exceedingly important photo in capturing logistics and flowpath.

Margaret 'Honey' Moody at the time of her high school graduation.

Newspaper photo revealing Tony Orsini (left) holding young Tommy Moody and Ronnie Moody (right) holding young Jimmy Moody on the day that the youngsters were released from the hospital. The baby Shawn would endure two more weeks due to the severe pneumonia that he'd contracted.

Marguerite 'Nana' Shea (left) with an unknown woman. This photo is, my guess, very early 1950's.

Ronnie and Honey's wedding in October, 1957. Nana is to the immediate left of Ronnie and Ronnie's sister Virginia is the dark haired woman to the right of Honey.

The Moody overturned car facing north, looking up into the Lake St. playground. The debris just outside the picture to the right is where Honey Moody's body was found. The DeMico residence is on the far right of the photo. Note the tall smokestack of the Turner Stanton Mill in the background.

The same area today. Other than the rebuilt wall and the absence of the mill, little has changed. Note that the original DeMico house is even still there.

The Longo Funeral Home with Bill and Katherine on their second story porch during the flood.

The extensive tunneling and flow induced damage on Pond St.

Another newspaper photo of the Moody car. The apex of the destroyed garage roof is right in the center above the car and the tree that saved them is to the right in front of the barn-looking structure with Longo's to the rear. The gentleman pictured is unknown.

The massive affect that water flow has is clearly evident here. This is the 'cave-like' tunneling that was carved into the roadwork leading from Lake St. down to Pond St. The very top surface was Lake St. as it ascended towards Boswell Ave.

A picture looking southward down Franklin St. presumably from atop Longo's Funeral Home. Note the large black fuel tanks and remaining ice chunks scattered about and the massive road erosion. The S&S Supermarket and H&M Package Store are the two businesses to the immediate right. The white Edsel that caused damage to the H&M Package Store has been removed at the time of this photograph.

The three story tenement house where William Zeitz watched the flood and destruction. Just down from the S&S Supermarket and H&M Package Store, the white Edsel is still here at the time of this photo.

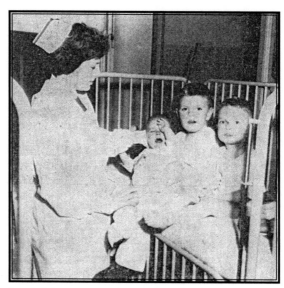

The Moody children at the Backus Hospital following the flood. Jimmy to the right with Tommy in the center helping the nurse hold Shawn. The two oldest would stay a week with the baby staying three weeks. This photo evoked national sympathy with an Illinois couple volunteering to adopt the children.

Ronnie Moody concluding his statement at the March 4th, 2006 memorial ceremony dedicating a stone for the departed at the rebuilt Spaulding Pond Dam. He was 70 years old at this time and although vibrant here, would soon start to deteriorate and pass away in September, 2009.

The Spaulding Pond Dam today . . . beautiful, majestic and most important of all, safe.

The house at 55 Lake St. as it looks today.

The 'Tree of Life' directly in front of the old Longo Funeral home as it looks today.

Shawn and Jim Moody in 2011.

Honey Moody's headstone at the St. Joseph's Cemetery in Norwich.

CHAPTER 8

Aftermath . . .
Subsequent Weeks and Months

B Y SATURDAY THE ninth, most downtown businesses had been cleaned and disinfected to a sufficient level that warranted inspections by the City Health Department. By Monday, the eleventh, most of these had been granted the OK to reopen. All of the sodden and potentially disease-ridden trash that had been compiled on the city curbs now had been carted away to the dump at Hollyhock Island and most of the main roads (upper Franklin Street all the way down to the square), although still showing erosion damage in some places, had been cleaned and swept and were starting to resemble the picture of the downtown that the locals were accustomed to. A handwritten makeshift sign taped to the inside window of Lamperell's Auto dealership symbolized the fortitude of the downtown area: "OPEN FOR BIZ."

For most of the townsfolk, the effort to clean up and restart had become cathartic; it was noted in the *Bulletin* eight days after the flood that only someone who knew what had happened here could ever suspect that anything had ever gone wrong—the downtown area now looked essentially normal. The large volunteer effort, so essential in getting the city's recovery complete, now refocused its efforts on the area homeowners who still required major assistance as few, if any, had flood insurance.

For the flood's victims, however, this quick physical recovery did little to salve the still-gaping emotional wounds that the destruction had created. The Moody family (with a front page picture in the *Bulletin* on March 13 of the three young children in a hospital bed that would evoke heart-wrenching testimony from the country [an Illinois couple seriously inquired about adopting the three children] and symbolize the urgency of the affected) still epitomized this pensive sensibility; Ronnie, in the ensuing days, had to quickly consider how he would maintain his family without a mother for his children.

His problems had quickly mounted—Tommy, Jimmy and Shawn were still hospitalized; his home was now an empty shell and one in which he had no real desire to return to (while nevertheless going through there in the near-term days following the flood, he discovered, ironically, that nary a drop of water had permeated his basement; had they stayed, everything, sadly, would have been OK); his job was, at best, less than rewarding; and he, suddenly, had no automobile. On top of this, he realized that a vapid melancholy had quickly overtaken him, one that would last, in one form or another, the rest of his life. This would also, in the long term, lead to mounting health and emotional issues that profoundly altered his personality and would make him an abjectly changed man.

Never remarrying, he would turn instead to an increasing proclivity to drink. Slowly at first and then more and more frequently, he found what little reprieve from the emotional trauma by "having a few beers with his friends." In fact, Ronnie's post-disaster personality became utterly defined by his deepening desire to drink with friends while discussing sports at a bar.

As a result, the children, although well taken care of and certainly shown a fatherly love for them, grew up with this behavior as "just normal for Dad." Ultimately, Ronnie's chronic and systemic alcohol abuse and lack of consideration for his health would evolve into a very visceral physical demise with graying and aging beyond his years while also being the main protagonist for some severe internal maladies and anxiety/ depressive disorders that would ultimately lead to his death at the age of seventy-three.

For Norwich's businesses and infrastructure, meanwhile, things slowly returned to normal. The J.B. Martin Company returned to limited business by the twenty-fourth, with its machine shop still facing repair and final cleaning. The firm had survived in Norwich for over seventy years and, with the hard work and fortitude of its employees, would return to full capacity, providing textile and velvet goods until an economic downturn forced the Norwich location to close its doors and move to Leesburg, South Carolina, in 1969, where it continues to prosper and provide upscale textile products to this day.

Over $100,000 in velvet and other goods that had been damaged in the flood was ultimately buried at the Norwich Corning Road dump site on the twenty-first—a symbol of the strong loss in earnings that would epitomize all the downtown locations directly affected by the disaster.

The Franklin Hardware Company on Franklin Square, meanwhile, had quickly determined that damage and cleanup was just too extensive to continue and decided to close its business (the lone downtown establishment of thirty-seven that did not immediately return to service). Phil Levin, proprietor, would later open a successful homeowners business (an early '60s version of Loew's or Home Depot), on Franklin Square but at a larger building, around the corner. Kay Jewelers, also on the square and suffering significant structural and foundation damage from the flood, undertook a major rebuilding and remodeling effort that would require two months to complete.

Much of the interior and exterior rebuilding of Kay's was performed with a complete store and business model redesign in mind, using funds generated from the Connecticut Small Business Administration and the Norwich Businessmen's Rehabilitation Fund. The elegant new store reopened its doors, substantially upgraded from its preflood guise, on June 15. Kay's would remain at this location and would be remembered as an important downtown entrepreneur until the 1980s, where it would finally surrender to the larger suburban economic forces as the entire downtown area would succumb to the giant malls and associated suburbs.

The significant street erosion on upper Franklin Street, in the meantime, was slowly repaired, and the slope where Lake Street turned into Pond Street (which had been carved into that large cavelike formation by the rapid outflow from the Lake Street playground) was also critically reengineered. This area, after intensive engineering inspection, required much more structural stabilization than most of the damaged areas in town and would require rerouting of major water and gas lines in addition to extensive concrete and rebar work.

Later in the year, the city was to endure some unexpected latent effects that the flood was ruled directly responsible for. On July 9 a comparatively large road cave-in or sinkhole occurred at the corner of Franklin Street and Bath Street, one of the sites of the rushing floodwaters of March as it had left the *Norwich Bulletin* parking area and entered the Thayer Building. No one, fortunately, was injured, but this unexpected structural failure brought back eerie and unshakeable memories of that night.

And then, as things always seem to happen in pairs, the same thing occurred on upper Franklin Street and Chestnut Street the very next day. Although smaller in size, this Chestnut Street hole was also directly the result of the significant saturation of the supporting groundwork that had been inflicted by the flood. Road repairs here and on Bath Street were performed quickly but had the familiar dread of rerouting traffic and reminded the townspeople, again, of what a calamitous effect the flood had.

The Lake Street playground was bulldozed of the flood waste and preliminarily graded while the city waited for warmer weather to administer the final repairs. It finally reopened for the area children, under the oversight of the Norwich Recreation Department's Playground Association, on June 26 with only minor fencing and final grading to be complete. Downstream, on southern Lake Street at the drop-off to the northern portion of the Lamperell's dealership area, the Moody's 1957 Ford Fairlane was removed by Saturday the ninth. Later, stored in a local wrecking yard, it was easily viewed from the passing road, and young Tommy recalled witnessing it many times, mangled and crushed sitting unobtrusively on the lot for many weeks thereafter while he and his brothers were often driven past it by their dad as they were out running errands.

This upper area of Lamperell's, where the car had landed, was never recovered, although most of the flood's debris and destructive influence was subsequently removed, and the stone-walled drop-offs, both from Lake Street and downward to Lamperell's, were rebuilt with nondescript cement facing. The area today remains virtually the same as it did in late March 1963 after the repairs, although now entirely in abandonment. In fact, an abundant amount of road debris and stone and glass from the flood, amazingly, still permeates the area, as it has become a passageway for the people in the area to shortcut their way from Lake Street down to Franklin Street.

The lifesaving tree, north of Longo's Funeral Home (which is today an apparent apartment house) that rescued the Moodys and Tony Orsini that night, is still prominent and, predictably, significantly larger today. The unmistakable V-shaped branches where young Tommy and his brother Jimmy hung on to still protrude outward and upward and it's easy to imagine the old garage roof of the Lamperell storage garage extending over to these outward reaching branches.

The Turner Mill building, predictably, was quickly determined to be unrecoverable and was summarily razed while the business moved to the former Saxton Woolen Mills facility on Clinton Avenue, a smaller building in Norwichtown. The remaining cleanup of debris at the site was followed, ceremoniously, by the implosion of the large Mill smokestack that thundered to the ground on July 7. The only remnants of the original structure today are parts of the foundation and a portion of the outside fence complete with rusted barbed wire atop it that was part of the original plant isolation from Broad Street.

This area also was never redeveloped and now is overgrown with massive tree and shrub undergrowth. The new Mill would last at the otherwise known Glen Woolen facility until 1974 when the onset of recession in the post Nixon-era coupled with the stalled area economic markets forced by the downturn of the national economy doomed its small market and forced it to close.

A little farther north of town but south still of Mohegan Park Road in the North Street and Baltic Street areas, the washout, although prominent during the flood, was surprisingly quick to disperse and return to normal. Ice blocks that had destroyed many a backyard structure and lawn quickly melted, and Mother Nature ultimately renewed the area with a lush green landscape. At Colonna's Field, however, the work to repair the extraordinary damage would require significant volunteer effort, much as it had required during the initial building of the ball field; and by late April the baseball diamond appeared to be ready for the upcoming Junior Major League season.

On May 1, however, a severe downpour overflowed the drainage brook from the skating pond once again (which had not yet been rebuilt to control this flow) and reflooded the field to where it eerily resembled the early after effects of the March flood.

Sal Colonna, irate again over the lack of assistance from the Norwich Public Works Department, complained heavily that the city-controlled drainage system would again ruin his upcoming baseball season especially since the dam at Spaulding Pond had been destroyed and would apparently not be rebuilt in time to block any rainwater from inundating his field for the coming baseball season.

With indomitable vehemence, he finally got a personal inspection of the area by Public Works director Walz. While touring the field, Walz explained to Colonna that the new flood watershed plan[8] would most likely alleviate the flooding that he was now seeing, but Colonna, typically, was still dubious and saw little in this conversation that would solve his near-term problems and continued in his fervent requests for action that would fix the flooding situation now.

The field was subsequently repaired (again) but the proposed opening date of May 5 had to be delayed. Finally, the following week and after further diligent work by the many local volunteers, youngsters were again playing league ball on an amazingly improved field. By the midseason all-star game (June 23), the field was in pristine shape, and the park itself had been enhanced with improved bleachers and an electronic scoreboard, all brought together by the efforts of the area people along with funding from the Norwich Rehabilitation Fund.

As previously mentioned, visitors to Norwich, in the first few days and weeks following the flood, arrived in droves to witness the damage firsthand and to see the gaping hole in the dam, but this curiosity soon tapered off to a relative few in the ensuing weeks.

The Mohegan Park officials, meanwhile, mindful of the still unsafe conditions there and along with security help from the Norwich Police,

---

[8] While a complete reengineering of the flood/flow conditions from Spaulding Pond all the way down to the skating pond would help to alleviate this field from flooding again, Walz also noticed that the field drainage system was severely undersized to handle potential flooding. The piping system to disperse the water was inadequate for its mission, and he informed Colonna of this inadequacy. Colonna, in typical fashion and nonplussed by this disclosure, said to the director that he'd spent enough money already and that the city needed to repair the skating pond drainage problem, and then he, instead, wouldn't have to worry about his field's pipes.

continued to keep these onlookers away from the site, surrounding it as the park announced a partial reopening on March 20.

Had the uninformed visitor been able to view the pond site now, however, he would have seen an empty, muddy expanse that would soon become a haven for deer and other wild animals to graze. By summertime, major outgrowths of grass and weeds in the drying lakebed would pervade, and, following spring rains, huge colonies of mosquitoes would reign in the area.

Meanwhile, in the heady few days following the dam break, a seemingly large rise in the number of dam inspections in the area towns, fostered by rumor of imminent break or fear of a Spaulding Pond-like disaster, was now observed. Earthen dams in Sprague, Waterford, and Windham that had little or no previous evidence of leakage or other known symptoms were now rumored to be saturated as well, requiring immediate inspections. These hurried inspections, as expected, found no saturation but did add an air of uncertainty and anxiety to the people in these towns.

These new and emergent dam inspections also put additional strain on the Connecticut State Water Resources Commission; during the post-Spaulding Pond Dam break, it was revealed during the town's investigation that the commission was severely understaffed. One man, amazingly, serving part time, provided dam inspections throughout the state. When additional inspectors were needed, consultants were contracted and brought in.

With this surprisingly small coverage, it was now thought to be only a matter of time before another catastrophic break were to occur somewhere in the state. One of the first postbreak initiatives that Governor Dempsey undertook, though, was to review the budget and staffing for the commission. Initial budgeting by the state did, in fact, increase, and manpower was supplemented; but by 1965, it'd petered out once again and was back to the same paltry 1963 conditions. It would not be until the 1980s that these area dams were provided the budget and inspection periodicities that they so desperately warranted.

By the end of March 1963, the first serious discussions of dam rebuilding at Mohegan Park were undertaken when the Norwich City Council opened talks with the Soils Conservation Agency of the Federal Department of Agriculture. The agency had hired a Hartford firm, Dewey and Kropper Engineering, to perform an early and in-depth analysis to determine the best course of action after receiving this inquiry from the town. All possible contingencies at this time were on the table including, remarkably, a plan to *not* rebuild the dam. Along with the immediate problem of the dam break and the downtown carnage, the city, for many years, had lived with a chronic underground plumbing problem (the result of inadequate flow of the original brook to the city) and many sewage drainage issues, and a new dam and flood control program was sorely needed to be packaged, it was determined, as a renovation to the entire system.

By April, it was hoped by city leaders that the Hartford engineering firm would recommend that not only the dam be entirely rebuilt but also that a new "watershed" plan for the city be undertaken as well. This plan, if adopted, would not only rebuild the dam and reengineer the flood controls at the skating pond but would also consider increasing the size of the "Franklin conduit," the underground plumbing header that was buried beneath Centennial Square, which the original Spaulding brook from the park flowed into.

The postbreak investigation had determined that this "conduit" was severely undersized and played a significant role in the profuse flooding in the square on March 6. Also the underground piping from south of Mohegan Park Road (the plumbing lines under Colonna's field and on down to Hickory Street), which had carried the original brook flow had been determined to be vastly inferior as well and exceedingly outdated, early twentieth century vintage it was estimated, and not nearly adequate for its modern mission.

This "watershed" plan then would be to increase the size of the brook flow piping as well as renovating and enlarging the conduit header. Also, an essential pumping/sewage treatment facility would have to be erected, preferably at Rose Alley, which would serve to separate raw sewage from the water and provide a constant clean water flow to the Shetucket River. If enacted, the city would then have sufficient flood protection designed to prevent another Spaulding Pond-type dam disaster as well as an alleviation of the lingering sewage problem.

By May, Dewey and Kropper had completed another study, this one more focused on the flood protection angle, so that by the twelfth of that month, the city council had a clear idea of the type of structures and updated watershed plans that would be needed and to be funded. First, requests were sent out for estimates of a new dam type that the Soils Conservation Federal Agency recommended. A Norwich firm, Chandler and Palmer Engineering, submitted to city manager Fitzgerald on May 30 an estimate and plans for what the new dam might look like and entail. At an estimated cost of $82,000 (for the dam only), a design was submitted that would have a sixteen-inch concrete core running the length of its base, over four hundred feet long, with large earth filler packed on both sides, which, in it's total quantity, would be three times the amount of the old dam.

A new and ultramodern level control system (one that resembled a large square cage, open at the top) would protrude from the northern face out into the pond and would drain to an eighteen-inch pipe passageway placed under the new dam structure, with valves and instrumentation that would automatically control the pond to predetermined levels. On paper, this appeared to be the modern upgrade that the city was indeed looking for.

At the top, the new proposal provided a forty-foot-wide causeway with a thirty-five-foot wide roadway, large enough to sustain automobile traffic, replacing the old road south of the duck pond. This road, after the dam was rebuilt, would, in the early 1990s, be permanently closed to automobile traffic and would finally harbor those same rose arbors and scenic views that the original dam had once attempted.

By July 13, Dewey and Kropper had now also assessed the flood control situation at the skating pond and presented a plan, whereby two smaller earthen dams would have to be erected here as well, at a cost of $90,000, with flood-control grading undertaken such that in the unlikely event of an overflow or break at the new Spaulding Pond Dam, the subsequent outflow would be all but mitigated by this new system. Design here would be such that only minimal flow and water damage would escape this new complex and ever get to the downtown area.

The upgraded skating pond would be built to account for a certain level of water, supplemented with an identical modern level control system and spillway as at the Spaulding Pond Dam, with the surrounding area graded and contoured such that any spillover would have to overcome the tortuous path to flow downward past Mohegan Park Road. This flow, in the analyzed "one-hundred year flood event" that would become the bounding criteria by which all flood accidents in the town would be measured (and would be much more devastating in terms of size and flow when compared to the menacing dam break that had occurred in March), would be quickly consumed, it was explained by the engineers, by the terrain's absorption rate and by the assumed manual emergency actions taken by the Public Works Department.

It would be many months, however, before any actual shovel to dirt activities would commence at the dam site, as the act of financing this extreme cost was, at present, in serious debate within the city's leadership.

An already complex and burgeoning financing scheme for the new dam/watershed plan was further complicated in September 1963 when Congressman St. Onge informed the city council that a grant of $41,000 was, suddenly and unexpectedly, available from the Federal Housing and Home Finance Agency. Moreover, this was federal subsidizing that St. Onge had personally bartered for, and it was this seemingly personal insistence of the district's federal representative that offset another, potentially more stable package that the city now had to weigh.

The "more stable" financial offer was a product of the Federal Department of Agriculture's Soils and Conservation division and encompassed a total award of $250,000. This grant could not be issued, however, until all engineering studies had been conducted (another study for an integrated dam and flood watershed analysis had been commissioned for November 1, 1963) and would require full review and approval by the Agriculture Department before issuance. The Housing and Home Finance grant was immediate, albeit limited in its financial scope, as it was targeted for the reconstruction of the Spaulding Pond Dam only, with the stipulation that construction would start no later than sixty days after the award.

With both of these potential sums to consider, the town now faced an absolute decision—should they take the immediate and sure money (albeit for less) from Housing and Home Finance, or should they rely upon the longer-term Agriculture Department grant, which had all the unknowns of federal government debate, voting, and possible extensions to approve an admittedly much more agreeable amount?

Clearly it was a gamble, but one that had numerous advantages in waiting. After all, the Federal Agriculture Department's Soils and Conservation Agency had already funded two earlier studies for the design and building of the dam and the downtown flood control scheme (and would subsidize another in August for a major engineering workup of the dam site), so it was assumed and hoped for by the city's leaders, that they would continue this seemingly focused interest in this project, along with the coincident funding, while working to close the final loopholes by approving the entire project that they had already invested so much in terms of time and money.

Now, while the financing for the rebuilding of the dam and the downtown watershed plan became a major issue for the city in early to mid-1963, predictably and inevitably, local lawsuits began being filed with the first one being proffered as early as May.

John and Yolanda Hurst, residents of Pond Street, filed for damages in the amount of $2000 when their car, parked in "a Franklin Street Garage" on that fateful night (most likely Lamperell's garage, although the record does not clearly stipulate) collapsed and was destroyed. Their suit accused the town, specifically Director Walz and police captain Casey, of being lax in adequately notifying the downtown area about the inevitable dam break and that they had inadequate time to move and store their car out of the flood path. The date for the defendants (Walz, Casey et al.) to testify was set for June 15, but by then, two more suits had also been filed.

Lawyers assigned to represent the city saw these early legal entreaties largely as dismissive, clearly fodder for an eventual larger and more integrated city trial that would call into testimony the actions and subsequent damages/liability of the town and its leaders. In the near term, however, these lawyers would advise Walz, Casey, and other city leaders who had been or would be subpoenaed for these lesser trials to avoid testifying, fearing that at this early stage, comments or statements would be made that would, at some future point, be taken out of context and that would only serve to excoriate them and the city later. Only until a full and thorough investigation was completed, it was advised, would the town's officials then comment.

Later, though, under extreme pressure to tell their side of the story from the local press, Walz, Casey, and other city officials cited in the Hurst indictment finally did respond and gave depositions on July 12. In their testimony, both Walz and Casey maintained that the dam breech was "an act of God", and that neither they, nor the city, had any liability in the subsequent damages to the Hurst's car or to the town.

These preliminary disclosures by Walz and Casey seemed to be enough to quell the storm of protest in the near term, but by September, with the J. B. Martin Company and the Turner-Stanton Mill now entering the fray with their obligatory lawsuits (alleging that the city was negligent with inadequate inspections of the dam while also failing to appoint proper and responsible supervision over the park's area, re: the dam), upping the total now to fifty-one cases being brought against the town, the onus shifted again back to these officials and their lawyers to explain and validate their actions.

By November, with the number of lawsuits now totaling sixty-five and with the Martin Company expanding that further by attaching a monetary value to their case by asking for $750 million in damages, and with the Turner/Stanton Company following with $250 million, lawyers for the city now advised "immunity" as a near-term defense against past and proposed litigation.

It was, however, becoming clear that the town was going to succumb to liability charges and pay out a considerable amount of money to quell these accusations and quiet the controversy—it seemed to be just a matter of how long they could delay the inevitable trial and then once into it, provide as much non-exculpatory evidence and testimony as they could to lessen the settlement payout.

But in the middle of all of these legal proceedings, some good news finally arose, when in November, a firm decision had been reached by the city with respect to the financing of the reconstruction for the new dam. On the fourteenth, the city council got word from Congressman St. Onge's office that the Federal Agriculture Department had approved all studies submitted to it from the Soils and Conservation Service and had agreed to a grant totaling $200,000, with an understood matching of $40,000 by the city. This federal money and subsequent city matching accounted for plans to not only rebuild the Spaulding Pond Dam but to also finance the entire watershed plan as submitted by the Soils engineers—extremely positive news for the town.

Additionally, the council had gotten early approval for a resolution that had been adopted in October to borrow $42,000 against the proposed federal grant of $200,000, so that now, only a formal vote needed to be conducted to confirm the acceptance of the Federal Agricultural Department money. A quick vote first, however, to formally withdraw consideration of the HHFA grant of $40,000 became an easy decision, as all councilmen had long ago decided that the gamble on the Agriculture Department's full funding was the wise and prudent course of action.

Now, to meet the requirements of the city government as spelled out in its charter, a public hearing would be required before the final approval of the federal money could be signed. This hearing, as tedious as it seemed to all involved, was scheduled for December 6, 1963 and was facilitated by N. Paul Tedrow of the Federal Agriculture Department. At this hearing, Tedrow ponderously read the engineering specs for the new dam and watershed program (110 acre/feet of floodwater storage, controlling 40 percent of the total watershed drainage area with the dam having thirteen acres depth and ninteen feet top width, etc.) to which our hero, Sal Colonna, undoubtedly thrilled to hear that his baseball field would now finally stay dry, exclaimed, "If the city is going to do a job, let's do it right!"

Following this hearing, Tedrow gave the final approval for the federal money to be added to the project budget on December 31, 1963, symbolically closing out the disastrous year on a somewhat high note.

Officially, the new dam's construction would not start until August 1964, but numerous and important precursor milestones were set to or were already occurring.

Soundings for ground rock determination for the new dam's concrete core had started at the devastated ruins of the old dam site as early as November, 1963. A. G. Macchi Engineering of Hartford, meanwhile, had replaced Dewey and Kropper, after formal approval of the federal money by the city council, as the designer of the new dam structure, with Raymond Skoglund of that firm being named as its lead design engineer.

The Connecticut State Water Resource Commission developed and issued its initial construction site permit for the dam rebuild on June 15, 1964, and city manager John Fitzgerald, after receiving the approved design and engineering specs from the Macchi firm also in June of that year, issued "invitations" for construction bids to prospective contractors, on July 10. These proposals were set for opening as "sealed bids" on August 4 and, with approval assuming to quickly follow, long-awaited construction of the new dam at Mohegan Park was set to begin no later than the end of August.

While the construction bidding process was now being formed, serious debate, meanwhile, roiled regarding the physical health of the dried lakebed at the pond. Following the breech and subsequent drainage of the pond, the inevitable outgrowth of wild foliage along with the wild animal occupation and the unforeseen and unbelievably heinous dumping of trash and refuse (mainly old tires and auto parts) into the expanse by some insensitive local residents gave the Public Works Department and city officials concern that when the pond was refilled, the combined rotting of this refuse and mixing with the fill water would cause pollution to the extent that the swimming area could become unsafe.

City alderman Stanley Israelite expressed hope in a council meeting that federal funding would somehow finance the cleaning out of the pond area prior to its reflooding; his statements would loudly echo those of most of the council when he stated that it would be a shame to "have a brilliant new dam but polluted and unsafe water behind it." He went on further to recommend that a "flow inducer" system to circulate the water be installed once the pond was filled. This system would act to filter the water and to help keep it from stagnating, thus reducing bacteria from forming and pollution from collecting.

The pollution concern would later become such a polarizing issue that Councilwoman Ethel McWilliams would seriously recommend that the pond become, instead, just a fishing and boating expanse and that a public swimming pool, the size and make equal to the Olympic-size pool that neighboring New London enjoyed at Ocean Beach Park, be built as an alternative. Later in 1965, an oversight group, the Mothers for Recreational Swimming (MRS), was formed with a Mrs. James McGill as its head, to spearhead this safe-swimming question. Querying experts at the Connecticut State Water Resources Commission and the University of Connecticut, she compiled data that formed a comprehensive report, which she then issued to then city manager John Iovino. This report, as suspected, showed no inherent health risks in refilling the pond as it was and allowing public swimming to occur there.

It would not be, however, until April 1965 when a Dr. Richard Benoit, the chief of Marine Sciences at General Dynamics in Groton, who was a limnologist (a limnologist is a scientist who studies the physical, chemical, and biological conditions at ponds and lakes) was consulted that the issue was finally put to rest.

Dr. Benoit reported that, after careful consideration and study, the pond area at Mohegan Park would in fact be completely safe for bathing and that no extraneous measures such as a separate recirculation system would be needed. Moreover, he recommended that the pond be allowed to fill "naturally" instead of pumping millions of gallons of city water into it as was also being considered by the town.

Dr. Benoit's prescription was that the "natural" composition of the ground fill, in large amounts, as compared to the chemical composition of the city water, would be better for the long term pond health. He did allow that the town should consider using the city plumbing supply as an "emergency makeup" in times of drought but thought that the groundwater fill would be adequate enough to more than make up for any evaporation losses.

Now as the July construction "invitations" were sent out, a total of sixty companies would eventually bid on the reconstruction of the dam. Seven of these companies appeared in person at the Norwich City Hall on August 4 at a meeting held by city comptroller Malcolm Quinlan to solidify their bids. Of these seven, only two would submit estimates below $200,000: the Geer Construction Company of Lisbon Connecticut at $113,000, and L. Becker Construction of West Willington at $132,000.

At an August 18 city council meeting, the Geer Construction Company was officially selected as the project constructor with the ensuing contract being signed on the nineteenth. Monday, August 24 was the agreed upon start of construction, and, at the dam site, the view on Saturday, the twenty-second, was suddenly one of major activity as four backhoes, a diesel shovel, and numerous trucks and loaders were now moved into position.

The initial construction work on that Monday consisted largely of excavation of the eroded remnants of the old dam and the digging of deep trenches for the concrete foundation for the new structure. This core digging encountered an immediate and unforeseen delay when a massive underground rock "ledge" was confronted, requiring much additional drilling and explosives and would result in a significant budget overrun and a month-long construction delay.

Massive clearing of overgrown vegetation and small trees, grown up in the year and a half since the break, also became a major undertaking for the crews. By the end of August, eight additional men along with two supplemental dump trucks, two bulldozers, and three bucket loaders would be added to the already significant amount of construction equipment.

Geer Construction foreman Robert Bitgood reported from the site on August 25 that the new dam, even with the initial setbacks, will "take shape within a month and two thirds of construction will be complete by December." Bitgood also intimated that soon they would be ready for the "thousands of yards of soil to be carried in." This soil would be the essential filler that would be packed around the concrete core and would make up the eventual framework for the dam proper and constituted a major milestone in its construction.

The design of this new dam, as summarized earlier, would be entirely different and far more rigorous then that of the relatively primitive structure built by Pedediah Spaulding and Henry Allen over one hundred years before. As mentioned, a concrete core base (essentially a wall) was poured that would penetrate many feet into the ground and would run the width of the pond from west to east. This wall would be over a foot thick and was consolidated in the middle where a raised concrete bunker/tunnel-like structure (formed in a north-to-south direction) housed piping and valves that would control the pond's level. On the north side, a boxlike concrete enclosure with small concrete slabs running north-south topped with three large slabs running east-west formed the new and ultramodern level control system.

The idea was for the pond water to enter the enclosure and, as it exited through the drainage piping, be measured by level instrumentation against a predetermined mark or "setpoint". This setpoint would then send an electronic signal to a valve to open or close, depending on the level, to maintain a certain level within the pond. The higher the level, the stronger the electronic signal and the more the outlet valve opened, draining the pond to that predetermined level. This seemingly simple system was an absolute mainstay in modern dam design and, as chronicled earlier, was a critically missing component (among many others) in the Spaulding/Allen dam.

Once the concrete structures were poured and dried, earthen material was heaped upon and consolidated over it. Pile after pile of dirt and stone was mounted and packed, essentially forming a large earthen wall, bounded to the north by the inlet cage and to the south by the outlet piping enclosure. Amassing to a height of thirty feet and a width of over 150 feet at its base, this new dam, ultimately, dwarfed the old configuration seemingly by double and gave a visceral security and protective effect to all who would visit the completed complex.

On October 27, 1964, Congressman St. Onge, in the midst of a reelection campaign, visited Norwich and the dam site that he was now so familiar with. Speaking with the Geer Construction workers, he was impressed with their progress but was noted to be a little melancholic after reliving the tragedy of that night. Later, after the press reported that his stop seemed only to be a ploy to further his campaign promotion and evoke voter sympathy, St. Onge angrily responded that his "visit was not trivial . . . I was proud to have proposed two avenues of financing for the new dam." He would go on to an overwhelming reelection victory and would serve the area until his untimely death in 1970.

By December, the promised construction progress had indeed been attained; all the concrete works had been completed, and a look at the surroundings now showed that the piping tunnel with its boxlike northern pit was the only portion of the new structure still exposed. The concrete core and area around it were covered and fully graded with earthen soil. Groundwater from the upstream springs now flowed through the new works, and it was evident that soon this spring water flow would be gated shut and become active only in filling the pond anew.

THOMAS MOODY, JR.

With the onset of winter 1964, dam reconstruction work was forced to break until spring. Recommencement, contractually, would be based entirely on weather and conditions at the site in the spring of 1965, but observers thus far were pleased with the progress made. A picture published in the *Norwich Bulletin* on the two-year anniversary of the break on March 6, 1965, showed the concrete piping tunnel from the south end looking north with the dried lake bed behind it. Groundwater flows through it toward the camera while earth filler and grading is clearly evident around the tunnel as proof of progress. Little of the previous area anatomy is evident. What is prevalent is change and change in abundance; it's clear to see that once the earthen filler is added atop the concrete core, this area will undergo a metamorphism that no one visiting the dam site and familiar with its previous layout would recognize.

As winter slowly eased into spring 1965, the weather in southeastern Connecticut predictably became unstable. Rain, snow, cold temperatures, and freezing rain pervaded such that the targeted construction restart date of March 22 would have to be delayed until April 5.

Making up for lost time now, Geer Construction had, by May 31, placed and packed earthen filler as high as the old dam and, importantly, laid stone riprap three-quarters of the way up on the northern/pond face side. This riprap arrangement (riprap is really nothing more than large rocks and stones packed strategically along the lower level of the dam) was crucial in the design to not only assist with wave resignation but also to help alleviate pressure buildup against the dam face such that the level control system and emergency spillway could easily handle any perturbations in level or pressure.

The designed emergency spillway, meanwhile, was really nothing more than an 80 feet by 115 feet concrete graded pathway around the dam on its west end. This channel, whose long-term use would prove to be lower-level visitor parking near the zoo, would be to divert overflow water downstream to the graded dam outlet such that it could be carried to the brook flow southward toward the skating pond. Future park renovations would remove this spillway concrete grading and, instead, install underground piping at various points along a beautifully upgraded western retaining wall that would, in the end, serve this same purpose.

By July 1965 the earthen content had been topped off; and on the seventeenth, construction was officially declared "complete." The finished dam's final inspection was conducted by city officials on the twentieth with formal acceptance being given by Whitney Ferguson and Donald Tierney of the Soils Conservation Service and Raymond Skoglund of Macchi Engineering.

The final product wasn't yet final though. Abundant grass planting was still needed on both the north and southern faces of the large earthen slopes. Bids were still required to go out for the roadwork and sidewalks that would become an integral feature of the top of the structure. Plants and other aesthetically pleasing accoutrements had not even been thought about, and the downstream strategy to repair the still apparent flood damage along with the leftover rugged terrain from the construction still needed to be addressed.

But the largest hurdle was indeed now past; the new dam was complete and a formal dedication ceremony date had been selected for September 17.

And as that day dawned cold and damp, with a brisk and chilly wind racing across the empty expanse of the still-empty pond and with cold rain showers intermittently enveloping the area, dignitaries and guests gathered on the west end of the new dam structure to view this technological marvel and to remember the tragedy that'd occurred here only two and one-half years ago. City council president Ethel McWilliams along with city manager Charles Iovino opened the ceremony by unveiling a concrete stone topped with a bronze plaque that beautifully summarized the physical details of the new structure (this stone monument today still stands as a testament to the dam rebuilding but is unfortunately buried in thick cedar ground cover and requires some extensive navigating now to get to).

Mrs. McWilliams then spoke of the memories of that tragic night and of the unrelenting support given by the city and its townspeople. "At 9:30 p.m. that fateful day the 45 million gallons of water in the 12 acre pond burst an antiquated 20 foot high rock and earth dam and roared down Franklin St. into the business district killing six persons, injuring six others and causing over $4 million property damage."

As the next day's *Bulletin* further reported, "The pond Friday gave no inkling of its death dealing capabilities. The water level was extremely low. Two white ducks, which earlier this summer built a nest at the foot of the dam, gazed up curiously at the ceremony."

Now as the speeches and ceremonial precepts wound down, Donald Williams of the Federal Soils Conservation Service, along with N. Paul Tedro, State Conservationist, and Norwich Public Works director Harold Walz all climbed out to the north facing, which housed the new and modern level control system and formally closed the outlet gate, thus stopping the flow through the drainage piping, thus initiating the formal refill of Spaulding Pond.

CHAPTER 9

The Trial

BY THE END of 1965 and on into 1966, with the new dam built and Spaulding Pond slowly accumulating water, and with the memory of the flood gaining time and perspective, the last pillar to be downed in this tragedy was its recompense. So who really was to blame? Was any "one" or any "thing" really responsible? Would or should "anyone's head roll", as a result, and if so, how far up the city management chain, or even state management chain, should the guilty be victimized?

To get to the true facts and to provide final closure to the victim's families, it seemed that the only proper mechanism would be to have a comprehensive and consolidated legal effort, launched with all the testimony and accusations judged. The earlier individual suits, filed from 1963 through 1965, brought against separate and disparate members of the city's leadership, were clearly not enough to coalesce into a strong legal statement or, most importantly, significant or permanent policy change.

For certain the families of the victims who were killed deserved not only an in-depth analysis and subsequent explanation of what had happened but also damage reparations and an understanding of the series of events that led to this dam collapse. The city, as maintainers of the dam, needed also to assuredly understand the break in an engineering and hydraulics perspective so as to better know the physical properties of the structure they had purchased in 1906 and to attach these lessons to the new dam to preclude it from occurring again. Moreover, inspection processes and inspection timelines would now have to be implemented and enforced now that the dam had been rebuilt to avoid any repeat of the disaster; even state and federal agencies would undoubtedly have to get involved now to preclude a reoccurrence.

How hard would it be and how many lawyers was it going to take to sort out the byzantine labyrinth of testimony, hearsay and circumstantial or direct evidence that was sure to be generated by this combined legal action? How much of it would (in the foremost of legalese) have any verisimilitude? And for the town, would Mohegan Park ever be the same sublime and relaxing area that it had been prior to the break?

It was with these lingering questions and doubts, along with, assuredly, many other thoughts and conjectures that the Norwich townspeople, still with a certain antipathetic opinion of the city's official stance, looked forward to the legal proceedings and subsequent search for justice. It was also, assuredly, with these expectations, that they hoped that the trial and litigation would get to the bottom of and settle the matter fairly while, ultimately, having a larger stake in putting this catastrophe, finally and resolutely, behind them.

And so a trial, in Norwich, under the jurisdiction of the New London County Superior Court, was, after almost three years of investigation, legal posturing, and the multitudes of smaller legal suits, set to open on Tuesday, February 8, 1966 with the seemingly elementary objective of judging three "pilot" cases that litigators had consolidated down from the large number of flood claims, both by the victims and those otherwise affected, and would be heard by a Superior Court judge, without a jury present, with the end result hopefully being a final and fair determination of liability and damages.

But before any courtroom proceedings could occur, the completion of the detailed and drawn-out investigation, initiated soon after the dam break, was required. As claims were amassed (viz., the fifty-one previous cases brought), attorneys Milton Jacobson and Allyn Brown, both of Norwich, had been assigned as litigators for the plaintiffs. It would ultimately be up to Brown and Jacobson to prove legal liability of the city and to extract whatever monetary damages they could, either via settlement or, if adjudicated, a superior court ruling in their favor.

With evidence clearly in their favor, Jacobson and Brown hoped to present enough damaging testimony to convince their counterparts representing the city that reaching a financial settlement would not only be in their best interests and best for all parties but also that avoiding a judge's ruling would be the most uncomplicated outcome and would avoid a long trial along with potential confrontational and accusatory testimony—and this quickly became their primary strategy as the trial date approached.

Brown and Jacobson would, as provincial lawyers, use their abundant local resources to supplement and enhance the detailed investigation that the city was still in the process of conducting, while, in parallel, supplementing the legal system to prioritize and compel affidavits concerning the who, what, where, when and why in the run up to and into the night of March 6, 1963.

Starting with the history of the park and the dam, these plaintiff lawyers were able to slowly piece together the story and record of the structure while also chronicling the shortcomings of the attention given to it in the fifty-seven years of town ownership. Using the official report submitted by Public Works director Walz and acting city manager Carashick, they melded the seemingly misguided earlier modifications made to the dam with the actions taken there by the city that fateful night and, by virtue, hoped to raise enough concern to question whether these facts, along with the infrequent inspections already recorded, proved liability.

Before the attorneys could make much headway, though, significant speculation as to what had happened and who was to blame had already been generated in the media. Following the seemingly dead-end litigation that the small individual legal suits postflood had brought, the subsequent still strong questioning by the town was enough to convince the local press that some form of strong legal strategy was indeed warranted.

Admittedly microscopic by today's standards, the media machine of the early 1960s could still nevertheless generate enough rumor and innuendo (whether warranted or not) to agitate the masses. Numerous editorials in the days following the flood excoriated the Norwich Public Works Department, the city council and the Norwich Civil Defense—all for lack of warning and, in the case of the Public Works Department, lack of maintenance on or attention given to the dam.

Attempting to respond, as witnessed in the earlier lawsuits, the city and its representatives realized quickly that the court of public opinion was an uncontrollable and unstable entity and that the onus of guilt was still clearly on them. The only way to maintain a semblance of objectivity, they'd learned, was to cooperate with the plaintiff's attorneys as they initiated their own separate and somewhat independent investigation.

Amid this period of investigatory trailblazing, not all the local press was "anti-city" however; the *Hartford Times* newspaper, in early March, attempted to assuage the assault by documenting the history of the attention given to the dam by interviewing past Norwich city leaders in a Monday, March 11, 1963, article:

AFTER A CENTURY . . . ACCEPTANCE

OFFICIALS NEVER THOUGHT DAM WOULD EVER BREAK

Ivan Robinson Times Staff Writer

"After 100 years you sort of just accept something."

That remark made by former Norwich Mayor Richard J. Marks summed up the experience of the city's past administrations with the Spaulding Pond dam that burst Wednesday night and brought death and destruction to this city.

Two former city managers and three former mayors whose administrations date back to 1941 all said they never were aware that the dam was hazardous.

It was periodically checked by park employees, they said, and the old Park Commission even held its summer meetings near it but no one ever recommended to them that it should be repaired.

Mr. Marks, who was mayor from 1948 until the mayoral form of government was replaced by a city manager in 1952 said park changes were often requested but there was nothing ever said about the dam.

Former City Manager Angus T. Johnson (1960-1962) said, "I never had occasion to have anybody point out any need for (maintenance on) the dam."

He said he had been "over it, around it and beneath it" many times and knows it had been checked in normal working duties by park employees.

Employees often worked around the duck pond just below the dam, he said.

Mr. Johnson also noted that the 13 acre Spaulding Pond is not affected much by runoff. It is 230 feet above the downtown area and is mostly springfed.

The earthen dam, he said, was substantial—40 feet wide at the base and tapering to 12 feet at the top—but it would be difficult to see cracks in it.

Former City Manager Jay Etlinger (1955-1959) also could not recall any requests for dam repairs. "I'm at a loss to understand what happened. Of course it's been a terrible winter with heavy frost. Thick blocks of ice built up the pressure. The weakening may have happened this year alone."

Former Mayor James J. Mullins (1944-1948) remembers attending Park Commission meetings in the summer at the dam site but does not recall any hazardous condition. He feels there should be appropriations in the future for inspection of dams both at the time of construction and in later years.

"A dam is either there or it is not," said former Mayor Richard L. Norman (1941-1944). "You don't think about it when its there."

A dam is part of a city's permanent physical equipment and since it does not depreciate, it receives little thought, he said.

Mr. Norman, who also was an alderman from 1951 to 1957 said the Park Commission was "very conscientious" but never reported that the dam needed attention.

A check of City Hall records shows the dam was built in 1853 by two businessmen to operate a machine shop and a woodturning shop. The city acquired it in 1906. Spaulding Pond held about 45 million gallons.

Although few and random, these attempts by the media to exonerate the city did offer some tangential reality to the tragedy. True, before the breech, there existed an acute lack of a program for inspections and monitoring, and, also true, the town officials were seemingly satisfied with or, at best, naive to this process. Moreover, when the floodwaters hit, there was an abject deficiency in an official process or direction from the city at the time when it was most needed, and the subsequent climate of chaos that this seeming lack of leadership exposed that evening certainly prevailed throughout the tragedy.

The larger point that many of the town's more vocal critics were failing to adopt, however, was that this dam, at the time of the breech, was 110 years old and had been under the city's jurisdiction for only fifty-seven of those years, meaning that the officials who oversaw it in 1963 had little in the way of a base understanding of its construction or of its design capabilities. As it was, the plurality of opinion among city leaders on March 6, 1963, was that the dam had always been there without issue and, it was reasonable to assume, would therefore continue to be there. This was, naturally, the attitude that the city and its lawyers would take as the trial started.

And now as a comparative microcosm of activity (investigation, blame, more investigation) that took almost three years to coalesce came to its culmination, legal proceedings for the initial trial of three "pilot" cases opened at 10:00 a.m. on February 8, 1966. On that Tuesday, New London County Superior Court judge William Barber took the bench with the self-appointed position of "specially named jurist," and he initiated testimony in a precedent setting legal proceeding that resembled a grand jury-like setting, albeit without the jury.

This "pilot-case" method had been chosen over other more-conventional legal methods as a somewhat novel but otherwise useful legal approach specifically for this litigation. Its inference was that it would combine the many claims already filed against the city into three "pilot" or summary cases. These cases would then summarize all the complaints offered thus far with a summary verdict being handed down by the officiating body, in this case, Judge Barber. This process was thought, and would become in the end, the most effective procedure for handling such a large and complex number of accusations in a fair and reputable manner ever seen in Connecticut law.

The first day's initial arguments started and, predictably, deteriorated to technical points; the plaintiff's lawyers were successful in adding five additional cases to the original three to make a total of eight pilot cases now before the court. Other technical points were argued, and when the initial session ended, it would prove to have been essentially an affair attempting to understand the breadth of the proceedings. "The pilot case method, believed by court authorities to be a precedent setting step in Connecticut judicial practice, is to determine legal liabilities and not financial damages." Lawyers named to defend the city were Ralph Dixon of Hartford and George Muir, also of Hartford, who, it was also determined, would represent the town's employees. John Dennis of Norwich, who was the city's insurance legal counsel, would also join the city's defense team.

The next day's (Wednesday) proceedings opened with Shepard Palmer, a Norwich civil engineer and a witness for the plaintiffs, testifying that the engineering view of the break was that of unimpeded saturation and that had a more rigorous preventive maintenance program been implemented, this disaster, most certainly, could have been avoided.

Palmer, with pictures and graphs as his evidence, unfortunately was an engineer of only minor stature[9] so his testimony would unfortunately go largely unheeded.

It would not be until many days later when a seemingly more reputable engineering source would give essentially the same testimony that the court would realize that what was suspected all along was true—that the Norwich Public Works Department and thus the city had been clearly naïve as to the dynamic and hydraulic design of the dam and that they were in fact culpable, notwithstanding its ignorance, for its demise.

It wasn't until Thursday, February 10, when Clarence Vantour, the Public Works employee who had been working with Monroe Cilley the day that the leak was discovered, took the stand for the plaintiffs that

---

[9]   The official courtroom record at this point for the entire trial (outside the Ronnie Moody emotional content which is uncontrived) is based on the surprising and gratefully detailed *Norwich Bulletin* account; the official courtroom transcript was destroyed, as was common practice, some seven years after the termination of the trial.

the court would begin to hear the exacting details of what had occurred immediately prior to the break. Vantour recounted his and Cilley's actions that afternoon—the discovery of the leak by Cilley, the opening of the relief valve by Vantour, and the initial breech inspection by Patsy Ferra. Vantour also testified to his opinion of the seemingly aplomb attitude exhibited by his leadership (re: Ferra) concerning the leak while he went on to also describe the exact location of the seepage that he and Cilley had initially observed.

After Vantour stepped down, Judge Barber called a short recess, undoubtedly for the defense and plaintiffs to internalize this first meaningful testimony in the trial and to regroup. When court resumed, Engineer Palmer was again called to the stand, this time for cross-examination of his previous testimony, but with no record of the outcome.

The next day, Friday the eleventh, park foreman Cilley was sworn in and began his statement that described his actions on March 6. Answering questions from plaintiff's attorney Brown, Cilley essentially mirrored Vantour's previous day's testimony when he stated that the two workers spent all morning and most of the afternoon digging ditches and clearing catch basins in the park area while monitoring the spillways at both the dam and the skating pond. Returning to the dam at about 4:00 p.m., Cilley stated that this was when he first noticed the small seepage from the eastern end and suggested to Vantour that they go out to investigate it.

Informing the court that he thought, after closer observation, that the leakage was significant enough to warrant higher-level scrutiny, he testified to asking Vantour to go down to the dam base and open the relief valve while he called Ferra on the truck radio. After Ferra departed following his now rather indifferent "well, it's seeped before" observation, Cilley then stated that he, Vantour, and Arthur Aldi, another park worker, became busy in "damage control." Cordoning off roads and setting up flares, Cilley then told of working on these efforts until seeing Director Walz at the dam at about 6:00 p.m. He then went on to say, curiously and as if seemingly to defend his work ethic, that this was the only time that he would stop work that day; this to explain the circumstances of the day's occurrences to the director.

Further, he added that he returned to the park at about 9:00 p.m. with his wife specifically to see if there were any new developments at the dam.

Out of his car and in the pitch dark, it was then that he first heard and then saw the "white foam-like stream" jetting from the east side of the structure. He stated that he rushed back into his car and made haste to the nearby Public Works office in the park where he attempted to call Director Walz at his home. Being unsuccessful, he then tried to contact him at the Brooks Street Garage and it was here that he learned that the director was already engaged in what little dam-break prevention measures he could muster at this late stage.

The record of the defense cross-examination of Cilley is, unfortunately, nonexistent, and subsequently, Judge Barber ended the session for the weekend. But with only two of the disaster's major players testifying this first week, it had already become brazenly clear with the evidence presented, that early on the day of the breech there were clear and efficacious symptoms of a serious problem.

The challenge now was for the city's defense to show that regardless of these seemingly telling portents, the town, that day, still had no concrete inclination to believe that a dam break of the proportions that were to come would, in fact, actually occur and, further, that the notion of even considering alarming the entire area based on this evidence was indeed impractical.

Lawyers Brown and Jacobson for the plaintiff's, meanwhile, undoubtedly now had the lawyer's instinctive sense of 'the kill' and decided to push the matter further by requesting records and documentation that they both strongly suspected did not exist. When court proceedings resumed Tuesday morning, February 15, Cilley again took the stand and, along with five subsequent witnesses, was immediately questioned about eight categories of records that, along with his March 6 testimony, he'd been subpoenaed for.

Other than photographs, Cilley stated that these records were either nonexistent or perhaps buried deep in obscure locations in city hall or at Mohegan Park and would undoubtedly take much time and manpower to locate.

Objections from the city's lawyers, mainly Dixon, led to the first of many lively and loud exchanges between the attorneys that required Judge

Barber to intercede in and referee. The records in question, and ones that Brown and Jacobson doubted the existence of, seemed to pertain to the specifics of the dam's maintenance, soil samples, and correspondence with the state's Water Resource Commission associated with modifications to the dam's structural dynamic. Minus this, it was felt by Brown and Jacobson, the ease of proving negligence and subsequent liability would become much clearer to the court.

Other witnesses, meanwhile, who'd been subpoenaed concerning documents were corporation council Orrin Caraschick (acting city manager on March 6 1963) and current city manager Charles Iovino. All those who took the stand pleaded ignorance regarding the existence of and/or location of these records.

Public Works director Harold Walz became the first key city official directly involved in the run up to and throughout the disaster to take the stand and was sworn in on the early afternoon of Wednesday, the sixteenth. With his highly anticipated testimony, attorney Jacobson immediately started challenging him with surprisingly belligerent and seemingly unnecessarily hostile questioning regarding the natural water flow from Mohegan Park to the downtown area while also badgering him somewhat on what was the quickest route from his Preston home back to the park (not, apparently and according to Jacobson, the one that he'd taken the evening of March 6) and why that particular route was the one that he did not use the night of the break, which brought, again, spirited exchanges between the competing lawyers. The question of available records, also predictably, was raised, and Walz indicated that he and his staff "were working on it."

Following the lunch recess, the issue of records and available documentation was finally put to closure when Walz and two of his staff walked into the courtroom and almost ceremoniously plopped boxes and large paper sacks down on the right-hand side of the court benches. Walz then explained to the court that these were the sum total of the available documents and evidence pertaining to the dam and its upkeep at the city hall, the Brooks Street garage, or at the Public Works Office at Mohegan Park.

The paper sacks covered old burlap bags that contained soil samples of the dam at various points in its history. These samples had ultimately proven inconclusive for saturation or anything dangerous to the structure after being analyzed. Moreover, the documentation, once analyzed and as Brown and Jacobson suspected, showed no evidence, formal or otherwise, of correspondence with the State Water Resource Commission for permission to alter the dam in any way. And now, as a result of this seemingly insufficient proof of approved dam alteration, the plaintiff's lawyers had (in their minds) seemingly clear and unmistakable proof of city liability.

With the city's defense now clearly shaken, Walz again took the stand on Thursday, the seventeenth for what turned out to be an extremely conclusive day of testimony. Recounting his actions on March 6, 1963, he explained in detail how he'd inspected the initial seepage and determined that it had appeared similar to previous leakage that he'd seen before. Returning to the park at nine o'clock that evening. and upon hearing and then seeing the torrent, he admitted that it brought on an altogether unforeseen terror that momentarily stunned him. Quickly regaining his senses and realizing that immediate action was required, he testified to quick, spontaneous acts all geared toward warning the immediate downstream citizens and to, hopefully, clearing the potential flood path to the extent possible. He testified to calling police chief Casey; of ordering Public Works nightshift foreman Yeitz to send worker Phoenix to the park to be their eyes and ears; he told of calling City Hall and speaking with city alderman Martin Rutchik and explaining the situation while also calling the *Norwich Bulletin* and confirming the now-dangerous leak.

He testified again, in almost morbid detail, of Phoenix's confirming radio call that the dam had breeched and of his (Walz's) and his son-in-law's efforts, on foot, to inform the people in and around Hickory Street (the road running west to east just north of the garage) of the oncoming floodwaters in a new disclosure. He also asserted that he solicited the help of two local teenagers to assist with notifying people in this area, including Lake Street, and, he stated, it was when he returned to the garage to call Captain Casey again that the floodwaters hit the building, making it impossible for he and the crew there to stay any longer, and it was while he was on the phone that he and several garage workers were forced to crawl through a small window to escape and where they subsequently sloshed their way up to Baltic Street.

Arguments and counterarguments during Walz's testimony again would get testy as plaintiff questioning attempted to pinpoint the definition of "acceptable seepage." Walz tried to point out that, in his limited experience, earthen dams "sometimes seeped," whereas Brown countered (with hindsight clearly as his ally) with queries as to how any dam leakage (earthen or otherwise) could possibly be acceptable and not be a harbinger of a larger problem. Attorneys Muir and Dixon for the city objected and snidely wished to see Brown's geological degree, which in turn brought more arguments and caused Judge Barber to call a halt to the day's heated proceedings.

Although certainly implying that the city was perhaps negligent in pursuing a more rigorous inspection plan and that they could be considered naïve with respect to the dam's capability and design, Walz's testimony, in the grand scheme, did little else than show that he and his department were not tendentious in their care for the dam and that they, as the responsible wing of the city's maintenance department, did indeed care about the park and the town and that they clearly did their best, under the circumstances that evening, to protect both.

Moreover, nothing is available as official record as to what lessons were learned as a result of the disaster and what became the new policies, postbreak, regarding inspections and leakage. Also, never brought out in the trial and what would have been fascinating to understand was what had been the understated requirements of the Public Works director position with respect to the dam when Walz took the job at the very beginning of his tenure.

With the trial now in full swing, other important players in the tragedy were quickly brought forward to testify before Judge Barber. On Thursday February 24, Public Works Department nightshift foreman Patrick Yeitz, park worker Leon Laisee, Public Works Department employees Louis Heller, Nicholas DaVanno, and Martin Anderson all entered important testimony concerning eyewitness accounts along with timeline-related evidence.

Although challenged by the city's defense regarding who specifically in the Public Works Department hierarchy gave him the orders, Yeitz nevertheless testified to his activities that early March evening relative to the dam. He spoke of the actual timeline when Director Walz came into the Brook Street garage and of him (Yeitz) being on the phone and overhearing Walz's announcement to the nightshift crew that he'd just returned from the dam and that "we might lose it."

Yeitz also recounted that he had followed Walz's specific instructions to move a large city truck, as the oncoming floodwaters were sure to damage it. While hurrying outside, Yeitz stated, he heard and then saw the oncoming torrent and "was stunned." While attempting to move the truck, Yeitz witnessed the floodwaters quickly surround the garage, and it was then that he decided to abort this vehicle-move and disembark. He somehow made his way back into the garage in the ever-increasing water level and flow, where he exhaustedly told Walz that "the truck, everything, was gone."

Mohegan Park worker Leon Laisee, meanwhile, next on the stand, testified to digging postholes on top of the dam and assisting in trench digging in September, 1962 and observing water "trickling from one spot in the trench while several of the post holes for the rose arbors were either muddy or had water in them", implying, of course, saturation of the type discussed in the engineering diagnosis as symptomatic of the earthen content of the dam losing its integrity.

Public Works Department employee Nicholas DaVanno meanwhile testified to witnessing abnormal water level at Calonna's ballfield and to observing "muddy water, trickling from the dam" on the afternoon of March 6, 1963. Louis Heller also an employee of the Public Works Department, said, curiously, that the spot that he'd witnessed seepage from was at a location on the dam not from the spot of the initial leakage sighting but from further up on the east side.

Public Works employee Martin Anderson was called next to the stand and he (also somewhat belligerently) testified to excavating postholes and digging trenches on the dam in September 1962, and of witnessing mud and water at both locations. While working his shift on March 6, 1963, moreover, he testified to overhearing radio conversations between park foreman Cilley and city foreman Patsy Ferra concerning the leak that Cilley had initially observed. Later, he stated that he heard Ferra give orders to Public Works Department employees at the city garage to go to the park and help Cilley and his crew with barricades and flares at the east and west end roads below the dam so that "no one would be caught below the dam if it broke."

Anderson, testifying that he himself was concerned at this point that an imminent disaster was about to occur, called Norwich police headquarters personally at 8:00 p.m. following completion of his work shift. Speaking with police captain Casey, he reiterated his fears and findings from his shift that day and suggested that he (Casey) warn area residents about the possibility of a dam break. Anderson then told the court that Casey explained to him in this phone conversation that "he didn't want to get involved in Public Works Department matters." Dumbfounded, it wasn't until Anderson's wife informed him a little while later that the dam had indeed breached that he realized that the worst had in fact come true. He went outside his house at Mohegan Park Farm, an area just to the north of the brook flow from the dam to the skating pond, and saw the torrent whisking by. Hurrying back inside, he called a neighbor to tell them to stay inside their house and that he would come by to see if they needed any help in getting out.

These damaging revelations from the day's witnesses, needless to say, brought about increasingly virulent challenges from the city's defense attorneys concerning timeline and veracity, especially in the case of Anderson who seemed to hold some form of vendetta against the city, even these three years later. Judge Barber once again was required to intercede in the sometimes internecine arguments between lawyers while still attempting to judge what was important in the way of exculpatory evidence and testimony that could be used to prove or disprove city liability. Regardless, if all that was said proved to be true, there were some holes in the city's timeline and defense that implied earlier knowledge of a leak and/or trouble at the dam, and these were discrepancies that would now need to be addressed.

Norwich police captain James Casey was the next key witness in the drama to take the stand, and he gave his testimony the next day, Friday, February 25. Recounting his version of the events of that night, he validated essentially the same story told by Director Walz—the Norwich Police Department's first true signs of trouble were when Walz contacted them at about 9:20 p.m. wherein the director declared that the "dam might go." Casey then confirmed to the court what his immediate actions then entailed; among them were initially ordering patrol officer Richard Paradis to the Mohegan Park Road area with directions to warn the citizens in that area of the potential dam break. Casey also talked about his personal acquaintances in that area and his subsequent phone calls to those folks warning them of the possible flooding.

In his two-and-one-half-hour session, Casey also testified to the technical problems with communications that would attenuate his staff throughout the evening, starting with the difficulty in establishing an emergency warning broadcast with the radio station WICH. Setting up emergency telephone lines would become problematic as well, he stated, since numerous calls into the station soon inundated the small telephone network and its tiny nightshift staff, requiring Casey to call in all off-duty officers for emergency duty.

Casey then discussed with the court the sheer magnitude of chaos that an unexpected catastrophe such as this played on his comparatively small nighttime police force. Coordinating manpower for traffic control while attempting to work with fire and rescue operations in addition to responding to the myriad telephone calls quickly depleted available forces and required much juggling of priorities, Casey testified. Moreover, protecting against looting and other subversive activities in these times of unexpected disaster made police work that evening much more precarious.

Questioned now by attorney Brown for the plaintiffs, Casey was asked about the existence of and/or availability of records that would document calls to the station validating warnings about leakage at the dam. Casey responded that no "blotter" was kept at the department as a matter of record and that a "radio log" was kept only as a matter of subjectivity, which is to say that the call receiver or "desk man" usually made the determination as to what was logged or not. Brown's point of questioning clearly was to further determine if earlier calls had been made to the station that day concerning any leakage problems at the dam and, if so, how much earlier. If, as earlier testimony implied, the police suspected, or worse, had been informed that leakage was occurring earlier in the day, then they too could now be held liable for the lack of warning to the townspeople.

Casey, though, vehemently denied all knowledge of any missing papers or of any early warnings of dam leakage, holding fast to his earlier statement that the first substantiated warning his department received of the potential disaster was at 9:20 p.m. When asked by Brown about earlier testimony from *Norwich Bulletin* reporter James Winters, who'd said in a previous statement that he had asked Casey about alleged weakened conditions at the Spaulding Pond Dam twice—at 7:00 p.m. and at 8:15 p.m., Casey responded that this was rumor and that he had heard "nothing about it."

Up to this point in the trial, the proceedings had taken on the certain dull legal drone that most would've expected. What little aversion from the normally staid courtroom decorum was the sporadic verbal sparring between attorneys Brown for the plaintiffs and Dixon for the city's defense. This malaise would, however, change suddenly over the course of the next twenty-two minutes on this afternoon of Friday, February 26.

When plaintiff's attorney Jacobson suddenly and unexpectedly called Ronnie Moody to the stand, it was met with an immediate and resounding objection from city defense attorneys Dixon and Muir who argued that Moody's testimony was clearly a stunt by the plaintiffs meant to play on the emotions of the court, particularly Judge Barber. Moreover, his testimony, in their opinion, would be skewed completely toward monetary damages, not liability, which, after all, was the point of these proceedings.

Jacobson countered that his witness's testimony was eyewitness with respect to the initiation of the floodwaters, hence it would certainly have liability connotations—how could the city's defense make such an absurd and uninformed assumption? Further, Moody was part of the original three complainants that made up the pilot cases and, like Director Walz, had contextual testimony that could be important in establishing the overall liability timeline. Convinced by Jacobson's counterargument, and undoubtedly nonplussed by Dixon's/Muir's "emotions" plea, Judge Barber overruled the objection.

Having just turned thirty years old (on February 6, 1966) and being somewhat more physically filled out, Ronnie Moody was now just starting to show signs of age with a small sprinkling of gray in his hair, which was otherwise seemingly frozen in time, still combed in the 1950s DA style (he would wear it this way, with only a minor diversion for the longish sideburns of the '70s, for the rest of his life) that he favored in 1963. Clearly nervous here in the courtroom in his dark suit and with hands folded in front, his brown eyes wide and his countenance furrowed with a focused concentration, he gave one the impression of a city-boy outsider, an ordinary guy out of his element in the big city where he had been asked to come explain something to these fancy lawyers and judges in his own simple language that they were supposed to then interpret and judge and which was very important, so he had better get it right.

Still exceedingly quiet by nature, it was formal proceedings such as these that made him abundantly uncomfortable. And as he now made his way to the stand, he took the oath while staring apprehensively at the floor of the courtroom. When finally seated, he was asked by attorney Jacobson to, in his own words, simply recount his actions on the evening of March 6, 1963—and this he now began to do, quietly and with only a slight ting of emotion, telling of arriving home from work at about 9:30 p.m. and settling in to watch television with his wife, Honey.

After hearing the loud banging on his living room window and then seeing water flowing down Lake Street from his front window, he and Honey bundled the children and attempted to make haste to Nana's house on the west side of town. Testifying to running up the outside stairs of his home and asking neighbor Tony Orsini for help, Ronnie then explained the logistics of who sat where inside his Ford Fairlane to the court as they drove down Lake Street.

Describing the wave that hit them as "a cloud of water and ice," Ronnie went on to describe how the car rolled over and subsequently became wedged against the garage roof at Lamperell's Auto Dealership. Explaining how Tony and he got out and how Honey extracted the children from the wreckage while standing in the overturned car, Ronnie suddenly stopped his testimony, for only a moment, while carefully gathering himself and his facts as he realized that this was clearly an important and consequential part of the proceedings.

Continuing, he explained that with the baby Shawn still on his arm (his left arm) and while turning to hand him off to Tony, he suddenly heard Honey shout. It was when he turned back around that the roof that they were standing on gave way momentarily and, he explained, that he, at this point, had his wife's hand in his own, but it slipped away and "she went down."

"I started to go for her with the baby in my arms, but she was gone," Ronnie continued and it was here, Ronnie went on, that Tony Orsini grabbed him and exclaimed, "Ronnie, she's gone." He then described to the court their harrowing escape to the tree, getting young Tommy and Jimmy to quickly "duck-walk" across the increasingly unstable roof with Tony now holding the baby Shawn precariously under his jacket before the wavering structure collapsed.

Ronnie also spoke of the seemingly interminable hour that they spent in the tree, soaked and freezing, before they were able to get the attention of Bill Longo who had gone out to the second-story porch of his funeral home. Ronnie then went on to explain the treatment that his children underwent in the hospital and the danger that the baby Shawn's pneumonia brought, which required a much longer and protracted stay there.

Asked now by Jacobson to describe how and where his wife was found, Ronnie stated that she was discovered the next morning by her brother Jerry Shea. Asked how he and the children were getting along, Dixon objected once again, this time as to relevance, but Barber once again overruled. Ronnie explained that he and Honey had been planning for her to go back to work at the Southern New England Telephone Company once Shawn was old enough to go to school and for his family to move out of the city. Now, three years later, the children were in a reasonably good state of health and lived permanently with Honey's mother Nana in a low-income housing project on the west side of town, while Ronnie, still working at the American Optical Company, was not allowed to officially "live" at the residence for financial reasons but was nevertheless still the boys' benefactor and provider and was with them every day.

With that, Jacobson indicated that he had no further questions. Judge Barber then turned to Dixon who, undoubtedly anxious for Ronnie to finish his testimony and get off of the witness stand, also stated that he had no questions, and Ronnie was excused.

Silence, eerily, now prevailed in the courtroom as Ronnie stepped down, and it was a few moments before Judge Barber called a brief recess. Ronnie's testimony, in terms of proof of liability, did comparatively little to further the plaintiff's case, but it was certainly an emotional bombshell—one that the plaintiff's attorneys felt they needed and one that the defense certainly feared. Virtually all of what Ronnie had testified had been available, in one form or another, as legal record prior to his taking the stand, but to hear it as an integrated oral statement made a resounding point and seemingly now represented a turning point in the case. In the days to follow, important substantiating and corroborating evidence would be introduced, but all of it would be hinged on and around Ronnie's groundbreaking assertions.

And with his exposing avowal out as public record, subsequent testimony would become even more revealing.

On Wednesday March 2 (the day young Tommy Moody turned seven years old while attending kindergarten at the now razed Falls Street School on Sachem Street), William Wise of the Connecticut State Water Resources Commission added another dagger to the city's defense when he revealed that the Spaulding Pond Dam had, remarkably, never once been inspected by his commission in the fifty-seven years that the town had owned it, even though it was required by state statutes.

Wise stated that, speculatively, the main reason for this omission stemmed from the fact that "less than half the dams in the state are inspected because my department lacks personnel," but, also nowhere in the official record was there an inquiry from the town to the commission as to why there were no inspectors coming to the dam on any regular basis nor was there any question as to why there were no programmatic inspection plans.

Wise, in still another revelatory disclosure, then went on to say that it was strict commission policy that if a town were to want any alterations to a dam structure, they would need prior written approval from the commission. Dixon, for the city, asked for clarification, and Wise stated that "ditches or trenches on the dam would require approval, but the planting of a rose bush, for example, would not need commission approval." Jacobson, now seeing an opportunity, then asked the seemingly obvious question, which was if the commission had received any documentation inquiring about the digging of a trench or postholes on the dam prior to the September 1962 project, six months before the dam break. Before Dixon could object, Wise quickly answered no.

Now, to further this line of questioning (and to dig the city in deeper [with no pun intended]), the plaintiffs again called Mohegan Park employee Martin Anderson to the stand. Anderson, recall, was the belligerent park worker who had earlier testified that he helped with trench digging and posthole erection the previous September and who'd noticed water in both. Moreover, he now contended that he'd also witnessed seepage at the dam a day earlier on March 5 which, Anderson said, was at the base of the structure. Dixon, of course, had objected to the novelty of this "previous seepage" testimony, but by now, the die had seemingly been cast; and when Jacobson countered with the argument that this Anderson evidence (the postholes and trench) was in fact known testimony and clearly showed that early signs of saturation were evident (notwithstanding the somewhat contentious early seepage assertion), no one in attendance seemed to doubt it.

Meanwhile, the volatile but ever-entertaining Sal Colonna was brought to the stand by the plaintiffs on Friday, March 4, with the clear intent of further pursuing the early and nonreactionary knowledge of the trouble at the Spaulding Pond Dam by the city on the day of the breech. Testifying to nearly waist-high water at his Mohegan Park Road baseball field on March 6, he told the court that he went to the Public Works garage and encountered Foreman Patsy Ferra. When he explained to Ferra that he'd "never seen water so high on my field," Ferra "sat down with bowed head with his hands between his legs and said 'You think you have troubles? The Spaulding Pond Dam's about to let go any minute.'"

Astounded and then somewhat fearful at what this disclosure meant, Colonna now walked to his house near Boswell Avenue and immediately called the *Norwich Bulletin* where he repeated what he had heard from Ferra to reporter Gordon Smith. Smith, also dumfounded, was puzzled with what to do with this information and finally decided simply to file it away. Colonna testified that he then called WICH radio station and spoke with an unidentified reporter there, relaying the same information.

Dixon, during the cross-examination, attempted to break up Colonna's timeline testimony by rapidly questioning the validity of his statements. Querying his actions on March 6 , Dixon, out loud, wondered whether Colonna was confused about when he saw the high water level on his field when he went to the Public Works garage and when, or if, he actually called the *Norwich Bulletin* or the radio station. Colonna, now completely flustered, countered back, "You're getting me mixed up. You're skipping around too much." Dixon was clearly trying to discredit Colonna's testimony by saying that he had previously stated that he was at the garage closer to 6:00 p.m. (which would match the discovery of the seepage by Mohegan Park foreman "Red" Cilley and the knowledge of the leak by Patsy Ferra) than the early afternoon time frame that he was now alluding to. Colonna denied this.

Attorney Muir now joined the fray by suddenly switching tactics and asking Colonna if he had been bitter toward the city because they hadn't done enough to alleviate the excess flooding on his baseball field to which Colonna vehemently retorted, pounding the railing in front of the witness stand "No! If I was I wouldn't be running for City Council now would I?"

After further bantering, Colonna was ultimately dismissed, claiming a doctor's appointment but, doubtless, not before making an impression (notwithstanding the volatility) of at least an honest attempt on his part to get answers for and to warn of a seeming problem near the skating pond and on his baseball field.

Norwich Bulletin reporter Gordon Smith now followed Colonna to the stand and the journalist, more or less, substantiated Colonna's frazzled testimony. Moreover, Smith added additional damning evidence when he testified to actually speaking with Walz at seven-thirty that evening and hearing the director respond that the dam indeed could break and that he (Walz) "planned to cut a hole in the ice and put up sandbags the next day."

Taking this information, along with the previously gathered facts from the likes of Colonna et al., Smith, at that point, considered writing a "what if" story of the implications of a Spaulding Pond Dam break and the damaging consequences to the city for the next day's newspaper. Forthcoming events, of course, made the speculations of such a theoretical work moot.

So now, with all of the facts garnered from this day's proceedings added to all of the previous day's nonexculpatory testimony, it was becoming more and more evident that the symptoms of disaster had indeed been adding up prior to March 6 1963. But what was also becoming clearly evident was the clear fact that these symptoms weren't as ostensibly evident to the right people as they should have been on that day—symptoms that would have most certainly spelled disaster if only they could've been compiled in a clear, integrated, and understood fashion.

First, we have the Norwich Public Works Department dealing with yet another leak at the dam—one that was thought to be understood but was nevertheless novel, requiring an additional burden on the city for having to establish and maintain local precautionary and preventative measures, with these being attended to by park workers in an entirely insular and contained manner and known only to the folks in that department and on that particular day.

Second, there are townsfolk living in and around Mohegan Park Road, near the skating pond, concerned about the abnormal water level that had accumulated in that area. Both Sal Colonna and Patti Pellegrini have been witnesses this day to uncommon flooding; Colonna, in fact and as previously mentioned, even went as far as to make a personal visit to the Brooks Street garage to complain while also calling the *Norwich Bulletin* later in the afternoon to voice his concern—with none of them being deemed grave nor troubling. These disclosures and Colonna's flood-day series of events wouldn't even become public knowledge until the trial, some three years later.

Third, we hear revealing testimony from a number of park workers attesting to mud and water being evident while digging a trench and after pulling up rotting cedar posts on the top surface of the dam in September 1962, only six months prior to the break, clear evidence of saturation of the dam's earthen content. This information at the time, and as far as we can tell, went nowhere and, again, only became public at the trial.

Further, we hear one park worker, Martin Anderson, attempt to warn the city through various means that day about the leak and about his concern of the dam potentially breeching. He even calls the Norwich City Police with this issue, but it is (arguably in the face of later testimony) met with a dismissive response about not wanting to "get involved in Public Works Department business" and his concern would go no further.

What we're led to conclude from all of this evidence, and what becomes frustrating to realize, is that even with these growing physical symptoms, none of it is understood or assimilated that day into an integrated problem such that the town's leadership could address it as a potential catastrophe.

Instead, it was now abundantly clear to the court that this became a fragmentary and fast-moving predicament, only fully realized late on that specific day by only a very specific few; becoming impossible to pin down or, for that matter, incapable of invoking responsibility onto anyone who could have had enough foresight to not only anticipate the coming onslaught but also, even more presciently, had enough intelligence or wherewithal to act upon it.

Sadly, the clear and obvious conclusion that could only be drawn from all of this was that there were just too many disparate and discordant sinews to this story for it to be focused entirely on one man or entity on the afternoon/evening of March 6 and that this tragedy would become, although catastrophically unfair and eminently unfortunate to the impending victims, completely and unalterably unavoidable.

So while the court proceedings extended into early March, it now seemed that a certain legal discourse was forming. Evidence, daily, was being introduced showing the city being clearly impervious of mismanagement of its asset and further, delinquent in its diagnosis of the symptoms that would lead to this disaster. But upon closer scrutiny and analysis and while being weighed against the provisions of wrongful death, it was also becoming more and more apparent that this was a much broader failure along many distinct and farther reaching bureaucratic lines and was in fact a failure that could not be confined to or confused with a particular town department or personage.

Making a judgment for liability against the city based on the available evidence, although becoming an increasingly intelligible proposition for Judge Barber, was becoming also a referendum on emotion—emotion that somehow needed to turn into equitable recompense.

With the victims of the flood being three years gone now, the only reasonable retribution for their families would be a fair and equitable settlement—and it was here that Judge Barber feared that no mutually accepted or appeasing amount would or could satisfy those disaffected by this tragedy.

A settlement still, resolved by the competing attorneys and then clearly explained to their clients with all the nuances spelled out, was nevertheless the cleanest and least vindictive for the court and the town. The limits of monetary availability, however, whether by adjudication or financial settlement, was sure to be vastly disappointing to all involved to whom, assuredly, would not understand the financial complexities of such an arrangement.

Simply put, this money for retribution would ultimately have to be funded, without any outside subsidizing, via the city coffers, which meant that it would ultimately have to be paid back by city taxes. This payout money, in comparison, for the amount seemingly fair and equitable for the victims, especially considering loss of life, would be an amount, unfortunately, that would also quickly bankrupt the city. City insurance policy liquidation would account for only a small portion, so the lawyers were facing the possible irony of not only having to explain the details of a favorable judgment or settlement, but more complexly, having to explain to a victim's loved one(s) why they weren't receiving an amount equal to that which they assuredly deserved.

When viewed under the fiscal microscope of the middle 1960s, this issue of monetary payout would prove to be a major polarizing event for the flood victims. With an unforeseen and drastic upturn in the national economy and the coincident anti-Vietnam War cultural explosion occurring between 1966 and 1970, a monetary settlement of even a few tens of thousands of dollars offered in 1966 would ultimately carry very little economic weight when measured against 1967 or beyond.

When valued in this inordinately changing economic environment, this mercantile-driven monetary difference would prove to be perceptibly unfair to the plaintiffs and a source of much angst and second-guessing as to their decision to settle. For the rest of their lives, the flood victims and their families would have the feeling of being short changed and exploited and whenever the subject of the flood and the city leaders of that time would come up, this was the general perception that would be passed down to the next generation.[10]

It was this complex cataloguing of financial payout options that was undoubtedly clouding the minds of the attorneys of both sides that the unexpected and sudden conclusion of courtroom proceedings occurred on Monday, March 7, 1966, almost exactly three years following the Spaulding Pond Dam break, following conclusive evidence, again, of city naivety of the dam's physical condition was presented, this time by one Steven Poulos, a Harvard professor of soil mechanics who would, this day, speak to the characteristics of earthen dams and saturation credulities that the town was under, and it was testimony that would prove vital, ultimately, in driving this case toward closure.

Dr. Poulos's mandate, when summoned to the court by the plaintiff's attorneys, was to answer a "hypothetical" engineering question that would speak to the circumstances surrounding the dam and its ultimate breech. Dr. Poulos, on the witness stand, discussed the cause of the break, ultimately, as one of "piping" that was attributed to four engineering factors:

1) poor dam design
2) poor dam maintenance
3) bad weather conditions on and prior to March 6th 1963
4) poorly chosen alterations to the dam

He then went on to disclose that his opinion was based on fifty-one suppositions given him by attorney Jacobson but was also supplemented by previous testimony.

---

[10] This, clearly, was how my father viewed the outcome; this "city was to blame" attitude was certainly very strong within him when he recounted this story to my brothers and I with the raging predilection that if the "city" (this mysterious "someone") had done something that day when the leak was first noticed, our Mom would still be here. Admittedly acquiring this same uninformed bias while growing up, it wasn't until actually delving into the detailed research for this book that I became comfortable with the notion that "the city" (re: the Public Works Department) certainly was not "to blame."

Dr. Poulos's testimony:

"On March 6th, 1963 there was an earthen dam approximately 27 feet in length and approximately 18 feet in height, running in an easterly, westerly direction and located at the southerly end of Spaulding Pond and was of a size and shape with slopes of a ratio of one to one. It was constructed of homogeneous soil and the dam impounded 45 million gallons of water on that date.

"The dam had a frost layer of 21 inches on the downstream face. There were several trees of varying sizes up to six inches in diameter growing on the downstream face off the dam with roots growing into the dam with at least two trees growing in the area that subsequently breeched.

"The upstream face of the dam was covered with stone rip rap and there was a concavity (ditch or trench) on the upstream face of the dam in the area that subsequently breeched. (author note: the previously mentioned "east side crest"). The lower one-third of the downstream face was an approximately vertical dry stone wall of an average height of 6 to 8 feet with a slight batter (author note: 'slope') of one foot.

"Beneath and at the bottom of the dam there was a six-inch outlet pipe controlled by a hand operated valve. Below the dam there was an area known as the "duck pond" with four walled sides and with pipes leading from the downstream base of the dam into the duck pond which was covered with gravel.

"On top of the dam, two parallel cedar post fences were located running from one bank to the other. The cedar post fences formed part of a rose arbor and on that rose bushes were planted, trimmed and cut back at various periods of time.

"The cedar posts during the summer of 1962 were placed down into the dam in holes which were dug to a depth of approximately three feet and secured by placing stones around the base.

"The cedar post fences replaced a cedar fence which previously had been in place on the dam and a number of previous cedar posts were rotted. Some of the previous post holes were filled with rock and dirt.

"Prior to September, 1962 there was a level gravel pathway across the top of the dam. About September, 1962, six months prior to the breech of the dam, the city of Norwich intended to put water pipes across the top of the dam.

"The city caused the commencement of the digging of a trench on the top of the dam to a depth in excess of three feet, with a width of approximately two feet, said trench having vertical walls and an approximately flat bottom with the spoil of the excavation being placed on either side of the top of the trench.

"During the digging of the trench, stones up to the size of a football were removed. During the course of the digging, the trench was left exposed and spoil washed back into the trench, requiring further excavation.

"Work on the trench ceased about December, 1962, at which time the trench extended from the westerly bank approximately three-quarters of the way across the dam and ended in the area that subsequently breeched. This trench was left exposed to the elements and spoil was washed down into the trench and remained in the trench together with an accumulation of rocks, leaves, rain, snow and ice, so that on March 6, 1963 the trench was from 15 to 18 inches deep.

"The dam has been owned and maintained by the city since 1906. The dam had a natural overflow channel prior to about 1930. The city constructed a concrete form with grooves on either side of the natural spillway designed to hold boards of one-inch thickness.

"It was the practice of the city to place a board or boards in the grooves after the annual spring thaws, until the summer, at which time the boards were removed entirely and the spillway remained in its natural state with no boards during the fall and winter seasons.

"In 1949, the city caused the placing of a permanent concrete block poured in two sections totaling three feet in length and 18 inches height above the bottom of the natural spillway thus raising the maximum height of the pond one and one half feet.

"By raising the water, the city increased the pressure on the dam at maximum pond level by 94 pounds per square foot.

"The city in 1949, through its employees, constructed a wading pool adjacent to the westerly end of the dam, at which time the level of the pond was reduced to about one-half its depth so the retaining wall of the wading pool could be constructed.

"Later, the city, through its employees, caused the height of the water behind the dam to be raised to the height of the top of the concrete block.

"The trench was begun by the city from September through December, 1962. Assume (author note: these "assumptions" were, in essence, the magnitude of the "hypothetical" testimony that Dr. Poulos was asked to provide.) the employees left the trench open from December to March 6, 1963. Assume the city did not trim or remove any of the trees on the downstream face of the dam and that ice covered the entire pond area right up to the rip rap and the pond drainage area.

"Rain fell from about 6 a.m. on March 6, 1963 to about 4 p.m. the same day with total rainfall about 1.75 inches.

"Water commenced flowing from the pond over the concrete block and into and through the spillway about noon on March 6, 1963. About 12:30 p.m. the same day, city employees began to clean the spillway of the dam of debris and leaves. The trench contained water and ice on that day about 4 p.m. Water in the pond did not overtop the dam on that date. The rate of flow through the spillway on March 6, 1963 was no greater than the ordinary flow to be expected for this time of year.

"Assume on March 6, 1963, about 4 p.m. employees of the city observed a pencil-line stream of water which was not collected with a container on the downstream face of the dam, about four or five feet from the top of the dam and above the top of the retaining wall on the easterly side of the dam in the area of the breech.

"Assume about 9 p.m. a large stream of water was observed gushing out from a hole in the downstream face of the dam above the top of the retaining wall and below the area where the pencil-thin stream had been observed. Assume at 9:30 p.m. a roar was heard and a large quantity of water was observed gushing through a hole in the dam. A little later the dam breeched."

Now as the attorneys from both sides conferred, Dr. Poulos sat tentatively awaiting follow-up questions. The gravity of his testimony weighed heavily on the defense, and he undoubtedly expected intense and deleterious cross-examination. Surprisingly though, the majority of the afternoon was spent on simple and benign explanations of technical details contained in his testimony. Unbeknownst to Dr. Poulos and those in the courtroom, the lawyers had already come to an agreement on preliminary settlement language, and these follow-up questions regarding the minutiae of his testimony were geared solely toward those finalization details.

When the trial resumed on Tuesday morning, March 8, 1966, attorney Dixon immediately requested a recess until noon, explaining that "some matters had developed on both sides" and he assured the court that "if these were resolved it would facilitate the termination of the trial." Lawyers for both the defense and plaintiffs then huddled jointly for a period of time before separating to their respective clients, clearly indicating a unified effort to bring the proceedings to an end.

Through on again, off again courtroom appearances, and subsequent requests for recesses, it was clear that a final resolution was at hand. When court was again requested to be adjourned until 10:00 a.m. the next day, it had been in session for a grand total of ten minutes this Tuesday, but neither the defense nor plaintiff attorneys had left the building. Lawyers then spent the rest of Tuesday explaining the complexities of the proposed settlement payout and personal injury monetary awards to their clients so that by Wednesday the ninth , a package was available to present to the city council. In it, the following points were noted:

1. Seventy-eight property damage suit claims were settled at 60 percent of amounts to be decided by a specially appointed referee.
2. Twelve personal injury suits would be settled on the basis to be outlined at a meeting of plaintiff's attorneys Brown and Jacobson.
3. The city of Norwich would pay off property damage claims over a five-year period.
4. Personal claimants would receive their share prorated from the insurance company within a short period after the settlement was signed and approved by the court.

It was also revealed at this Wednesday session that the testimony of Dr. Poulous had, in fact, been the conclusive evidence that completed the picture of all the evidentiary statements, and it was substantiation of these facts that apparently added the resounding finality that the plaintiff lawyers needed to close the courtroom portion and to proceed onto the settlement phase of the trial.

Now in a series of seemingly clandestine meetings with clients and opposing attorneys, the final details were worked out such that the final summation would be presented to the court on Thursday, the tenth and followed up with a special session to be presented to the city council later that evening.

CHAPTER 10

The Settlement

BY REACHING A settlement in this case in the manner in which they had and with the lawyers subsequently convincing their clients that the determined method of payout would "save the city from bankruptcy", the estimated savings to the town would ultimately exceed $1 million dollars. By "preventing too great a strain on the city", the plaintiffs, alas, agreed to accept an amount far lower than initially implied, indeed lower than they deserved.

"After all," the two local attorneys pointed out, "every plaintiff and ourselves are tax payers in Norwich. Though the city has the responsibility of paying the claims, we and our clients want to make it possible for Norwich officials to absorb the debt and the method of payment will not create too great a strain on the taxpayers."

And so it was on Thursday, March 10, 1966, before the largest crowd to date in the Norwich Superior Courtroom, indeed a "somber crowd" in the words of the *Norwich Bulletin* court reporter on the scene, that the details of the settlement were explained to the plaintiffs and to their loved ones. In eerie particulars, attorney Jacobson recounted each victim's plight followed by the total summarized cost for all their hospital, doctor, and medicinal expenses. These costs (miniscule by today's medical standards) and the breakdown associated with them were then to be "refereed" by Judge Barber (basically analyzed for discrepancies or abuses), and a final award amount would then be handed down the following day.

Now in front of the large courtroom crowd and with attorney Jacobson being the defacto spokesman for the attorneys of both sides, the terror of that dreadful night was again relived as each victim's heart-wrenching account was retold. Recounting how Ronnie and Honey had planned to finance their children's education while Honey went back to work after their youngest Shawn was at school age, Jacobson explained how that plan was irrevocably thwarted after those tragic events unfolded. He "told of the car being turned over by the flooding waters. As the third of the young sons was handed to the neighbor (Tony Orsini) and safety, the husband (Ronnie Moody) turned to see Mrs. Moody yell as the battering ice-filled water pulled her under. Physicians viewed the body the following day after it had been recovered wedged in among the debris at a wall. The doctor said Mrs. Moody sustained a broken leg and arm as her body was dragged away from her loved ones. The doctor said the bones were broken prior to her death by drowning."

Honey's sons, it was reported, were in the hospital for varying periods of time. Tommy and Jimmy were admitted to the Backus Hospital for a total of six days and were treated for shock, "exposure" (a term used throughout the 1950s and '60s to describe hypothermia and the onset of pneumonia), with both of their body temperatures below ninety-five degrees for an extended period and with abrasions and bruises resulting from the trauma of the car crashing over the Lake Street drop-off. Also, as a result of their extended time in the floodwaters and elements, Jimmy would suffer some latent asthma symptoms in his early childhood while also experiencing some believed early physical developmental problems. Tommy, in turn, would incur migraine problems of his own in mid-to-late adulthood that doctors conjectured most likely could have resulted from the exigencies associated with the flood.

The baby Shawn, although becoming fully recovered in adulthood, suffered the most from his flood-related afflictions. Staying at the hospital for fifteen days, he would become the most at risk medically of the Moody children. Having an extremely low body temperature when admitted and having ingested a large amount of the disease-ridden mud and water, the infant easily contracted pneumonia and the obvious initial fear was the spread of bacteria throughout his underdeveloped systems. Fortunately, in time and with intense antibiotic treatment, he responded quickly and reverted to a healthful recovery within a few days

After his release from the hospital and during his youth, however, he would endure many severe migraine-related headache episodes of his own and head-related impairments that were feared would have permanent repercussions throughout his life. These incidents of migraine-related pain were so intense that Nana, as she became the demonstrative "mother figure" for the boys, would actually place him in her bed on the first floor of the Western Avenue home that she and Ronnie provided for the boys postflood and sit with him as he cried himself to sleep. Tommy and Jimmy would also solemnly observe these occurrences, as young children, and offer as much empathy as young brothers could muster, but the two boys would ultimately feel a huge sense of emptiness and even guilt as they would watch their young brother lying in bed crying, in great discomfort, trying to sleep to ward off the pain.

Now as attorney Jacobson continued to read the Moody's saga, the medical costs of each was also revealed allowing Judge Barber to note the amounts required to be paid by the city's insurance. Shawn's hospital bill was $337.05 with additional treatment by the family doctor, Imogene Manning, totaling $150. Tommy and Jimmy both had hospital bills over $140 and similar treatment from Dr. Manning totaling $85. These costs, when measured in the comparatively low medical economical environment of the early 1960s, and when added to the overall award for the city settlement sum, goes a long way toward understanding the ultimately low final settlement payout to Honey's children. The court stipulation that this money be withheld from them until their eighteenth birthday, and, with an interest accrual, resulted in an amount barely enough for each of them to purchase a reasonably priced used car. Amazingly and sadly, no educational benefit was ever realized by any of the children from this catastrophe.

Tony Orsini's losses were totaled at $70 for a week's wages and a $102 hospital bill for exhaustion, exposure, and a badly bruised knee, which had him confined to a wheelchair for two days. He also received treatment from his private doctor, Anthony Tramantozzi, for $65. His settlement payout totaled approximately the amount that Tommy and Jimmy received, but nowhere was there mention of his heroics that night nor any award pertaining to it. He would nevertheless be spoken of in reverence in the Moody household for the rest of Ronnie's life. Whenever Tony's name was mentioned or brought up, an almost reverential moment of silence ensued, and Ronnie would always recount Tony's heroics once again to the Moody children who would then listen in respectful silence.

Ronnie, as husband and father to the three children, would obviously be the executor of Honey's estate. The complete award, ruled on by Judge Barber the next day, would total over $29,000, with this amount including all the monies for both Ronnie and the children. When viewed again in the vastly subdued economic times of the 1960s, this, at first glance, appeared to be a substantial amount of money. But when the children's amount was subtracted, funeral costs were considered, and the hospital/medical costs were extracted and when the family automobile was replaced, there was, predictably, little money left. Ronnie then used the remainder to purchase school clothes and other necessities for the children, and when this amount quickly dissipated, he would find himself running up an enormous bill at the Sears Roebuck department store downtown for clothing and school supplies that would take many years (the youngest, Shawn, would be at high-school age) before he was able to pay it off.

His low-paying job at the American Optical Company was enough to basically keep the family afloat, and this income, coupled with Nana's Social Security and her small Veteran's benefit from her husband's wartime service, plus some kindly low rent assistance from the Kennedy Heights housing projects where the family settled, were the primary provisions for the children.

When looked at, in the final analysis, Ronnie and Nana had been able to heroically keep the children together and provided for—certainly meeting and exceeding Honey's "if anything happens to me, I want you to take care of my kids" predeath premonition. This outcome, of course, in hindsight, would add another layer of admiration and respect to both from anyone associated within or outside the family, and it would become a level of reverence not fully nor completely understood by the young Moody boys until much later in their lives, unfortunately, not until Nana and Ronnie were either ill and/or had passed on.

Continuing on now with the settlement summaries, attorney Jacobson read the stories of the Turner Stanton Mill victims. Alex Pobol was the forty-three year old in charge of the night-shift at the Mill when the floodwaters hit. His wife, Anna would be the administrator of his estate. Attorney Jacobson recounted how Alex had been working in the basement level of the structure that evening when he observed, without warning, water and ice suddenly pouring in. Making haste to the highest point, the third floor, while being certain to warn fellow workers along the way, he was one whose cry for help went unheeded. When the building collapsed,

Alex was driven back down to the basement level where he was discovered the next day under debris, crushed to death.

Alex's funeral costs totaled over $1,500 with Liberty Mutual Insurance (Turner-Stanton's insurer) paying $500 toward that amount. Alex's final award as deemed by Judge Barber was $44,694 to his estate.

Anna Barrett was a braider at the mill and at forty-six years of age had two daughters who, like the Moody children, were suddenly without a mother. A mill worker, like Alex Pobol who was thrown mercilessly from the third floor to the darkened basement below, Mrs. Barrett survived, as attorney Jacobson explained, only to die, without regaining consciousness, in the emergency room at the Backus Hospital. The mill's insurer also paid $500 toward Anna's funeral expense, which totaled over $1,100, and Judge Barber would rule the next day that her settlement amount would be $25,701, to be overseen by her husband, Edward.

Helen Roode, Jacobson continued, faced the same fate as her co-workers Alex Pobol and Anna Barrett, falling to her death from the third floor of the crumbling structure. At forty-four, she had three children, two of whom were minors, and she had been employed at the mill for over fifteen years. As with Pobol and Barrett, the mill insurer paid $500 toward her funeral expense, which totaled $1,172. Her final settlement award as judged by Judge Barber was $23,790 and was administered by her daughter Phyllis Howard.

The case of Carol Mae Robidou, although familiar to those knowledgeable of her tragic circumstances, was still shocking, nonetheless, when read to those sitting in on the settlement hearings. Attorney Jacobson, still providing the settlement results to the courtroom, explained that she had been a braider at the mill for some nineteen years and had gone, on that fateful night, to the third floor of the mill with her co-workers when the floodwaters hit. Somehow surviving the collapse of the building and the fall of three stories to the murky waters below, Mrs. Robidou was subsequently dragged along in the flood flow down through the Lake Street playground only to be slammed up against Longo's Funeral Home where she somehow managed to open a door and drift into the first floor area only to drown as this room filled up with the flood waters and having no means of escape.

The mill insurer paid $1,000 for Mrs. Robidou's funeral expenses, some $500 more than her co-workers. Mrs. Robidou's daughter, Caroline Murphy, administered her estate, which was judged at $23,790. Mrs. Robidou was also survived by another daughter, Mrs. Dorothy Foley.

Finally, for the Turner Stanton victims, sixty-one-year old Madeline Atterbury's story was read. Another veteran braider at the mill, Mrs. Atterbury, as previously described, was near retirement when the floodwaters hit. Racing also to the third floor with her co-workers, her death was as tragic and violent as the others. Sustaining multiple fractures as she too was crushed under the crumbling building, Mrs. Atterbury likely suffered a similar severe and painful death, attorney Jacobson offered as he continued reading. Liberty Mutual Insurance, the mill insurer, paid the entire total of her funeral expenses of $1,400 and her estate was awarded at $22,815 the next day by Judge Barber to her husband, John Atterbury, her administrator.

Jean Bujnowski and Madeline Gordon were the miraculously fortunate mill workers to somehow survive the fall from the structure's third floor only to find themselves configured in such a way that the crashing wood and brick had formed a safe haven. Mrs. Gordon would be found nearly frozen three hours later after the collapse and would spend eight days in the hospital being treated for shock and exposure. She would be awarded $4,758 in Judge Barber's ruling the next day.

Mrs. Bujnowski would, unfortunately, accrue significantly more medical costs while suffering chronic back pain from the ordeal. She would require over $1,000 in future medical costs from three private doctors of which the mill insurer would pay $750. Additionally, she would need over $2,000 in medicinal costs that the insurer would pay $705. Dr. Christopher Glenney, a local physician, testified that Mrs. Bujnowski was, in his estimation, 25 percent disabled of which one-half was the result of the injuries suffered in the flood.

When all of the victim's final awards were added up, after thirty-one days of litigation, the grand totals amounted to a staggering cost of $1.5 million, a state superior court record for fiduciary payouts in a judiciary case.

This total, however, initially extolled by the press as an amazingly generous settlement and a seemingly astronomical amount by 1966 standards, would prove, unfortunately, to be an altogether small payment when separated into installments for the victims and an unending source of frustration for its payees.

When interviewed in 2006 and asked about the amount, Ronnie Moody exhaled piteously and remarked with a tone of dissatisfaction, still after forty-three years, "It wasn't much . . ."

CHAPTER 11

Epilogue: "A Few More Seconds . . ."

"**A**LL WE NEEDED was a few more seconds, and things would have been different. There were many acts of bravery that night, and I was with one of the bravest on that cold, damp Wednesday night. Margaret 'Honey' Moody. Margaret made sure that her children were brought to safety."

It was yet another unbearably cold March day in Norwich, Connecticut with inches-deep snow covering the frozen ground and a bright, clear sunlit-sky overhead. The date now was March the 4th and the year 2006, with the occasion being the dedication of a memorial monument at the Spaulding Pond Dam, in remembrance of those who'd died now some forty-three years earlier. The Norwich Public Works Department, with backing from the city council, had agreed to finance and erect this stone memorial to be displayed as a permanent marker on the northwest side of the dam, near the location of the old 1949 wading pond and retaining wall.

The wading pond was now, of course, an artifact of the distant past, replaced, in one of the many contemporary park upgrades, with a small grass-meadow viewing area at the northwestern section of the dam. The old retaining wall was gone now as well, torn down in the construction for the new dam to make way for its emergency spillway, which itself was now gone, having been later modified into a newer, ornate, and larger retaining wall. The park center had also been greatly enhanced, indeed recently (long gone was the zoo and convivial monkey house), to hold a beautiful fountain with manicured environs that lent a beatific ambience to the surroundings and which added a special aura and significance to this dedication ceremony.

The snow drifts, this day, had been dutifully plowed away from the meadow area, making the frozen green grass stand out in the sun-drenched whiteness of its surroundings. A microphone and stand had been erected at the southern end and city dignitaries were scheduled to speak. This dedication to those lost in the flood was becoming a rather important event.

Dan Kelly, a local retiree and close friend of Ronnie Moody, had decided, after hearing the story of the dam break for many years and himself a habitual walker in the park, to approach the city, in September 2005, about erecting some remembrance to the victims there. Surprised at the immediate and positive reception that his request received, Kelly was soon notified that not only would the city honor his request but that the Public Works Department would pay to engrave the stone monument while also agreeing to finance a ceremony to dedicate it. Kelly, needless to say, was delighted and immediately sought out his friend to inform him.

Both men, somewhat overwhelmed now at the city's benevolence and while envisioning only a small, family-oriented ceremony, soon realized that this was burgeoning into something somewhat larger—especially when press coverage surrounding it and the long-suppressed details associated with the flood became, once again, public news.

It wasn't until WTNH TV channel 8 in New Haven requested an interview for their nightly newscast, though, that Ronnie would realize just how large it would get. While responding to the reporter's questions, he typically and humbly stressed that he thought it was finally time that some permanent marker would be established to honor the unfortunate and forgotten people who had lost their lives so long ago now.

As the stone was being completed in early 2006, the city event schedulers looked to an early March weekend, one that would coincide with the anniversary of the dam break, for the dedication ceremony. After verifying that the date would not conflict with any of the city official's schedules, March 4, a Saturday, was selected, and the news of the ceremony was announced in the local newspapers

Now, as the memorial gained further traction in the press, the community and the affected families also realized that this was more than just a simple remembrance ceremony. A celebration of loved ones and another step toward forgiveness with perhaps a small closure component added would probably be realized as well, all after being thought long dead. All those who thought to attend now believed that the news of this ceremony would be wonderfully cathartic and remarkably inspiring.

As the March date approached, the younger members of the Moody family looked upon this as a redemptive occasion as well. Having dealt with some minor physical and health-related aftereffects of the flood for a portion of their childhoods, the Moody boys, all adults now and with families of their own, were indeed anticipating it with perhaps renewed optimism. The story of the flood had certainly dominated their lives, but the details and exacting emotion had been kept, in one respect or another, almost secretly from them.

Looking back upon their childhood, whenever the subject of their mother's death was mentioned, both Ronnie and Nana certainly would muster the fortitude to explain what had happened and answer any lingering questions that the boys might have, but it would, even into their teenage years, become obvious to them that this was an abundantly sorrowful subject for them and that it was never a topic that was deliberately expanded upon nor voluntarily brought up in normal conversation.

As a result, all of the Moody boys were left with somewhat incomplete memories and unknown details which, it was felt by not only Ronnie and Nana but also all of their relatives and others who were close to the children, that this was the best of all possible emotional outcomes for all three of the boys.

For Tommy, Jimmy, and Shawn then, it would become a somewhat atypical early childhood but one in which Ronnie and Nana were nevertheless determined to preserve all appearances of normalcy. After being released from the Backus Hospital, Tommy and Jimmy stayed with their aunt Jackie, Honey's brother Paul's wife and her best friend, at Jackie's home on Laurel Hill. Nana, meanwhile, was making it abundantly clear to all in the family that the children were going to live with her (fulfilling Honey's desire and prophecy) while finalizing the terms of their living conditions on Western

Avenue at Kennedy Heights[11], after which the children were guaranteed a

---

[11] Kennedy Heights was and still is currently, a low-income housing project on the west side of Norwich that, in 1963, had numerous contemporary and small two-story cottages, designed for dual-family occupancy and was arranged geometrically around a large underdeveloped wooded area.

This housing project was in a prime location that Honey and Ronnie were actually seriously considering relocating to at the time of the flood. Situated close enough to the city and, importantly, to Nana's west-side home, this was the proverbial escape from the city environment that they'd envisioned and, consequently, presented a perfect climate in which to raise three young children.

After the flood, Nana, with much assistance from many empathetic relatives and siblings, was able to work out a deal with the city management of Kennedy Heights whereby she would be the prime renter and where the three young children would live with her in the project housing. She would pay a substantially reduced monthly rent with her Social Security money and her monthly government check remitted to her for her husband's military service and, mostly, from large "contributions" from her sons and others anxious to see Honey's family succeed in her wake, as the primary rent income source.

Ronnie, meanwhile, would have unlimited access to his sons of course but could not officially "live" at this house on Western Avenue as his income, low as it was even by 1960s standards, was still significantly above the state limit that bounded the "low income" policies that Kennedy Heights operated under. He would, however, spend most of his time there and support his boys financially to the extent possible, and although they certainly weren't spoiled, they would lack little in terms of necessities while being brought up. This devotion to his children, combined with Nana's passion for family, gave the boys as loving and sincere a childhood as one could hope (with Ronnie running up a large debt throughout this period to keep the children clothed and supplied for school).

Western Avenue and Kennedy Heights in particular, as can be imagined, expanded in later years with, in the 1990s, the abundant backyard and wooded surroundings that the Moody boys and neighborhood children enjoyed and explored being summarily plowed under to make room for another roadway

THOMAS MOODY, JR.

home with a father and mother figure filled with all the familial love and devotion that Honey could have hoped for.

When the baby Shawn was finally released from the hospital, they all moved into the house on Western Avenue with Nana to begin their life anew without Honey.

It would not be easy.

Struggling, as young children are wont to do without their mother for comfort or to console them while often screaming for "Mommy" throughout the days and nights to assuage their discomfort, it became exceedingly difficult for Nana, as now their primary caregiver, and Ronnie, as both were grieving in their own right, to continue to muster the determination and emotion necessary to calm the three young children and still present a solid front with which the children could grow to depend upon. Nana in particular, at sixty-one years old, was fortunately still very vigorous; she'd learned through raising her own seven children all the subtleties needed to raise small children, and although it had been many years since she'd been the predominate mother figure, she quickly regained her stride with Honey's boys.

Ronnie, at twenty-seven meanwhile, was still learning the nuances of child raising, and in Nana, he could not have asked for a better ally; together they would struggle to get past these initial hardships and go on to instill a set of values and principles that most knowledgeable of the tragic circumstances of the boys' early childhood would marvel at in their late teenage and early adult years. Indeed, when confronted in the late 1970s and early 1980s, both Ronnie and Nana would be consistently complimented on their ineffable efforts in raising such 'meritorious' young men.

---

that would accommodate additional housing. A visit to the area now reveals the depression that present day low-income housing projects seem to project. The old Moody house, in particular, with the tall tree in its front yard and the trees in the front of the surrounding houses cut down, is currently symbolic of this downturn such that it represents little of the significant and wonderful childhood spent there.

It would certainly be medically safe to say that none of the Moody children suffered any permanent or disabling health effects from the flood. The baby Shawn, though, in his early childhood, had, perhaps, the most visible signs of trauma when he would experience those chronic and excruciating migraine headaches that he gratefully grew out of. These episodes, as recounted earlier, were sporadic and unpredictable, but traumatic nonetheless, peaking between his seventh and tenth years. Keeping with Nana's upbringing in early twentieth-century medical lore and culture, she would faithfully place raw potato slices directly onto his head, wrapping them in kitchen towels so as to "absorb" the pain with the inevitable darkening of the potatoes being "evidence" that the pain had in fact transferred to the potato slices.

Of course the exposure to the elements had resulted in the blackness to the raw potatoes, and the resulting sleep that Shawn would finally fall into would cause the pain to go away, but these homespun anecdotes that Nana so lovingly undertook to relieve the pain were absolute signifiers of her devotion to Honey's children and showed to what lengths she would go to assure their health and safety.

The baby Shawn would go on to become a rather large and healthy adult man. Initially, in his youth, remaining small and thin, he would eventually fill out by his high-school years (he graduated from NFA in 1981) and would continue to grow, eventually, to nearly six-feet four inches and weigh 230 pounds. He married Patricia Lambert in 1991 and would have two children, Travis, born on Christmas day in 1991, and the beautiful Erica, born in 1994.

Jimmy, by comparison to his brothers, was and would remain relatively small in physical stature. The only remotely "flood related" illness that he would suffer from in his youth would be some asthma related symptoms that would require him to take some breathing medication as a young child. Growing, eventually, to six feet tall, he would graduate from NFA in 1978 and, like Shawn, would go on to work at the Stop and Shop grocery chain immediately after high school, advancing to a management position over a thirty-year career.

He married Christine Przekop in 1986 and would have two children of his own, Eric in 1988 and the equally beautiful Alyssa (the Moody boys were apparently prolific in producing beautiful daughters) in 1991. Both Jimmy and Shawn would see their post high-school careers advance at Stop and Shop. After becoming employed almost immediately following their graduations, they both progressed upward to management while maintaining their residences in the southeastern Connecticut area, close to Norwich—Jimmy in Canterbury and Shawn in Colchester.

Young Tommy, meanwhile, would also graduate from NFA (in 1977) but then take a somewhat different career route, going on to and graduating from Thames Valley State Technical College (now Three Rivers Community College) in 1982 while pursuing a profession in nuclear power. Eventually, after being the peripatetic nuclear power plant worker, he would arrive in Texas in 1988, starting work at the Comanche Peak Nuclear Power Plant.

While there, in early 1988, he would meet and immediately fall in love with a beautiful and sassy young Texas lady, D'Ann Ballard, and would go on to marry her in 1989. Moving her to Phoenix, Arizona, soon after their wedding to work at the Palo Verde Nuclear Power Plant, he continued the life of the nuclear power plant contractor.

There, Tommy and D'Ann's first son, Ryan, was born in January, 1990, an event which would prompt an immediate move back to Texas, in July 1990, to be closer to D'Ann's mother and brother Joe; and it was in Stephenville, the town where they would ultimately settle, that they too would have a daughter, the equally beautiful Brooklyn D'Shea (born in September 1992 and endearingly named after Honey and Nana by D'Ann).

For the Moody boys now, life in the 1990s had congealed into a normalcy and routine that made the dam break and flood seem a remote and mythic image of their past. Other than sporadic and obscure reminders, the death of their mother and the heroics of their dad and Tony Orsini that fateful evening were but a distant part of their past.

By 1993 however, the tenuous structure to life and its seeming unfairness would come roaring back. This time it was Tommy who would come to understand the vestigial nature of life's circumstances. His young son Ryan, after turning three years old in January, soon started awakening each morning with the alarming habit of immediately vomiting before continuing with his daily childhood activities. In February, while continuing to vomit each morning, he would become noticeably somnolent at points throughout the day and then, toward the end of that month, become even more lethargic, with subsequent doctor visits revealing nothing clinically abnormal.

As he persisted in this upsetting behavior, Tommy's wife, D'Ann was finally successful with getting him admitted to the hospital. Facing a confrontational and staggering amount of resistance from the doctor who was responsible for Ryan's condition, she would persist nevertheless, and upon the marked worsening in Ryan's condition in February, was finally given a CT scan, which revealed a large brain tumor.

Fortunately for Tommy and D'Ann, Fort Worth, Texas (about sixty miles northeast of their home in Stephenville), has a nationally renowned children's hospital that specializes in cases of childhood oncology. Upon arrival at the hospital (Cook's Children Hospital), Ryan was diagnosed with a highly malignant brain cancer, medulloblastoma, an aggressive and usually fatal disease that specifically attacks the brain stem. Ryan's cancer, at this point, had also metastasized into his spinal fluid and settled into the lower portion of his spinal column. This initial diagnosis was tragically fatal, as any spread of this aggressive cancer, as explained to Tommy and D'Ann, was virtually always terminal.

Ryan was quickly admitted to Cook's and subsequently underwent surgery for removal of the tumor in March 1993. The neurosurgeon was, as expected, unsuccessful in completely removing all of it, which made his case far more complex. The hospital oncologists, being made up of marvelously experienced yet empathetic doctors, explained to Tommy and D'Ann that, based on the results of the surgery, Ryan's period of survival was possibly one year and that they should now concentrate on his remaining quality of life.

Devastated at these recent events and prognosis, D'Ann and Tommy were nonetheless determined to make Ryan's remaining time as pleasant and memorable as possible. Enduring the subsequent chemotherapy and radiation regiments, they saw their beautiful three-year-old son undergo a marked and agonizing physical change, one in which the brain surgery required him to relearn basic humanistic skills such as walking and speaking, along with a vigorous steroid treatment, giving him an obligatory puffy-faced look that most childhood cancer children must unfortunately endure. D'Ann, reaffirming again that she was the amazing woman that Tommy instinctively saw in her before they were married, worked tirelessly with the hospital staff at helping to return Ryan's motor skills to as close to normal as they could become.

Balancing this unbelievably stressful work with her son while continuing to raise her baby daughter Brooklyn, and with the grateful help of her wonderful mother Judy, D'Ann went from being a young, earnest bride to drastically responsible mother in seemingly very short order. Responding magnificently, her instinctive mothering skills and devotion to her children would remind Tommy of his own mother and would, again, only reinforce his decision that he'd married the right woman—indeed he could not imagine enduring this nightmare without her.

Ryan completed his treatments and physical rehabilitation by September 1993, and Tommy and D'Ann celebrated Brooklyn's first birthday (September 4) with Ryan's release from the hospital. Alas, aware that the inevitable return of the cancer was irrevocable, they held Ryan close, realizing that they were spending their last moments with him. Sitting in the living room of their Stephenville home in December, Tommy heard the telephone ring one afternoon and D'Ann answer it. Hearing an eerie silence for a long moment, he instinctively and suddenly knew that this was the bad news that they had been awaiting.

Ryan died on February 15, 1994, at home after just turning four years old (January 9). As if providentially, even with the large number of people gathered at their home for many days as Ryan had been set up for hospice care, Tommy and D'Ann were somehow alone with him, in their living room seated around the large hospital bed and breathing machine that had been set up for him when he breathed his last at 4:25 p.m. After a moving and heartfelt funeral and memorial service, Ryan was buried at the Gardens of Memory cemetery in Stephenville.

Being still relatively young at the time of Ryan's death (Tommy was thirty-five) and with a recuperative three years, he and D'Ann still decided to go forward with their pre-marriage plan to have their third child, giving birth to Evan Marc, in August of 1997. This of course added greatly to the healing process, as Evan would provide a loving addition to their family that Brooklyn would be a big sister to and a wonderful reflection for both Tommy and D'Ann on how big brother Ryan and Evan would have interacted and bonded as brothers.

Nana's condition throughout this period, meanwhile, was one of a slow, but abiding physical deterioration. The "old girl", as she'd often referred to herself, was giving out and, after having now seen two generations into adulthood, was clearly and affectionately entering the dimming twilight to her life. By 1988, with Jimmy now married and with a child on the way, and Tommy immersed in nuclear power and travelling to earn his living and living in Texas, and with Shawn now becoming more mature and independent as well, her need as a "mother figure" had finally been exhausted.

With the flood and its preternatural living arrangement being a thing of the long-ago past and with new management having replaced the old order at the Kennedy Heights Housing Authority, Nana's rent, as the children had slowly moved out of that household, had been on a cumulative increase. Realizing that with no young children living there (Shawn at this point was twenty-six years old) and the economy being what it was, a boost in rent payment was rationalized as an economic decision. What it clearly was, however, was a "force-out" maneuver to free up space for younger clientele who were clearly more in need and better prepared (with young children and with state and federal financial need requirements of their own) to pay these larger amounts.

With this intractable and seemingly coldhearted policy, Nana was now forced to move out of the house which she'd raised Honey's children to a home in Colchester, with Shawn, one that Tommy had purchased a year earlier when he'd envisioned, in his myriad nuclear plant moves, a re-settlement in Connecticut.

As Nana was acclimating to this new Colchester home and as the Moody boys grew and expanded their lives to include their own families, her physical symptoms of disability were becoming increasingly more pronounced. While living with Shawn at this Colchester house, she would show the first pronounced signs of her inability to get around on her own—sometimes falling down and becoming unstable even with a doctor's prescribed walker. It was clear now that her mobility, challenged even in the boy's later years at Western Avenue, was now clearly denuded.

As Shawn and Pat, meanwhile, became more serious as a couple and decided to live together in the Colchester home, it made the decision to move Nana to her son Peter's new Broadway apartment best for all; she, typically, did not want to burden Shawn or hinder his life with her slow demise, and a small apartment setting would be better for her, it was thought by all, from an attenuated physical standpoint.

Nana's downturn would, unfortunately, become much more acute while living with her son back in Norwich. Peter, fresh out of alcohol rehab himself, was at first primarily concerned with finding employment, and this left Nana alone in the apartment for many hours a day, a condition that proved to be the worst of all experiences for someone notably physically dependent. As the 1990s progressed, Peter recognized clearly that she was now beyond his capability to care for her. He now, together with his brother Jerry, made arrangements for her to be transferred to the Hamilton Arms living assisted home in Norwich. Never once complaining, Nana looked upon this, with her intense New England practicality, as an inevitable consequence of life. Essentially an "old folk's home", her demise, as the now rapid onset of Alzheimer's complicated her physical disability, was flourishing. By 1999, she was relegated totally to a wheelchair, and her once acute memory had deteriorated rapidly as well; to the point where on October 25 she passed away, at ninety-seven years old, peacefully in her sleep.

Nana's funeral, instead of being immensely sad, would become, conversely, a milestone and celebration of the woman who had remarkably raised two families while exhibiting the utmost in loving care and principled guidance. Symbolizing a fortitude and loyalty to family that would go beyond contemporary compare by having taken on the upbringing of the young Moody boys at sixty-one years of age, she'd demonstrated an ingrained devotion to her daughter that was symbolic of her deep-rooted singularity that humanistic sacrifice justified the familial end result; the responsibility of raising Honey's boys and bringing them into adulthood was clearly the same to her as if she were again raising her own children.

Now, as Nana was being laid to rest in the same cemetery as her beloved daughter, her life could now be reflected upon and recounted with an affirmation and acknowledgement of supreme resoluteness, indeed a moxie that seemed to symbolize her tough upbringing while representing her extreme desire for her family to excel while avoiding the tribulations of her own childhood.

Raised, unfortunately, in an unloving household and shuttled around as a child while being reared in a Protestant convent, she would become nonetheless tough as a "warhorse" (as she would sometimes self-avow) and, at the same time, tender as a lamb.

She could be unflinching in her views, particularly on religion and morality, while at the same time flexible and far reaching in her acceptance on racism and religious fairness (on contemporary issues, for example, she would certainly be far left on gay rights but would straddle the fence, I believe, on the pro-life/pro-choice debate). A true believer in the humble respect of others' viewpoints, she would pass on this dogma to the Moody children in earnest—a conviction that would add greatly to their ethical makeup and allow the boys to see clearly and indelibly (and thus allow them to make clear and thought out choices) on how best to manage their lives.

She would instill in them a toughness and compassion that undoubtedly would have been missed or lacking had the boys been separated following the flood. Indeed, the greatest gift that Nana gave them was a familial component that would be viscerally passed on to their own families; any observation of Tommy, Jimmy, or Shawn's interaction with their own family later would be all the evidence necessary that Nana "did her job well."

Ronnie, meanwhile, and as chronicled earlier, was never the same man that he undoubtedly would have been had this horrific tragedy not occurred. Many who'd known him prior to the flood and who became certain of his convivial personality now saw a subtle but nonetheless marked change following Honey's death; a definite darkening of his forbearance, a defined cynicism, and reluctant acceptance of the despondency that life sometimes administers seemed to pervade his day-to-day existence now, giving him a somewhat stark and demoralizing demeanor of defeatism (that became most pronounced to his family) that would unfortunately permeate his everyday personae.

Continuing to work at the same American Optical Company (with the self-defeating but clearly uninformed and unmentored guidance that even being in his late twenties, he would never be able to recoup the same salary that he was currently earning, and that if he attempted school or training outside of his current skillset, it would be too late for him), the additional stress of his sudden new life as the sole responsible parent of three young children and working at this less-than-satisfying job were all factors that would drive him to a sort of repressed depression while progressively causing him to drink more heavily.

Slowly at first, but then more and more often, this chronic consumption would noticeably affect his health and stability. Although never deterring his ability to provide for his children, he would only engage in "beer drinking with the guys" initially, talking sports and town gossip at some of his preferred spots in town. Escalating eventually to harder liquor to supplement this beer consumption, he, by the 1980s, would get completely off track such that by 1984, after getting arrested for DUI, he would, under the terms of his arrest, require the assistance of a rehab facility to "dry-out." This visit, to an in-town state funded rehab program resulted, predictably, in only three months of sobriety.

One of the lessons that Ronnie did learn while there, however, was that moderation, as difficult as it was for him to execute, was absolutely vital to recovery; and although he would still drink and drink comparatively heavily throughout his life, Ronnie would never return to a rehab facility nor require tertiary medical help for his drinking until the final years of his life.

While never fully realizing the dangers of his addiction, he would always rationalize his drinking by attributing it to family genetics—indeed the Moody and Kirby family history was fraught with alcohol-laden illnesses and deaths, and Ronnie's immediate family history was sobering proof; his older brothers Andy and Cliff would both die in their early '40s from alcoholism, and his sister Virginia was accelerated into her early death by alcohol. His parents, although both officially dying in their early '40s of cancer, were alcoholics as well, and Ronnie's outlook on life, subsequently, took on an ambivalence that seemed to acknowledge an early alcohol-driven demise.

Occasionally he would even remonstrate, either sober or inebriated, that "*His* family died young and *he* was going to do the same." This he would unfortunately announce in front of the children when they were young, and it would seal in an impression of sorrow and fear such that it would require Nana to try to soften with anecdotes of "Mommy, in heaven wouldn't let Daddy die until you're all older and can take care of yourselves." These allegorical fables would help them somewhat, but it, nonetheless, instilled, especially in young Tommy, the distressing notion of what a world without his father would be like from an extremely young age.

Subsequently, as he grew older, a psychological fear of losing his father would ensue in Tommy that would pervade most of his preteen years, introducing a behavior pattern that would necessitate overscrutinizing his father for signs of illness or degradation. This, then, would be a condition that would continually affect him emotionally and, to a large extent, psychologically, throughout his high school, college, and adult years.

Now as Tommy matured and moved on with his postscholastic life, he would become more and more circumspect for signs that his father was regressing either physically or mentally. Entering the mercurial world of nuclear power, Tommy quickly adopted this maniacal, workaholic-driven ethos and the requirement for extensive travel, as the 1980s proved to be the heyday for those willing to relocate in the post-1979 Three Mile Island accident influx of contractor employment.

As he would go from nuclear power plant site to site (ultimately living in Ohio, Arizona, and Texas), Tommy, working on average sixty to seventy hours per week, was nevertheless religious in his commitment to stay close to his father, and Nana and would try to contact each of them often, at least weekly.

Looking, in these conversations, for nuances and inflections in his dad's voice, anything that would indicate a change, Tommy was able at this point, and with the help of his brothers Jimmy and Shawn, to piece together a profile of his father that would provide (into the 1990s) at least a somewhat satisfactory peace of mind that his dad was at a minimum "keeping it together."

THOMAS MOODY, JR.

Later as Ronnie, surprisingly and counter to his earlier morbid pronouncements, aged into his late sixties (although, frustratingly, never stopping his alcohol consumption), acute symptoms of deterioration now started to manifest. Always being atypically high strung, Ronnie now started to show even stronger symptoms of anxiety and nerves, and, combined with age, alcoholism, and his predominantly slight build, these now seemed to converge suddenly into a period of rapid downturn as he entered the new century.

He would, at first, complain of insistent digestive problems and upsets coupled with light-headedness and, at times, severe dizziness. Numerous doctor visits in the early to mid-2000s determined a mystifying allergic reaction to normally processed food that resulted in a requirement for Ronnie to undertake a "gluten-free" diet.

Next and alarmingly, he was diagnosed with and would require surgery for a stomach/digestive tract problem (found, curiously, to be an abnormally reduced small intestine tract, a condition, doctors noted, to be genetic but also exacerbated by his progressive drinking) that would neither stabilize nor improve. His renewed anxiety over this condition and subsequent attempts at recovery would prove intolerable as well, requiring increasingly larger doses of antidepressants to get him back to a semblance of stability.

Ronnie's obstinacy in the face of the gluten-free diet requirement meanwhile, coupled with his other mounting health problems was predictable; "I've been eating what I want to all my life and I'm not stopping now." But from about mid-2006 on he never felt good", complaining increasingly of internal maladies.

Having been essentially driven out of the American Optical Company in 1994 when downsizing forced him into early retirement (after thirty-eight years of service) Ronnie took a "retirement" job at the Big Y grocery store chain in Norwich in 1996 and subsequently enjoyed a period where the minor physical work there appealed to him while the personal interaction with customers, who would search him out in the store, for social calls and talk was somewhat cathartic. Not at a point yet where his medical problems would interfere with his work (he worked only part time, thus he was able to fit in his doctor visits around his schedule), he prospered here for twelve years, and it was something that he enjoyed and which clearly added time to his life.

By 2009, however, his health was clearly worsening. Still not abiding by the gluten-free diet and still drinking, his intestinal problems now became untenable. On top of the internal upsets, Ronnie was now suffering blood-clotting difficulties (his blood was somehow now too thin), and he was diagnosed with clots in his legs and extremities. Being prescribed injections for this condition and feeling worse and worse physically, Jimmy and Shawn administered these shots twice a week to which Ronnie obstinately soon refused to take. Having left his job at the Big Y grocery store the year before (when new management "gently" forced him out because of his age), Ronnie now "saw no real purpose to live" and, again, was not shy about sharing it with his sons. Saying over and over again that "he was ready to go be with Honey", it became agonizing for the boys to listen to, especially Jimmy and Shawn who were living so close by and felt duty bound to take care of Dad as best they could.

For Tommy, listening to his father listlessly describe his health problems over the phone each week, it was indeed a dark period as well, heightened by a frustration that there was absolutely nothing he could do for him. Having rushed to the Backus Hospital emergency room a considerable number of times in the last few years (all for the same disparate internal upsets), it was no surprise then that he'd heard from his brothers that he had gone in again on Friday, September 25, 2009.

Unbeknownst to anyone, however, this time it would prove to be fatal. Ronnie's internal problems had been severely compromised over the last few months by his having hardly eaten while still continuing to drink, a condition that resulted in a painful swelling to his extremities that quickly resulted in renal failure and a subsequent shutdown of all of his systems. Once admitted, Ronnie this time deteriorated quickly and fell into incoherence and then a coma, finally passing away on Sunday afternoon, the twenty-seventh.

As with most weekends, Tommy was completely unaware of his circumstances and had tried to call him at his apartment earlier that morning. Knowing that he'd gone in to the emergency room again that

THOMAS MOODY, JR.

Friday, Tommy hoped that there were no lingering effects from this latest visit and that he had been released and was somehow home again.

Finally hearing from Shawn later that morning that not only was Dad still in the hospital but that "the end was near", Tommy, instantly in shock, suddenly had to make hurried and immediate arrangements to fly to Connecticut and was actually driving to the Dallas/Fort Worth Airport with D'Ann and the kids when he got the call from Jim's wife Chris that his father had passed away.

Externally, Tommy had long ago established a method to mask his emotions. The ordeal with his son Ryan had reinforced a long-held pretense that outward and demonstrative showings exhibited a behavior that just did not make things in any way better, so that to look at him or converse with him now, as he continued to drive toward the airport, would not have registered the sadness or deep sorrow that was completely enveloping him.

In his mind, though, he was racing through old memories of his dad throwing a football or baseball in the backyard on Western Avenue and passionately watching a Cleveland Browns football or Cleveland Indians baseball game on TV while listening to him demonstrably preach the value of education (even though he had little to offer in terms of experience or guidance himself). He thought of every little conversation or nuance of his father that he could muster; his dad's love and support, he realized, was total and unconditional, and it suddenly dawned on Tommy, sadly, that he would never again hear his father's voice.

Not nearly possessing the education nor being the egalitarian that would have furthered his boys in terms of intellect, what he could and did pass on was an ingrained sense of integrity—that basic component of right and wrong that had forever burned deeply and passionately within him and would become a personality trait that all who knew him recognized immediately, indeed drew people to him; he was "real", not a fraud; you knew what you had and what you were dealing with when you talked with Ronnie Moody, and this he preached as a credo to his boys time and again. "You might not be rich, but you can always treat people right," he would say and this was by far his lasting legacy.

Tommy now was almost totally incapacitated by these images and thoughts of his father—a sudden and profound sadness and loss that, although well disguised externally, would be a condition that would cause an internal depression, which, time and again, would manifest throughout the coming days and weeks whenever Tommy found himself alone or in an introspective mood.

In Connecticut, as Tommy, Jimmy, and Shawn now assembled to discuss funeral arrangements, a small and subtending emotion of relief and thankfulness, strangely, pervaded the three brothers, somehow integrated within their grief. "It's over for him . . . and for us" they realized and it would become a common conversational thread, and, far from being disrespectful or cruel, it was meant to be, as it was when Nana passed away, a period of celebration and remembrance of a man who had been so influential to all of them.

True he'd been extremely callous with his health, especially late in his life but as the boys now remembered their father, they thought about how he had somehow managed to survive longer than anyone ever thought he would, notwithstanding the "early death" rhetoric that he had preached so long ago.

Because his wife, Honey, had died so young and so long ago, her burial at the St. Joseph's Cemetery in Norwich had, necessarily, been rapidly arraigned. Her burial plot site had been chosen and purchased under the Shea family jurisdiction, as nobody else at that time had the financial resources to consider other burial strategies, certainly nothing to arrange a burial plan in which Honey, Ronnie, and their boys could be buried in the same place (this was something similar to what Tommy had gone through in 1994 with his wife, D'Ann, when having to confront the sudden burial requirements for their son Ryan).

But since her death, this area had become increasingly populated with Honey's brothers. William "Bud" (March, 1975) and Paul, a 1982 cancer victim being laid to rest here, essentially surrounded her, thus there was no room, heartbreakingly, for Ronnie. A sad decision and one being thrust upon them by family history, the Moody boys now were faced with finding a proper burial spot for Ronnie close enough to Honey but with the upbraiding knowledge that husband and wife would be eternally separated.

THOMAS MOODY, JR.

This to some would seem a minor detail, but it was one that, Tommy knew indirectly, always meant a lot to Ronnie. Always mindful of Honey's birthday, the flood anniversary, and of the Memorial Day holiday, Ronnie had been religious with flowers and prayers for her on these occasions, even chastising his then-teenage boys about missing an opportunity to "go to your Mother's grave and say a prayer for her." Never really mentioning it and seemingly aware that, under the circumstances, the Shea family and he had done the best they could when she had died, Ronnie knew, in the end, that he would not be laid to rest by her and seemed to accept this somewhat sad inevitability. Nevertheless, it was always an unsaid desire to be as close to her as he could, and the boys now felt compelled to meet that wish.

During the funeral and burial arrangements, Shawn and his wife, Pat, did an extraordinary job coordinating with the St. Joseph's Cemetery plot organizers and, together, they found a wonderful spot only about fifty yards northeast of Honey's headstone for Ronnie. Although not right next to her, and under the circumstances the best that they could have hoped for, and also by chance located near his older brother Bill, whose headstone (Bill had died when his diabetic condition overtook him) was about thirty yards northwest of his, this location was in a centrally located area and could be easily reached on foot when visiting the memorials for Nana, Honey, and Ronnie.

Ronnie's funeral was at St. Patrick's Cathedral in Norwich on Wednesday September 30 2009, the same church that he would frequently go to pray for Honey, Nana, and his boys while lighting a votive candle in remembrance of his wife. One of his strongest spiritual beliefs and fervent desires was to be reunited with Honey in heaven upon his death, and he talked of this many times, especially in his later years as his illnesses overtook him and he neared the end. Now, it was hoped by all who'd known him and as the Mass got underway, that he was now somehow realizing this dream. The service was a strict Catholic affair, as Ronnie would have been devout in his wishes for, and Tommy was further comforted by having not only his wife, D'Ann, and daughter Brooklyn in attendance with him but also his son Evan (now twelve years old) seated next to him, also being a casket bearer.

At St. Joseph's Cemetery, while the officiating clergy were administering the final measures of the funeral Mass, Tommy, standing off to the side of his father's casket with D'Ann, Brooklyn, and Evan at his side and in a deep, pensive mood, now tried to recall the last time that he had personally witnessed his father truly happy. It would take some time and, in the end, hard introspection, but he would ultimately determine that it had occurred over three years ago at that seemingly now-distant memorial ceremony for Honey and the others who had died that tragic evening in 1963.

Remembering his dad on that cold March 4th day in 2006, talking in great gestures to everyone and walking around among the guests both before and after, being visibly proud that recognition was finally forthcoming for Tony and especially Honey, this, Tommy thought, was how he wanted to remember his father, a man who this day had seemingly reached the emotional apex of his life.

Thinking back again to the run up to that ceremony and the day when it'd finally arrived, Ronnie, he recalled, had been very nervous, realizing that he would be asked to speak in front of a large gathering, something he definitely was not comfortable with. This was a task, though, that he felt was consequential and important and even though he was shaky, he had remained resolute throughout—this was an absolute for him, prioritized in his mind just as testifying in superior court forty years earlier had been, and it was something that simply had to be done, and he was now determined to do it.

As the large crowd now filled the small meadow area just west of the dam, a gathering much more substantial than expected on this bitterly cold Saturday, Norwich mayor Ben Lathrop, with stocking cap pulled down tightly over his head and heavy overcoat buttoned to his chin to protect against the chill, opened the ceremony by thanking all the attendees, giving reverence to "this solemn occasion" and thanking in particular, members of the city council who were all present.

Asking Dan Kelly to come to the podium next, Mayor Lathrop then stepped aside as Kelly, looking appreciative and somewhat surprised at the turnout as well, pronounced that this was indeed a project that had "blossomed after starting off small." He thanked Snow's Memorial for the beautiful job they'd done on the yet-unseen memorial stone and the Mohegan Park Advisory Committee for being the conduit that had channeled the city funding efficiently such that this event could be staged in the manner that it deserved.

After speaking, Kelly summoned his friend Ronnie to come forward; and together the two men ceremoniously unveiled the stone from under the blue tarpaulin cover that had masked it since it'd been delivered and set. Amidst loud applause, the crowd now edged closer to read:

IN MEMORIAM

THIS MONUMENT IS DEDICATED TO

THOSE WHO LOST THEIR LIVES

TO THE SUDDEN FLOOD CAUSED BY

THE COLLAPSE OF THE SPAULDING POND DAM

MARCH 6, 1963

MADLYN ATTERBURY	ANNA BARRETT
MARGARET "HONEY" MOODY	ALEXANDER POBOL
MAE ROBIDOU	HELEN ROODE

Now, as the applause slowly died down, Ronnie apprehensively stood at the microphone stand. "I want to thank you all for what you're doing for me today . . ." he opened in a clearly nervous voice. Rushing his words somewhat, as he was wont to do when he was tense, he thanked the Public Works Department and then Tony who he said "he and his three boys would not be here today" without. "Have a good day and God bless all of you" were his closing remarks, and he went straight to Tony and embraced him amid loud applause again.

As Mayor Lathrop returned to the stand after witnessing the emotional exchange between Ronnie and Tony, he now introduced Tony, formally, to the crowd.

The years had certainly been kind to Tony Orsini. Still thin and wiry strong, he had the athletic build that marked his younger days. With his shaved head, he seemed to be braving the bitter cold as though he was on a mission. Unfolding a prepared statement from his topcoat, his voice was firm and strong:

March 6 1963 is a long time ago but to me it seems like yesterday.

I don't remember every detail because everything happened so fast. I found myself taken from a warm safe bed to the realization of my own mortality in just minutes. I recall the overall picture of the raging floodwaters, struggling to get to safe ground and being terrified.

There were many acts of bravery that night and I was with one of the bravest on that cold, damp Wednesday night.

Margaret Honey Moody.

After the car we were in was flipped over by a wall of water and landed on its top, somehow we managed to escape the vehicle through its front door. We then were surrounded by ice-cold water trying to sweep us away. Honey handed her three children, Tommy age four, Jimmy, two-and-a-half, and Shawn, five months old; to her husband who passed them to me perched on a building. Margaret made sure her children were brought to safety.

All we needed was a few more seconds, and things would have been different. I know the Moody family are very proud of their mother. I'm sure she is with us today and looking down lovingly on her husband, three children, six grandchildren and the entire Moody family.

Today, we honor her and all the brave people who lost their lives forty-three years ago on this devastating and unforgettable day. Thank you.

The loud applause, of course, and the site of Tony himself, freezing cold and leaning into the microphone while still holding his windblown speech papers, was enough to strike emotion in virtually everyone there; but it was what he said and the way he'd said it that struck a deeper and more-affecting chord with those who were closest to him. For Ronnie and the Moody boys, this speech had been very typical of Tony, deferring any acknowledgement of his own heroism that night while placing it squarely on Honey.

One of the most profound missing components of this memorial, it had occurred to Tommy while standing there, was the need for someone to speak on Tony's behalf—of his heroics that night. All the speeches and retrospective accounts that day still did not come close to grasping the enormity of what that scared nineteen year old boy, agreeing out of the kindness of his heart to venture out with his downstairs neighbors and, with little regard for his own personal safety, help save three very young children, had really done that night. His bravery in the wake of an immense and sudden life-threatening event, kindness and overall personal forthrightness throughout the ensuing years had, as previously chronicled, made him a hero to the Moody family; and it was here, at this memorial, where it should now should have been demonstrated and appreciated.

As Tony stepped away from the podium and embraced Ronnie once again and as the many cameras snapped picture after picture, it seemed suddenly proper and just that, as a sort of final closure and with the memorial stone now shining brightly in the afternoon sunlight, these two heroes would gather here at this place, the site of profound sorrow and tragedy in their lives, with Tommy, Jimmy, Shawn, and Nana (spiritually) present as well, to remember and honor Honey for her magnificence and bravery that night and to lovingly give thanks, for having had her, even if for only a short time.

And yet even now, in the midst of this celebratory atmosphere, if one gazed out upon Spaulding Pond, with its inches-deep ice layer and snow covering, the would-be observer could only think about how similar it looked to this same pond some forty-three years earlier when tragedy and death had destroyed six lives and left untold others in emotional ruin. Then, while maneuvering to the south side of the dam and listening even closer, you would hear the ever-present brook flow, constantly gurgling from below the dam, meandering its way, as it'd done for hundreds of years, downward toward the skating pond while flowing further onward in its inevitable path toward the city.

AFTERWORD

I N A YEAR when the youngest ever-elected United States president would be so violently and tragically sent to his death, the correspondingly sorrowful passing of Honey Moody seemed to, tangentially, symbolize the onset of a period of radical national change. The staggering and assailable assassinations of Malcolm X, Martin Luther King, and JFK's own brother Bobby five years later eponymously embodied what the '60s later represented and exemplified in modern history. These inane and uninformed acts of seeming rebelliousness and unwitting violence would indeed become milestones of American culture change and the start of a social revolution.

Certainly not implying that Honey's death held the same relevance nationally that Malcolm, the Kennedys, or King's did, rather, with these deaths, the 1960s, in addition to being this bellwether historically, also incited a period of profound and extreme culture change only previously seen at pronounced periods in history. These moments had severely altered society's view of "routine" such that any heretofore notion of a "normal life" had shifted suddenly onto a new and unforeseen course. And now for the Moody family, this seemed profoundly true as they embarked on this new path much as the nation had—with an engrained and profuse sadness and guarded sensibility that would require much fortitude and adaptation to get through.

But unlike much of society that entered the 1970s without their measured leaders or a seemingly concerted moral compass (the hippies had completely contorted the moral fiber of this country!), the Moodys had seemingly turned the corner after losing Honey and gotten back on track due to the amazingly focused and loving efforts of Nana and Ronnie. Surviving the numerous national recessions and inflations that the '70s were renowned for simply by living within their means, the boys, Nana, and Ronnie progressed through childhood and public school and, in the case of Tommy, used their low economic standing to help with college, simply by being "poor" and without letting any of the ongoing cultural or national financial disasters significantly affect them.

While the Moody children were able to grow and move on without their mother and establish lives of their own, even prospering to a degree in adulthood, the same, unfortunately, could not be said for the downtown area of Norwich. True, thirty-six of the thirt-seven businesses destroyed by the flood were initially able to recover and go back into business, and the area did resume industry as best it could for a while, but the loss of the Turner Stanton Mill (from the downtown area) and the J.B. Martin Company soon thereafter (in 1969) slowly caused the town's leaders to come to the startling realization that this once-mighty industrial and manufacturing giant had irrevocably seen its demise.

With small, colloquial stores taking over as the main engine for the downtown industry, major Norwich employment became thrust outward to the suburbs and beyond, south to New London and Groton. Large plants outside the city limits such as the Thermos Company on Laurel Hill and Electric Boat in Groton now employed many of the town's inhabitants while the onset of large shopping malls and suburban commerce, which would become so prevalent in the '70s and '80s, took over the main entrepreneurship of the area, leaving the downtown area stagnated in terms of economic growth and expansion.

As a result, a predictable downtrodden climate soon replaced the vibrancy of the '50s and early '60s, giving the area an ever-increasing aura of downward mobility that has continued to this very day. Indeed, a visit to downtown Norwich these days is not, shall we say, an uplifting experience.

As far as the major players in the flood dramatis are concerned and what eventually happened to them, I've concluded that a tidy summary of those disparate characters and the divergent paths connected with them would be a near impossibility—and that would assume a best of all cases, a scenario where I could somehow get unfettered access to and, most importantly, unlimited ability to converse with those who are now, unfortunately, no longer among us.

THOMAS MOODY, JR.

For the contemporary historian (and please believe me when I tell you that I rank with the lowest of the amateurs in this category), the record of and track-ability of this event and its participants becomes marginally weaker with each passing year. There is, however, still a substantial amount of information regarding the actual event and developments soon after March 6, 1963. This documented information resides almost solely in the existing newspapers of that era.

In those bucolic pre-internet days where newspaper reporting largely constituted the written news, the reading, today, of these ancient journalistic relics has been a charming alternative to the present day, twenty-four hour confrontational type of reporting that we've become accustomed to. Here in these yellowed sensitive copies of the early 1960s *Norwich Bulletins*, I've discovered what it was like to read editorials concerning the latest town gossip at Sabby's Barbershop or about open-air art exhibits on the sidewalks in Franklin Square or about how local shoppers felt at the Five & Ten store on Saturday November 23 1963, the day after JFK was assassinated. I believe this congenial vernacular and bourgeois reporting has made my research for this project and thus my writing of this event seem hopefully more expanded and enhanced. It certainly made for some fun and interesting research.

While these existing newspapers document the events as they occurred, the personal and emotional content of this tragedy can only be recounted, obviously, by personal and emotional memories or discussions; and these can only be delivered by those who were there, either at the time or somehow connected. This is what I hope that I bring to this subject that few others can. My intent with this book was to juxtapose my family's experience onto this drama and, hopefully, provide the reader with a twofold experience—a history of the event that is somewhat comprehensive and unique and one that hopefully answers some long-held questions while also being a literary account of the heroics of my mother, father and Tony Orsini that can be internalized and appreciated by anyone compassionately attuned to tragedy and its recovery. I've learned through these three years of writing though, that this is an immensely difficult job.

In the course of developing this history, I've spoken with many who have distinct memories of that day while also having to seriously tap my own memory bank of all past discussions that I've had with my father and grandmother to help recreate that time. Tony Orsini, who is the only one of that night's "first line participants" that is still thankfully with us, has obviously been an immense help to me, placing things in perspective, walking the Lake Street area with me a number of times and sharing his memories time and again—he was a true hero that night and remains one, to me, today.

There is, unfortunately, much that I haven't covered and most probably missed and/or left out—a "complete" record of all that occurred that night and in subsequent days simply does not exist. My apologies, especially, go to the families of the Pobols, Roodes, Robidous, Atterburys, and Barretts for any omissions or poignant stories that would have, certainly, fit perfectly here. I purposely did not pursue any of those stories that did not appear in the newspapers of the day and, again, apologize for this, but my objective was insular and entailed simply superimposing my own parents' and Tony Orsini's heroics onto this tragedy.

This, of course, in no way diminishes the bravery or sadness in which all of the Turner Mill workers died, nor does it lessen their worth or relevance; I simply had a smaller and more-focused agenda and, moreover, had no real means to gather any of those meaningful stories.

What I did learn about the people and places and what became of them, however, I'll share now, but it is, admittedly, spotty and by no means comprehensive and may mirror some of the information that I've touched on in the text already:

Spaulding Pond today is still the large, popular water expanse located in the same rustic Mohegan Park. The city of Norwich, contrary to all of the criticism of the downtown area that I've heaped upon it here, is to be highly commended for its upkeep and beauty. Held in place by the equally beautiful and, more importantly, highly reliable and safe Spaulding Pond Dam, it remains today the highlight of the park area. The areas immediately surrounding the dam and on top of it have been closed to normal automobile traffic since the early 1990s and now this uppermost surface has seemingly realized its long-sought-after-goal, decorated with beautiful rose arbors and a people-only passageway throughout with small resting areas to the side that have amazing views of the pond and the

THOMAS MOODY, JR.

wooded park area surrounding it. This expanse simply has to be the most scenic and beatific region in the Norwich area, and one indeed in all of southeastern Connecticut.

Downstream, the post-flood watershed program changes can be seen starting with the rigorous southern face of the dam and drainage plumbing. This intricate and high-tech amalgam of piping and instrumentation diverts the overflow and necessary outflow of the dam down a rocked pathway under another pipe-way (where the old "duck pond" used to be) that routes flow under a large parking lot covering the old brook that leads it onto its natural flow path through the southern woods and on down to the skating pond.

At the skating pond, another beautiful viewing area now exists where the brook flow empties into the small pond area, which is held in place by another equally high-tech level control gateway. Large grading and earthen dams now surround this pond that was reengineered in 1968, also as part of the postflood watershed plan. Walking out to this area now from a gravel parking lot off of Mohegan Park Road, is, again, to view another site that the town has retained as a beautiful getaway for recreation and gazing for those so inclined.

As research for this book, I've walked the path from this pond back up to the Spaulding Pond Dam through the woods where those floodwaters once careened; the Public Works Department has laid manicured woodcut paths here for hikers and walkers, and one certainly enters a sort of deep woods melancholy along these trails. They unquestionably give one an appreciation for nature and what the downtown area is lacking in terms of visit-ability, it more than makes up for here. I was delighted to discover (having lived in Texas for close to twenty-five years now) that this pathway existed and that it essentially marks the brook flow path from the dam down to the skating pond and in such a scenic fashion.

The multiple dam structure at the skating pond and downstream piping/under-road plumbing that leads to the southern side of Mohegan Park Road was also part of the watershed refurbishment of the 1968 skating pond plan; in fact much of the rock-strewn disorganization leftover from the flood north of the road is, incredibly, still visible here with large boulders rendered haphazardly on the steep slope leading from the dam grading buildup down to the road. A simple drive into the park on this road goes right past this small piece of history.

On the south side of Mohegan Park Road where Colonna's field once provided the area youth with a summer baseball league and the Public Works Department a constant thorn in its side with the field's owner, there now resides a multibuilding low-income apartment complex, the Mohegan Apartments. Fully landscaped and contoured with large parking areas, the spot now looks to me to have adequate flood-control accommodations, as the water from under the road is now plumbed using large bore pipes that could seemingly handle large water flows. This is of course the view of an amateur observer, but a quick library review of the past few years' news reveals no obstinate complaints a la Sal Colonna of flooding in this area.

On the subject of Sal Colonna, I admittedly did not pursue his fate postflood; I suspect, though, that the Junior Major League program that he ran there was no longer in existence by the early '70s as the large Norwichtown Little League complex had been built on Otrobando Avenue on the northwest side of the city by then, and it was here that most of the city youngsters (including this author) went to become involved in organized league play and to show off their baseball talent. Neither, though, am I certain as to when Colonna's field was removed to make way for these apartments, but I would be fascinated to find out.

Moving farther down the flood path, the contoured area downstream of the Mohegan Apartments between North Street and Baltic Street that harbored the floodwaters so well that night and channeled them onto Hickory Street and through the Public Works garage remains almost entirely the same today as it was in 1963. This area is still largely residential with seemingly the same houses that existed during the early '60s, including the Makowiecki residence at 14 North Street which saw its owner Richard and his backyard devastated by the rapid ice chunk-filled flow. Some cosmetic ditch digging and levy type erection in the late 1960s was done here, I'm told, to help alleviate the constant flooding that large rains brought, but I've no documentation to this effect. Due to privacy issues, I purposely did not walk through this area to see what, if anything remains of the culvert system that was so affected by the flood.

At the site of the old Public Works garage on Brook Street, there is now emptiness. An open grass field exists where the garage once was with a worn dirt path south of it that the area residents have carved while crossing the field from Baltic to Brook streets. This dirt-and-glass strewn path also now gives access to a leftover and seemingly forgotten small cement wall and fence enclosure that houses sand and other piles of fill like materials that, long ago, provided the Public Works garage with snow and ice storm road cover, while an ancient city truck, rusting and rotting, still sits, abandoned, outside this wall at lease as late as 2009.

The Public Works Department building and staff moved, long ago, to Clinton Avenue on Norwich's northwest side (near Otrobando Avenue) into a modern-style building and the garage structure here on Brook Street was plowed under leaving this small field/park area that is now simply an open and abandoned expanse.

A short distance away at Centennial Square, little, remarkably, has changed in fifty years. Try as I might, I could not find records or documentation of major rework of the "Franklin conduit" as part of the 1964 watershed design plan here. The roadwork in and around this area is extremely well paved now, though, with numerous new-looking manhole covers, so I will go with the assumption that some sort of major rework to the ancient underground plumbing occurred since the flood and has been contemporaneously maintained along the way.

The houses around the square look exactly the same 1963 vintage, and the western road branches to Broad Street as it did then with the major attraction today being, in the proper New England vernacular, a large package store (a place to purchase beer and liquor) on the square's western side.

Boswell Avenue still veers sharply upward on the square's eastern side and Labenski's Funeral Home, the site of the area's major flood relief effort, is still in business across from it. Moving south toward the lot that encompassed the Turner-Stanton Mill, large trees and vegetation now pervade. A disorganized dirt parking lot with an abandoned eighteen-wheel moving truck trailer sits unobtrusively behind a small section of rusted chain-link fence with barbed wire atop it. This fence is the only outward remains of the old mill structure that still stands and, moving deeper now into the parking area and farther past the overgrown vegetation, the old mill concrete foundation still protrudes slightly upward, barricading the large and abrupt earthen drop-off down to the Lake Street playground.

Where once the prominent three-story brick structure of the mill dominated, there is now trash and junk in and among the trees and overgrowth strewn throughout the large drop-off area. Old mattresses, appliances and other assorted waste items have been dumped here and it is literally dangerous to walk about the area on foot without an understanding of the terrain before entering.

Lake Street itself, predictably and even if taken in the context of the downtrodden and malaised inner city, is an imminently disturbing, even dangerous, enclave that nowhere nearly matches the cheerful and welcoming community that it was in 1963. The old Moody/Orsini residence at 55 Lake Street still exists, although painted today in a garish orange/yellow. It still, however, has the same porch and small yard structure leading down into the playground and, amazingly, still with the prominent "O" on the black stair banister leading to the upper apartment from the street.[12]

At the bottom of Lake Street where the road veers sharply left, the playground is still prominent to the left and the steep drop-off visible to the right. A poorly supported chain-link fence now nonsensically attempts to separate the road from the plunging landscape while the locals have literally removed it from the concrete support base upon which it was built, leaving it languishing unobtrusively and rusting in the backdrop.

Gazing down, one notices the stark emptiness of the surroundings. Weeds, vegetation, and more junk/waste is the predominant perception, and it is remarkable to note that the only thing that has seemingly changed here since the flood is the rebuilt washed-out walls of these drop-offs. With

---

[12]   During a visit here in 2011 with my wife, D'Ann and as I was revisiting the area across the street, she spoke with a small child who was at that time actually living in my old first-floor home and explained to him that we were there (as we certainly appeared to be out of place) to look at that house as part of research for this project. Describing to the youngster that we came from Texas, and with her accent being a dead giveaway, he suddenly looked up at her and exclaimed "You came all the way from Texas just to see *this* house?"

only a little climbing and digging, one can still find small amounts of road debris and stone from the old wall structure, amazingly, on that barren drop-off landscape.

Looking a little to the right now, the old Longo's Funeral Home (now an apparent apartment house) still stands on Franklin Street. To the north of it is the tree in which we strove to get to and subsequently climbed up into to survive. Today it appears to be a very healthy and now rather tall Connecticut elm with its branches elbowing outward and upward. My inner desire to historically mark it or protect it somehow overcomes me every time I stand and gaze at it.

Looking left, the massive building that housed Lamperell's is now a boarded-up warehouse-looking structure, long devoid of any inhabitants. It's not certain to me when the auto dealership closed down or if any other businesses were housed there afterward but my teenage and early twenties memories are of this building being largely abandoned.

Across Franklin Street, the structures that housed the S & S Supermarket and H & M Package Store survive (with them now of course being under different ownerships), but the old three-story tenement house that young William Zeitz gazed out of that evening is long gone, torn down many years ago, and replaced with a do-it-yourself carwash that encompasses the remainder of the block to Chestnut Street.

Before leaving Lake Street, a quick view to the left notes the rapid upturn in the road toward Boswell Avenue and the curved slope downward to Pond Street. This was where the flood did some of its most visceral damage as it carved a huge twelve-foot deep cave in this rise as it continued to charge its destructive path downward toward Franklin Street, eviscerating Pond Street while leaving pipes and cars dangling in its aftermath. Today a well-paved rise still exists while the seemingly exact narrow features of Pond Street still empties onto Franklin Street. One can't help but imagine that if another flood were to come, it would do the exact same damage here as it did in 1963, as the area geometry, buildings and all are amazingly identical.

A drive down Chestnut Street today, meanwhile, would offer a vision only slightly different, I imagine, from, say, a couple of days following the flood. The structures that housed the Connecticut Beverage Company, the Franklin Press, and Lords Manufacturing are now falling apart, long deserted, and with all the outside windows broken. This area, in essence, is the apotheosis of Norwich's industrial downfall as these buildings, it would seem, will remain in this crumbling disrepair until they are allowed to just rot away and collapse to the ground.

To the east, on Franklin Street it is only marginally better; most of the actual buildings that were here in 1963 still exist, and many even have businesses in them, but these structures are, today, exceedingly old and in apparent need of upgrade. The redeeming stalwart on this section of Franklin Street is of course D'Elia's Grinder Shop, which is charmingly still the same small eatery that it was that night. While paying for your "grinder", you can actually read a copy of a newspaper article about the flood taped to the underside of one of the product viewing windows, and, if curiosity strikes further, you may even be able to speak with someone working there knowledgeable about and willing to exposit on the flood.

Farther down Franklin Street, the massively cold, dark, and desolate factory that once housed the J.B. Martin Company still sits like an albatross, similar to the rest of the old downtown industry, bare and abandoned. This gloomy and looming complex was vacated when the Martin Company closed up shop in 1969 to merge with its sister factory in Leesville, South Carolina. Again, I have no immediate memory of this place ever being in production again after 1969, and it is now a monstrosity and huge city scourge—another massive testament to the long ago removed downtown industry.

Just across Willow Street where longtime Norwich business inhabitant Goldberg's Appliances saw its entire appliance inventory lost that night, a new contemporary office building now resides (Goldberg's having lasted I believe into the 1990s) while across Chestnut Street from it where the old Norwich Fire House saw inches-deep flood waters pervade, The Spirit of Broadway Theater (the fire station having since moved to a large new building on the west side of town) now resides.

The *Norwich Bulletin* newspaper meanwhile, housed in the same Franklin Street offices that became flooded in 1963, still remains the intrepid downtown stronghold that it was that night. Delivering not only a daily hardcopy newspaper but also servicing its more—popular online mediums, the building today appears to have survived these fifty years rather soundly. Although, admittedly, not having ever entered the structure, to me, from the outside, it still looks rather modern and, with the addition of some modern offices attached to its southern side, even somewhat upscale. I suspect (hope?) that the *Bulletin* will be here, in downtown Norwich in these same Franklin Street offices, forever.

Farther down at the corner of Franklin and Bath streets where the One Hour Martinizing did profitable business for many years, there is now a seemingly forlorn parking lot that ironically provides parking for many of the nearby *Bulletin* employees.

Louis Zeirler's Package Store is long gone and, I'm sure, so is Louie, the gregarious owner who would loudly proclaim "Hey Tom, Dick, and Harry . . ." every time my brothers and I would walk into his store with my dad. This establishment today, like virtually all of the other small businesses in the area approaching Franklin Square, is a tiny local affair that is migratory at best and will almost assuredly not last and then another in the long string of small owners will incorporate the small shop.

Directly across Franklin Street from the old Zeirler store is the Thayer Building, still standing and looking, even after some relatively recent cosmetic upgrades, much like it did in 1963. The charming walk-in businesses that predominated the structure on the ground floor in the sixties have long since vacated as have all of the upstairs offices. This building was the location of the old Cooley & Company offices and the point where the young Bill Stanley was attempting to get to on that night. Sporadic small and local enterprises have started here over time but, for the most part the structure, as it does today, has laid bare since the 1990s, again a bleak reminder of the disappearance of the downtown industry.

Sadly, this can also be inferred for the entirety of nearby Franklin Square. All of the physical structures that once housed a thriving downtown scene today still remain upright but seem mired in misfortune, either boarded up or supporting small itinerant businesses situated around a cretinous traffic circle that has since become so burdened with traffic lights and signs that it has completely stripped the area of any of its former charm.

The Five and Ten store building, still displaying the same prominent red billboard-type stripe above the doorway and windows that was its trademark for decades, now has, as of this writing, "Madonna Place" emblazoned over the old gold lettering of the valiant 1963 store; other businesses in the square of the same ilk now inhabit the same structures that once were the home to Reid and Hughes and Kay's Jewelers—none of these, seemingly, with any substance or longevity.

Rose Alley, meanwhile, is still the same small road to the south of the square that terminates at the Shetucket River. At its end, a small but somewhat modern pumping station resides, undoubtedly the culmination of a large sewer system upgrade undertaken since the flood. Prominently missing, though, is the old Palace Theater where the floodwaters raced by its glass doors that night on its way to the river with not a drop, miraculously, entering its lobby. Torn down sometime in the recent past (I would again be fascinated to know when, strictly from a personal curiosity viewpoint), it today, predictably, is nothing more than another city parking lot, incredulously with no marker or otherwise historic signifier of what once stood here.

Now as for the flood's personae, the group that I would have most loved to speak with (outside of the departed of my family of course) is the Public Works Department workers who were so diligently involved with the dam's health that day. Director Walz, park workers Cilley (who would later become Public Works director himself) and Vantour, Foreman Ferra (who unfortunately died before the 1966 settlement trial), Brooks Street garage workers Yeitz, and especially Charles Phoenix (he the lone witness to the dam breaking) are all participants in this drama who would have assuredly added consequential insight and perspective if I could have somehow tracked them down.

These people, as individuals or as a group, would later be maliciously blamed for the dam break and although admittedly faulty with their diagnosis of the problem that day and naïve as to the signs of threatening degradation from September 1962 on, they would also prove, in the final analysis, to be just victims themselves, doing the absolute best they could under circumstances completely and utterly beyond their control. And while researching this book, I've discovered that to a man, I have no further knowledge, nor did I pursue vigorously, as the whether these gentlemen still survive today.

Indeed, I've often been asked over the years if I blame or hold them in some form of contempt; I can say now that after learning the true details of this event and reaching an age at which I can attach some measure of perspective and, most importantly, empathy to this story, the answer is of course emphatically *no*. I'm now convinced that had these folks an inkling that the leak that they were scrutinizing would actually expand to the horrific break that ensued, they would most certainly have acted to do all that they could that afternoon and evening to evacuate the downstream and make the immediate area as safe as possible.

And even as it is today, a look at their actions just prior to the break should be enough to convince even the most dubious of their honorable integrity. We see Director Walz certainly going above and beyond the call in leading his department once he grasps the enormity of the situation. We watch as the Public Works Department garage workers coordinate the Hickory Street area evacuations by gathering local volunteers (mostly area teenagers) to go door to door to help spread the warning about the dam break in the short interim between the actual breech and the oncoming floodwaters.

We even witness park worker Monroe Cilley actually returning to the dam later that evening, well after his work shift, to check on its status and while there, to his imminent surprise, spotting that "white foam-like stream" spewing from it, and then frantically calling Walz to inform him of this new and dangerous development.

No, I really don't believe that the continuing criticism that is often, at times, directed at these Public Works Department folks is warranted. Their only stigma throughout this entire episode, in my view, is of a naivety and a lack of a process pertaining to the when or of how-often to inspect their dam. And with virtually no ancillary expert guidance pertaining to the dangers or nuances of this structure, these otherwise competent folks, in my opinion, were left completely exposed and in the dark as to the imminent disaster that was to ultimately ensue.

No, I believe that if a perceived tragedy still exists within this drama it is with the fiduciary outcome for its victims. And this I can only really expound on in the context of, shall I say, my father's rather denuded outlook. The easy conclusion and the one that my dad certainly maintained throughout his life was that he was "cheated by the lawyers and the city" and that they "took advantage" of him and the others by talking him and his fellow complainants into a quick settlement.

My view though, after nearly three years of careful review and the weighing of the facts, is drastically less moribund. It is true that my family's total settlement amount did not go very far in terms of financial security, but when considered in the larger scope of accident liability, I'm now convinced that its payout was, when judged pragmatically, actually fair and equitable.

Removing emotion from the analysis, let's consider for the moment that had my mother survived, she, as noted earlier, would have gone on to reemployment when my youngest brother Shawn had reached an age where my family could have afforded it. This new job however would undoubtedly have not been exorbitantly high paying, leading my family to struggle financially, essentially as it ultimately did. I believe that, notwithstanding my father's strong feelings, this post flood financial settlement actually served to restore my family onto a more stable financial footing while providing us (my brothers and I) with some monetary security later in our teens that would decidedly not have been there.

As sad as it is to admit and accept, my brothers and I actually did better monetarily after this settlement; the money certainly did not, nor could not replace our mother, and our lives would have, of course, been better had she survived, but a review of just the strict financial argument concerning whether my family was "cheated" or not, to me now, just does not hold weight.

And just for the record, I've never really been a champion of that "pain and suffering" epithet that the legal community seems to throw about now in many of its contemporary cases, but I can see that if a circumstance ever deserved that rather vapid designation, this is the case that could very well embody it.

This notion then logically brings us to another question—Could there have been, in actuality, a "pain and suffering" payout component that was missed by the city for this elusive aphorism? "Pain and Suffering" was, after all, where virtually all of the subjective arguments and the emotional turmoil about the final settlement began, and continues to eat away at its victims, and their families, to this very day.

While, again, immersed in the evidence, what I needed to understand (and I admit that it is a value virtually impossible to quantify) is what, in the 1966 legal worldview, was seen as a fair recompense for the loss of a loved one and in such a tragic way? Moreover, what, in any year can be considered a fair payout for such a horrific loss?

Today, of course, lawyers are able to extract exorbitant sums for this rather evasive intangible and, certainly, had this tragedy occurred in today's society, the fiduciary outcome would have been markedly different, but, given the era that it actually did occur, and with the benefit of the evidence, I've now had what I consider an ample opportunity to reflect on this important point.

And the conclusion that I've reached, perhaps propelled by this insular view of the economy of those times, is that the final award, this "record-setting" settlement, really did account for this intrinsic estimation. Newspapers in the days following the settlement even boast about how well the court awarded these victims and it is clear to me when reading these reports that the town honestly felt that they were going far beyond simply compensating the victims for damages.

Of course we now know that those economic norms soon swiftly and dramatically turned upward and that this award amount, even only two years later, paled by its 1966 comparison, but my feeling still is that if anyone, victims or family, were asked on that March 10 1966 day at the courthouse about their individual case, they would have assuredly evoked at least a composed sense of satisfaction at its outcome. It wasn't until later, when the money started to curiously dissipate that my father, at least, and perhaps some of the others started to consider that, maybe, they'd been "short-changed."

So for my dad to get this bereft absolution, the town would have somehow seen the need to go beyond the record settlement amount and, by some further means, decide to offer an additional and exorbitantly larger payout to the victims, one clearly beyond its capability. This larger financial encumbrance, which would have required applying for long term loans (along with the assuredly attached high percentage interest rates), would have added greatly to their financial burden and, in an ironic twist, would also have raised tax rates such that the city tax payers (re: my dad) would have then had to pay more.

My rather ameliorated view of this whole proposition and what, sagaciously, did not occur was that they chose not to do this. The final legal settlement of over a million dollars for the plaintiffs was, patently, as far as the town was willing to go—bankruptcy, which could have assuredly ensued had they attempted these "pain and suffering" payouts, was simply never an option.

My final thought and determination, having lived through all of this from my early childhood and into my adult years now is that the lawyers for the plaintiffs, in actuality, did their best under the circumstances and ultimately proved to be predominantly successful, perhaps even heroic. Within the bounds of not having bankrupted the town, they did a remarkable job of gathering testimony and evidence while expertly refuting every counter argument that the larger city lawyers threw at them. This, as they'd announced before hand, had been their "going-in" strategy and they accomplished it in relatively short order, an outstanding legal victory and one which should have left no doubt in anyone's mind as to the cause or effect of the dam break and subsequent damages.

I may be in the minority today, but I now thank attorneys Allyn Brown and Milton Jacobson for their staunch efforts at reaching this settlement and for all that they did for my father and the other unfortunate victims of this disaster. My father's worldview was never really cosmopolitan enough to see it, but I'd like to believe that mine now is, and I trust that I understand enough to know that my brothers and I were able to start our lives, even without our mother, due in large part to their efforts. Lastly, I feel somewhat obligated to state that I am not one of the survivors or persons intimately involved with this tragedy who, in any way, hold these lawyers in any form of scorn or malice.

As mentioned earlier, all of my uncles on both the Shea and Moody sides, absent my Uncle Jerry, are now gone. In his eighties now, my uncle

THOMAS MOODY, JR.

Jerry is still amazingly sharp intellectually and still even works part time. My Aunt Rita and he still reside at the same house in Lisbon that they'd moved to soon after the flood and one which I have many fond memories visiting and swimming when growing up.

Tony Orsini is in his seventies now, still healthy and with a magnificently high energy level. Maintaining an almost spiritual relationship with my dad after the flood, Tony also stayed involved with area athletics, as previously discussed. Either playing or coaching, he seemed ever present at a myriad of events around town, which resulted in him becoming well known by many who would then discover the wonderful personality with the remarkable sense of humor that he possesses. Having just recently relocated to Niantic with his wife, Jan, he still remains active in the Norwich area while in "retirement."

Patti Pellegrini, my dad's cousin and one of my favorite people in the world to talk with, was a very involved mom postflood. Immersing herself in her son's Boy Scout troop and volunteering at the St. Mary's Catholic Church in Greenville, she gave of herself, typically, in a sweeping fashion. Divorcing from "Chic" in 1982, an emotionally trying and traumatic experience for such a loving person, it nevertheless still didn't slow her down as she followed that agonizing period with an involvement at the Plainfield (Connecticut) Greyhound Racing Park where she fell in love with that breed of dog while also discovering a hidden passion for family genealogy, discovering a path all the way back to the Mayflower for her family.

Dennis Riley is retired today after a distinguished career in local journalism. He still resides on Otis Street in Norwich, his same home as it was in 1963, and my fondest memories are of him and NFA teacher Jack McCady broadcasting the NFA high school varsity basketball games live over the radio on WICH.

Bill Longo now resides in Tennessee in retirement. Divorced and since remarried, he reopened the Longo's Funeral home on Franklin Street postflood and continued there until 1973 when he decided to close it down. He then went to work for General Dynamics at Electric Boat in Groton for another twenty-five years before permanently retiring.

Roberta Delgado went on to marry her high-school sweetheart Robert Howard who would tragically lose his life in Vietnam in 1969. Remarrying in 1972, she also worked at Electric Boat in Groton for twenty-six years, retiring there in 1991. Traveling all the way to the Cape Verde Islands in 2006 to pursue and uncover her heritage, she now sponsors an NFA senior scholarship for the St. Anthony Chapel rebuild on those islands and is active in the Norwich Historical Society and the Hospice Care of Southeastern Connecticut while maintaining a staunch interest in Norwich history and culture.

My Aunt Jackie Shea today is Jacqueline Dows and still lives in Norwich. She and her husband (my Uncle Paul) divorced in the 1970s, and he would ultimately succumb to lung cancer in 1982, with his headstone being right next to my mother's at St. Joseph's Cemetery. She also lost her eldest son and my cousin "Chipper" in his early twenties, but she has her daughters and my cousins Robbie and Linnsie to comfort her today. A wonderfully caring and compassionate woman, it is easy to see what drew my mother to her.

The city leaders and lawyers of the time went on, as was necessary, with the business of the city and of the law. I'm told that, of the 1963 upper-tier city echelon, only Stanley Israelite survives today. Attorneys Allyn Brown and Milton Jacobson, meanwhile combined forces post trial to form the Brown & Jacobson law firm that still practices in Norwich to this day. The whereabouts and outcomes of Allyn Brown and Milton Jacobson, to my chagrin, are a mystery to me though, since inquiries to the firm about their eventualities went unanswered.

BIBLIOGRAPHY

T HE DOCUMENTATION AND historical backdrop to this storyline have been drawn almost exclusively from the real-time reported accounts of the *Hartford Times*, *New London Day*, and, in most cases, the comprehensive day-to-day coverage of the *Norwich Bulletin* newspapers. Those near-term and, later, extended accounts of the dam break and subsequent flood were my baseline source for the technical matters and, in the case of the *Bulletin*, my secondary source as well. Contemporary interviews and, importantly, past discussions with my family and key participants were, of course, vital to the overall emotional makeup of the story, while contextual supporting evidence of the newspaper accounts was consistently solicited and constantly approbated. In the final outcome, I think it would be fair to say that this narrative is made up of reportage from the newspapers of the era, documents obtained either via research or left behind/donated to me, and, largely, interviews and memories of discussions with key individuals or of my own.

An important and perhaps controversial point; I've chosen, within the storyline text, to not formally denote or credit each source, line by line, by which I obtained information simply because, in many cases, I'm simply not able to do so. For example, I have copies of articles and accounts of the tragedy that I reference that I have virtually no idea where it originates. Also, other information that I use and might even recognize as being from a particular organ, I, unfortunately, have found no further way to substantiate what specific day, or year, that it was published. As a survivor of this tragedy and one who aggressively solicited information for this project, I had the good benefit of receiving an assorted amount of material, most of it, unfortunately, without the requisite contextual backup. Moreover, and as mentioned above, scores of this information has been a part of my family for my entire life, with absolutely no source data or supporting reference stated.

What this amounted to then was essentially a pile of critical information without any idea of its origin. Notwithstanding, I chose to go forward with the story using this sometimes unsubstantiated information, since I also knew that I was going to use other undocumented accounts in the form of conversations and memories to establish many other important milestones; these conversations, in many cases, had occurred long ago with now-departed family members for which you'll just have to trust my memory. In the case of my memory, though, I did attempt corroboration whenever possible with my brothers, family or anyone else pertinent that's still alive.

For specific written sources outside of the newspapers mentioned, I used a wonderful book of Moody family genealogy written by my distant cousin Valarie Sullivan, *Samuel Moodie of Ireland & Scotland,* January 2004, for information on my father's parents.

A visit to the Norwich Public Works Department one rather mild winter day uncovered much information on the history of Mohegan Park and of the post-flood watershed program undertaken since 1964. I was courteously assisted there by Public Works employees Suzanne Cicarelli and Teresa Hanlon in the search for these records and with copying. I was unfortunately not successful that day with learning of the modern-day process that determines the physical health of the dam (i.e., the normal inspection periodicity). Most of the officials, or the director, were not on hand at the time that I was there and my time was short. Notwithstanding my weaknesses in uncovering this program (as stated earlier, I am an avowed low-ranking historian), I am, however, nevertheless certain that one exists as I've personally witnessed, on more than one occasion, a certain inspector out on the dam's north face level control "box", and this being an observation of a visitor currently living in Texas who only now sporadically returns to his home area.

As for personal interviews, I was truly honored to speak with many who were involved that night and gave of their time to share what constituted to be, in many cases, unpleasant memories.

Tony Orsini, of course, has shared with me through these many years his memories of that night, and I've constantly contacted him for clarification on certain points that my father or grandmother hadn't made clear to me.

My Uncle Jerry Shea was absolutely essential in establishing certain timelines of that night and, of course, disclosing the details of searching for and discovering my mother the next day.

A family videotape of the March 4 2006, ceremony to dedicate the memorial stone at Spaulding Pond allowed me to transcribe Tony Orsini's and my dad's speech along with all the other official speakers. It was also immensely poignant to see and hear my father again in such a wonderful and meaningful manner; his presence that day seemed to give off just the right aura that I needed personally at that time to believe that he was in fact flourishing healthwise and that I could travel back to Texas secure in the notion that he was, for the time being, stable.

Bill Longo was actually responding to Wally Lamb, whose work *We Are Water*, uses the flood in a fictional sense, when Wally steered him toward me. I spoke with Bill over the telephone twice from his Tennessee home and was able to extract not only the facts as he remembered them but also an emotional perspective of that night that I would not have otherwise obtained. His breathtaking account of the tragic death of Carol Mae Robidou was made even more horrifying by hearing him personally tell it.

My Aunt Jackie (Jackie Dows) spent the better part of a day with my wife, D'Ann, and I and answered untold questions about that night and subsequent days. Her memories and emotional feelings about that period were key components to the story as were her insights and loving memories of my mother and their time together.

My father's cousin Patti Pellegrini was a virtual gold mine of information. Living so close to the action that night and having such vivid memories, she became a major source of perspective and information regarding, among many things, the goings-on at Mohegan Park Road that day and night. She also gave me a much-needed viewpoint on a young mother's protective instinct with respect to her children that I was hopefully able to translate into my own mother's outlook.

Dennis Riley was another unforeseen and welcome Wally Lamb contact that provided a heretofore unknown angle to this tragedy. His story was absolutely fascinating, and he also surprised me with his unique personal viewpoint and interactions with Public Works director Harold Walz, one that this story desperately needed as a humane counterbalance to the otherwise vilifying information of the man that is rampant in the survivng documentation.

Roberta Delgado Vincent was yet another key component to this work provided by Wally Lamb. A marvelously erudite woman, she shared her emotional story with me while providing timely context about her young life on Boswell Avenue and the Lake Street playground.

William Zeitz was another who'd contacted Wally Lamb about his book. Quizzing him one summer evening over dinner at the Norwich Country Club, William related his story in rather colorful terms, almost as if he were a child again, describing the onrushing flood waters as they poured over the Lake Street drop-off and then saturated Longo's Funeral Home. Describing the disaster as it appeared to a young boy also added immensely to the emotional content of this story.

Speaking with Frank Majewski Sr. was a marvelous experience. In his gruff New England accent, he described his actions that day and night while recounting the marvelous story of having to destroy the Connecticut Beverage Company beer inventory at the dump. His son Frank Jr. was also immeasurably helpful and courteous in providing a DVD copy of his father's 16 mm film of the aftermath. For those interested, a viewing of this revelatory short film can be found at the following link: http://www. youtube.com/watch?v=11ofJr5iyV4

Ned Carlson was one of the young NFA volunteers assigned to the downtown cleanup. In a telephone interview, one facilitated by my brother Jimmy who had spoken with Ned while working at his Stop and Shop grocery store, he added to the grim next-day outlook of the downtown area that lent a depth to the narrative while his description of the damage at Chestnut Street, not wholly covered in the newspapers of the day, added another personal perspective that I so actively sought.

My beautiful and way cool nieces Alyssa and Airickuh (how 'bout that spelling, girl?) Moody provided photographs and assistance that are included in the insert . . . I love you guys! My equally beautiful and abundantly cool daughter Brooklyn provided much assistance to her severely technically challenged father with cropping and formatting the really old, yellowed

THOMAS MOODY, JR.

and degraded pictures that also appear in the insert . . . Thanks, Snooks, I definitely owe you a white mocha!

A quick word is needed on the maps that appear throughout the text. They are *not* drawn to scale and are meant simply as a visceral guide to help the reader (hopefully) follow the sometimes complex road structure that I'm describing. My son Evan did the best he could with his computer "unsavvy" father and made them look as professional as they could—thanks bud! I was basically forced to hand draw them and would love to ruminate on how charming hand drawn maps are and how heartfelt this effort was, but the truth of the matter is that I was facing a serious deadline and needed to get them included in the text in the most expeditious manner possible; Evan is the one who made them look as good as they do. I hope, as rough that as they appear (yes they do represent my most able artistic talent), that they are still helpful and convey a picture of what I'm describing in the book.

One day in September 2012, I received an e-mail response from the Frank Majewski YouTube video mentioned above concerning a Dam Safety Project and question concerning whether I'd be interested in "collaborating?" It was from a Mark Baker who was on some sort of dam safety committee. Always dubious about these kinds of requests, this one though had a ring of authenticity and I responded back saying that I would like to help. Turns out that Mark is the chairman of the Association of State Dam Safety Officials, a professional engineer associated with the Federal Department of the Interior's National Park's Service.

Through numerous (now) e-mails and telephone conversations, Mark has read a draft of this narrative and has provided editing (he really should be a professional editor) that I would have never otherwise had and has graciously provided numerous comments and inputs to the structure of this narrative.

In my association with Mark, I was also able to connect with a Dr. Steven Poulos, he being the same Dr. Poulos who actually testified in the postflood trial in Norwich Superior Court in 1966. He did a presentation for the ASDSO in 2005, and some of the pictures of that presentation are included here. Also, in a telephone conversation, Dr. Poulos, still amazingly razor sharp after all these years, explained his thoughts about the breech and the activities leading up to it, and those conjectures and thoughts led to many of my conclusions throughout.

The interviews that weren't really interviews at all were conducted, of course, over the span of my life. These consisted of an unquantifiable amount of conversations, sometimes extensive, sometimes minute, with my grandmother and my father. As with any family, these abiding stories over time, although purposely measured in their detail, built a base of understanding and perspective from which I grew to view this story. The untold number of heartfelt accounts of my mother extolled to my brothers and I by my father and grandmother, certainly provide the intimate underpinning to this work. All of the documentation and research for this project would prove to be meritless without these consummate family memories, and this project would not have carried nearly the same emotional weight without them.

Also true are the lifelong reminiscences shared with my brothers Jim and Shawn. Numerous phone conversations and personal talks started with "Do you remember . . ." and these would ultimately evolve into much-needed clarification of my ever-cloudy and failing memory. They both are as responsible for the emotional content of this narrative as I am.

THOMAS MOODY, JR.

ACKNOWLEDGEMENTS

I N ACTUALITY, THIS project started out as nothing more than a few-page, hand-written account for my children, Brooklyn and Evan, and for my wife D'Ann, that sought to document the heroics of my mom, dad and Tony Orsini. I particularly wanted all of them to appreciate the specific heroics that every one of them undertook and that it was entirely because of them that their dad and husband was alive today and for my children, in particular, to carry this story forward since they never got to meet their grandmother Moody and have fond but, now, rather distant memories of their grandfather Moody. Also, with our family living so far from Connecticut, this legacy, seemingly, has a way of dimming over time.

Many things, however, have added to the largess of the production of that small intimate project that has since blossomed into this book. Following my son Ryan's death in 1994, my outlook on family and its ever-tenuous state took an amazingly strong hold of me and made me reevaluate how lucky, even in the face of such a sorrowful occurrence as watching my son pass away, I've been in my life. Naturally, contemplating that, the circumstances of the flood and the miraculous outcome for my brothers and I were ideals that I realized led to this wonderful life, so much so that I became resolved to learn exactly what'd occurred on that March 6 1963, evening. Remember though, many of the details had been purposely kept from my brothers' and I, so in my weekly telephone calls to my father, I now started asking him some of these harder and more-pointed questions.

While mustering the fortitude to answer them and definitely challenging his memory, it was also at about this time that renowned Norwich historian Bill Stanley started publishing articles about his memories of town history in the *Sunday Norwich Bulletin* under the marvelous title "Once Upon A Time." And seemingly always at the beginning of March each year, he would discourse on the Spaulding Pond Dam break and flood, discussing his destroyed Cooley & Company offices, his time spent on the Norwich Businessmen's Rehabilitation Fund, and his view of the water-damaged downtown scene the next day.

Also he would talk about the six people tragically killed—five at the Turner-Stanton Mill and the heroics of one Margaret Moody who died saving her children. In it, he, undoubtedly with his best intentions at heart, inevitably would miss a detail or misplace a point. As my father would cut these articles out of the paper and send them to me, I would scrutinize them and discuss these discrepancies with him. Always dismissing my detailed concerns as trivial, I nonetheless wanted more from him . . . Where exactly did the car land? Where did the roof terminate in relation to the car? How long were we in the tree, and what did you do right after you descended from it? Where exactly did Mom go down and how?

When my Texas family visited Norwich, I would quiz him more and more now, taking him out to Lake Street time and again such that my interrogation got to the point where my wife finally had to admonish me that these were painful memories for him and that I needed to stop; but how could I explain to her or to anyone else that it was too late? I now had to fully know and understand everything.

Finally, after further badgering, he wearily asserted to me in another long telephone call that the details that I sought would probably never surface; "Put yourself in my place," he said. "I was just trying to rescue my family in a flood. I wasn't looking at where a roof was or a tree was. I was just trying to survive." And there suddenly it sunk in. Neither he nor Tony were, of course, noticing details that night; they were only trying to get to safety. What I was asking for was far beyond their capability to remember because it was happening so fast and in the middle of such a sudden and life-threatening catastrophe.

To get to the answers that I so desired, I now knew, would require a lot of self-determination. Fortunately for me, two photographs, along with my Uncle Jerry's timely help, would prove to be the essential components in piecing together the specifics of my mother's death and, ultimately, my understanding of what had happened to my father and Tony Orsini that night.

THOMAS MOODY, JR.

Both photographs, I believe, were taken by *Norwich Bulletin* photographers, but neither appeared in the immediate flood aftermath of the 1963 newspapers (this first one did appear about a month later in the newspaper and in Bill Stanley's contemporary books and also in an article on the 2006 memorial stone at the park). This first one is an aerial shot undoubtedly taken the next day via helicopter showing the destructive flood path from just north of Centennial Square at the top of the photo to the Lamperell parking lot as it connects to Franklin Street at the bottom. In it, the Lake Street drop-off is clearly visible as is the crushed roof that led my family to safety. A magnified look even reveals our overturned car and it is clear to see that the garage roof, even crashed downward, but extended far enough to the east, would have prevented our car from cascading down to the floor of Lamperells, thus supporting the sometimes debated theory (within my family) that my mother was found down at that lower level.

The other photo, given to me by Tony Orsini, is one taken on the first drop-off level looking north with our smashed and overturned car to the immediate left. This photograph looks upward toward Lake Street with the massive wash-out that destroyed the supporting wall structure leading from this level up to it. The basketball courts of the Lake Street playground, importantly, are noticeable in the background, and it is this photo that I would take with me to the area for perspective (using the basketball courts as a vantage point) to also help me determine the exact location of our car in relation to the garage roof and subsequent drop-off to the garage floor. After reconnoitering using this method, it is also clearly evident that the car had crashed much too far to the east with the garage roof behind it for my mother to have fallen down to the next level.

These photographs, in context, not only helped me in determining the location of my mother's death but also were instrumental in providing the logistics and locations for the answers that I sought.

Now I could determine exactly where our car crashed in relation to the garage roof and drop-off to Lamperell's dealership floor. I could now reasonably estimate how far we had to "duckwalk" to get to that tree at Longo's on this unsteady roof while also visualizing what my father probably saw and the amazing tribulations that he went through in contemplating going in after my mom that awful evening as she "went down."

I could also now envision the torrent flowing downward from the playground, over the Lake Street drop-off and then coursing around us with our car being held in place tenuously by this roof, shifting to and fro in the current with the nighttime freezing temperatures settling in upon us and the confusion and disorientation taking hold. Why shouldn't my dad hop off this roof and go in after my mom? She was probably just right there, goddammit!

Now knowing and understanding these logistics became tantamount for me in understanding and finally internalizing what these remarkable people went through that night and should have, in fact, provided that elusive "closure" component that so many seek in tragedies of this sort.

After the 2006 memorial ceremony at Mohegan Park in which I was fortunate enough to meet my dad's cousin Patti Pellegrini and learn her story, I started soliciting more and more information with the now-determined idea of somehow further documenting it. The idea of actually writing a book, however, did not become fully realized until after my father passed in September 2009. It would take me until May 2010 to organize my thoughts and information to a point where I could actually put pen to paper, or actually keystroke to screen, and what you're now reading is the result.

The first person that I absolutely need to thank, obviously, is Tony Orsini. I should start, I suppose, with a statement of undying gratitude for saving my life and work my way down from there. Tony, seemingly, has always been an intrinsic part of my life, and my respect for him is only exceeded by that for my father. His participation in this work has been unconditional and vital, clearly, and he has cooperated at every turn. I most assuredly could not have written this without him; with my dad now gone, he remains the only link that I have to that awful night, and he shares what he remembers with an amazing grace and strong personal forbearance that's been inspiring and influential throughout. Thanks, truly, for everything, Tony.

I owe a large and indelible debt to my friend and novelist Wally Lamb. The peculiarities of our meeting and subsequent convergence on this project is eerily ironic. I am, for some reason, fascinated with historically tragic places and, if lucky, hope to one day publish a series of essays about the strange aura that comes over me when visiting them. While researching the tragic shootings at Columbine High School, I came across Wally's novel *The Hour I First Believed* and was completely enthralled with his main character's fictitious meet-up with shooters Eric Harris and Dylan Klebold. After literally just finishing that novel (another outstanding work by Wally), my cousin Nora Shea Kaszuba e-mailed me to tell me that she'd heard that "famous" novelist Wally Lamb was working on his new book and planned to use the 1963 dam break and flood as a trigger for one of his storyline starting points. Knowing that I was working on this book also, she determinedly worked up the courage to call Wally to see if she could get us together.

Suddenly I received a funny and gracious e-mail from a "wlamb01" and we were off and running. As an aside, I should point out that as great a writer as Wally is, he's an even better person. Soon he was paying to fly me to Connecticut to walk the flood path and to meet Tony Orsini; later, he set up a radio interview/call in over WICH radio station to help me obtain contacts and other information. As previously discussed, he directed numerous people who had contacted him for his book my way and those contacts turned out to be absolutely essential to completing this book. The thought of two Norwich natives and NFA graduates first being interested enough in Columbine to want to write about it and then, at virtually the same time, writing about the Spaulding Pond Dam break is, to me, almost providential. Thank you so much, Wally for everything you've done for my family and I and for being a great friend.

Another person who was absolutely vital to this work is my cousin Ellen Shea Larson. If anyone needs a research assistant, trust me, Ellen is your gal; long interested in how "Aunt Honey" died, she initially shared her memories and thoughts of what happened that day and night with me. Later she became dogged in her research of *Norwich Bulletin* newspapers at the local Otis Library, making copies and sending them to me along with e-mail updates. A marvelously intelligent and insightful woman, she and I later discussed details as I learned them, which seemed to spur her on even further. At the library one day, she met a gentleman named Frank Majewski Jr., and that per chance meeting turned into the amazingly illuminating DVD copy of Frank's father's 16 mm film of the next day's surrounding area that's mentioned in the bibliography. In the end, a large amount of the documentation that I have now is due to her passion and perseverance, and it is documentation that I could not have completed this project without. Ellen, I've told you many times how awesome I think you are and here's one more.

Ellen's sister and my cousin Nora, as previously noted, was responsible for connecting me with Wally Lamb, and I would not have been able to speak with people such as Bill Longo, Dennis Riley, or Roberta Vincent (to mention only a few) without that connection. Also, Nora was essential with providing me with some key history on our grandmother Nana as well as being kind enough to read a draft of this book and provide some thoughtful feedback. Like her sister, Nora is also exceedingly intelligent (their parents, my Uncle Bud and Aunt Jean always struck me as having an amazing intellect; I particularly remember my Uncle Bud speaking with Nana when I was small and thinking that I would never be that smart) while having a remarkable personality, and I thank her for her help from the bottom of my heart. Her brother Mark, my favorite cousin growing up (he took me to my first NBA game at the Boston Garden!), is a lawyer in Connecticut and helped me with some legal language and advice. While writing this, he became a newlywed, so I didn't get to discuss as much of the flood as I would have liked to with him, but I thank him also for his help.

To say that Patti Pellegrini was an important part of this project would be a huge understatement. Unfortunately, getting to know her only since the 2006 memorial ceremony, she has, nonetheless, been an irreplaceable source and confidant for this book. Having gracefully shared her story with me time and again while adding to my mother's memory with many emotional targets was remarkable enough, but as it always is with Patti, her passion and involvement is total, and she would contribute a whole lot more.

The picture of her, in her seventies now, talking with me with her aluminum walker for assistance out at the dam site and skating pond, with a self-made photograph board, is priceless to me. Driving the entire flood path and pointing out many of her memories of downtown Norwich added much depth to this narrative, and her subsequent follow up e-mails and written accounts and consistent involvement have been truly inspiring. She also read a draft of this book and provided essential corrections and feedback, and I feel as though this is as much her book as mine. I love you,

Patti, for your help and passion, and, although I've been saying it a lot in this section, I could not have completed this without you.

My Uncle Jerry always scared me when I was young; very pointed in his conversations with me then, I thought he was very severe and trenchant. Later, being a rather tall man himself, he would sidle up to me whenever he saw me to compare heights (he's perhaps six-feet two-inches and I'm now six-feet eight-inches); when I finally outgrew him, it was then that I noticed the sparkle in his eye and the beguiling nature of his personality. What's amazing to now realize is that, back then, he had a certain hard kidding/joking approach with all of us kids that I never appreciated and that I've since naturally adopted and I've horrifyingly realized since interviewing him for this book that I've essentially turned into him!

And it was only after speaking to him for this book that I truly understood that it was he alone who'd discovered my mother the next day. My father always asserted that "Uncle Jerry found her," but it was under the pretext of a group finding. In fact, in numerous visits to the Lake Street site, my dad always, and erroneously, thought that she was found at the floor of Lamperell's, at the bottom of the next drop-off, and told me this several times. It wasn't until I spoke with Uncle Jerry and actually went to Lake Street with him that I learned the real truth.

Noting the contradiction and asking him over and over if he was sure, he repeatedly pointed to the general area on the first drop-off where he found her, explaining his actions that next morning and walking around the area with me to rekindle his memory. Showing him the picture of the overturned car looking north into the Lake Street playground, he regained his bearings and confirmed his statements.

Leaving me, at that time, absolutely confused and without my father to verify, it was not until I scrutinized those two informative photographs that I realized that there was no way for my mom to be anywhere but where my Uncle Jerry said she was. Fate left him as the only living son of my grandmother, but it was my personal gain and this book's essential benefit that he was available for me to speak with. Helping me on several occasions and having me up to his ever-familiar Lisbon house with my Aunt Rita, I realize what a remarkable person he is and how very proud I am to have him as my Uncle. Realizing now how very much alike we are makes me prouder still, and I thank you Uncle Jerry for revealing an important point in this drama and for everything that you and Aunt Rita have done for me over these many years.

My Aunt Jackie (Dows) is simply one of the most loving and caring people to ever inhabit this planet. Sharing an important part of her emotional past with me while connecting me with my mom in such a way that I could not have otherwise obtained, she most closely appends me to her. Detailing her and my Uncle Paul's actions that night and in the subsequent days, she provided me with still another perspective that I've been lacking these many years. Sharing her feelings and observations prior to and during the funeral also furthered this narrative, and I cannot thank her enough.

I wish also to thank Bill Longo and Dennis Riley for providing me with exceedingly important testimony. Their story became absolutely essential to my account leading into the dam break and to the tragic and chaotic turns later that night. Of course, if Wally Lamb hadn't connected them to me, I never would have spoken with them, but once I did, they both were extremely cooperative and spoke with me on more than one occasion. Thank you both, gentlemen, for your important and heartfelt input here. I will certainly never forget it.

Roberta Delgado Vincent is another of my fervent and ardent sources that I feel completely indebted to. Speaking with her via telephone and e-mail, I sense an immense grace and personal confidence that befits her story that I've learned since the flood. Her assistance with this work, in addition to sharing her passionate story of that evening, has been uplifting and, to use another cliché, inspiring. She, as a member of the Norwich Historical Society, has kindly promoted this tragedy to that board as a matter of significant Norwich history, which, in the end, has been one of the goals of this endeavor. Thank you Roberta—you've been a great friend and confidant.

This work would be significantly less without the input and passion of Mark Baker. An amazingly insightful reader and editor, he provided a much-needed "outsider's" view to this manuscript along with almost "nerve-wracking" section and chapter change suggestions. He really made me think and see the reader's viewpoint, and I thank you, Mark, very much. Also, having never met me, he asked me to be a member of the Association of State Dams Safety Officials (ASDSO), of which I am now proudly one of, and to be a part of the ASDSO 2013 New England Dam Safety Conference. As I've said previously, Mark, I owe you a lot. My association with the ASDSO has consequentially and immeasurably furthered this book (there are pictures and documentation that this group has gathered that I never would have had access to had I not known them) and I have Mark to thank for it. I wish I'd known you and this organization when I first started this project and, more importantly, I truly wish the ASDSO had been around in 1963.

Ditto for Dr. Steven Poulos—another late find for me in the writing of this work but absolutely key nonetheless. His 2005 ASDSO conference presentation pictures are absolutely discerning, breathtaking and important for my understanding of the dynamic of the dam prior to the break. Also, his picture uploads to the 2013 ASDSO Safety Conference web page were absolutely heart-stopping to me. Most of my descriptions of the old dam and the breech are actually attempts to describe these pictures. Having never seen the old dam nor, of course, the actual breech, these pictures give me now an understanding and an emotional target far beyond the normal viewer. Looking upon these photos as a survivor and as one who lost a loved one, they provide a context and aspect not ordinarily understood by simply viewing a photograph; "This is what killed my mom," is the ever-present theme that I have in every viewing. It, really, is difficult to convey my total feelings when I look upon these rather morbid old photos, but, they do go an enormous way in providing me with a "closure" component that, I thought, was long ago "closed." Thanks so much, Dr. Poulos.

Micah Muir, my daughter's boyfriend and a supremely intelligent young-man majoring in geology at the University of Texas at San Antonio was an immense help with reviewing maps and being a sounding board for the geological anatomy of the dam break one Thanksgiving weekend. He reviewed some of Dr. Poulos's 2005 graphs and offered insight into his thoughts as to the cause of the breech. I hope to someday bring him and Brooklyn up to Connecticut to talk with him in depth about what happened and perhaps walk the flood path with him. Thanks Micah, very much for your help.

I really enjoyed speaking with Frank Majewski Sr. and sharing his memories of the flood and the following days. He was the Public Works employee who overheard the somewhat frantic radio traffic about the dam leak from his truck that day and who was active in the cleanup the following day. His marvelous story of destroying the contaminated beer of the Connecticut Beverage Company is one of my favorites, and his 16 mm film of the surroundings is absolutely surreal. Frank Majewski Jr. is also to be absolutely commended for taking this film and converting it to DVD, and the irony of his meeting with my cousin Ellen is providential indeed. Thanks Frank Sr. and Frank Jr. for your surprising and incredible addition to this story—if I ever meet up with you guys the beers are definitely on me!

Ned Carlson is my dad's cousin and another who had entered this story by way of casual contact. As mentioned earlier, Ned would periodically encounter my brother Jim in his capacity as dairy manager at the Stop and Shop grocery store in Norwich and, upon open discussion concerning family happenings, particularly the writing of this book, one day suddenly disclosed that he'd been involved in the postflood cleanup operations.

Upon hearing this and determining that it may be perhaps revelatory, Jimmy gave me Ned's telephone number, and the resulting conversation relayed not only personal memories of his NFA volunteer efforts but also an abiding recollection of the almost-morbid downtown destruction the next day. He too added to the comical destruction story of the Connecticut Beverage Companies stock, particularly the "damaged" beer, and I thank him for his time and contribution.

Stu Bryer of radio station WICH in Norwich was kind enough to dedicate an entire show to Wally Lamb and I to discuss the flood while answering call-in's concerning it and our books on the subject. Stu has been a staple at WICH since the 1960s (my grandmother Nana loved his mid-morning program *Potpourri*) and his show is still exceedingly popular, so to get quality time on it was, for me, an extreme honor. Thanks very much, Stu.

I was also honored to have the following friends read this narrative in draft form and offer some enlightening feedback. Thank you, Patti Toler Burris, Kim Mitchell, and Jennifer Moody, my nephew Eric's wife (my brother Jim's son).

My brothers Jim and Shawn, I hope, know my feelings and gratitude for them; any sappy thanks or drawn-out platitudes would only draw more good-natured ire and ridicule from them, and I've certainly had my share of that over fifty-plus years!

Seriously, though, they both took responsibility for Dad when he absolutely needed them during his time of rapidly failing health (along, thankfully, with great help from Shawn's wife, Pat), taking him to the doctor and hospital, babysitting when required and doing anything and everything to get him to feel as well as he possibly could. And they did all this while balancing their own family priorities and getting absolutely no help from me.

I, from a distance, marveled at their aggregate fortitude and mature handling of a sometimes immature situation. My father was most assuredly difficult and unpredictable in his final years, and Jim and Shawn stepped up to take control and provide him with the best possible care right to the very end. To say that I am proud of them only conveys a fraction of the connection that we share. Solidified, assuredly, due to Nana's doggedness in keeping us together, and with her and Dad's otherwise stalwart upbringing, we as brothers, I feel, are as close and inseparable as any could be. Staying in touch as much as possible, it seemingly takes only a few words or utterances when we're together before we are back conjointly to where we were fifty years ago, and for that, I'm forever thankful. I truly love them and forever look forward to either seeing them or speaking with them, and I believe my Mom, Dad and Nana could not have asked for more.

Thanking my children, Brooklyn and Evan, and my wife, D'Ann (to whom this book is dedicated), is like being thankful for the air that I breathe. My core existence depends solely on them, and I could not ever imagine a life without them. This project, as previously noted, was started to enlighten them as to the heroics of their grandparents, and I daily draw strength and inspiration from them. Brooklyn and Evan, I now empower you both to keep this legacy alive and to pass it on to your own children. I love you both with all my heart and am eternally grateful that I have you both in my life and that I can share this story with you.

D'Ann, honey, I've told you many times how much you've influenced this project and, by virtue, have been my inspiration going forward. For this book to have ever come this far, I've needed your total support, and you've given it to me in both loving and intellectually essential ways. With you behind me and to lean on, I've been able to exceed my capability, I feel, as a writer, capturing the essence of this story and hopefully doing justice to my parents. This most assuredly would not have been possible without you. You've been my shepherding light, my heart, and my total inspiration and I love you for everything that you've made me. I'm exceedingly fortunate to have met and married you, and the only regret that I have is that my mother never got to meet you. That picture, in my mind, of you standing with her truly completes the emotional arc of my life.

Thomas Moody Jr.

11/19/12

Stephenville, Texas